NEZ PERCE
COYOTE TALES

▼▼▼▼▼

NEZ PERCE COYOTE TALES

The Myth Cycle

Deward E. Walker, Jr.
in collaboration with Daniel N. Matthews

Illustrations by Marc Seahmer

University of Oklahoma Press
Norman

Library of Congress Cataloging-in-Publication Data

Walker, Deward E.
  [Blood of the monster]
  Nez Perce coyote tales : the myth cycle / Deward E. Walker, Jr. in collaboration with
Daniel N. Matthews ; illustrations by Marc Seahmer. — Oklahoma paperbacks ed.
    p.   cm.
  Originally published: Blood of the monster. Worland, Wyo. : High Plains Pub. Co.,
c1994. With new pref.
  Includes bibliographical references and index.
  ISBN 0-8061-3032-6 (pbk. : alk. paper)
  1. Nez Percé Indians—Folklore. 2. Nez Percé mythology. 3. Coyote (Legendary
character) 4. Trickster. 5. Tales—Northwest, Pacific. I. Matthews, Daniel N.
II. Title.
E99.N5W27   1998
398.24'5297725'0899741—dc21   97-40106
                                                                                      CIP

This book originally was titled *Blood of the Monster: The Nez Perce Coyote Cycle.*

The paper in this book meets the guidelines for permanence and durability of the Committee on Production Guidelines for Book Longevity of the Council on Library
Resources, Inc. ⊗

Oklahoma Paperbacks edition published 1998 by the University of Oklahoma Press,
Norman, Publishing Division of the University, by arrangement with High Plains Pub-
lishing Company, Inc., P.O. Box 1860, Worland, Wyoming 82401. Manufactured in the
U.S.A. First printing of the University of Oklahoma Press edition, 1998.

1   2   3   4   5   6   7   8   9   10

To Richard A. Halfmoon
mentor, exemplar, and friend

▼▼▼▼▼

Contents

PART ONE COYOTE MYTHS

Coyote and Monsters

Coyote the Transformer

Coyote and Fox

Coyote and Grizzly Bear

Coyote and Women and Children

PART TWO
A DESCRIPTIVE INTERPRETATION
OF COYOTE'S CHARACTER

▼▼▼▼▼

Acknowledgments

WE WISH TO ACKNOWLEDGE the contributions of the following people whose work has been particularly valuable in the various phases of researching, writing, and producing this book. Our deepest gratitude goes to the Nez Perce Tribe, especially the Tribal elders and Allen Slickpoo, Sr., for their generous cooperation and support and to *Wáyi'látpu*, Elizabeth Wilson, and Samuel Watters for sharing their versions of Nez Perce myths. We are indebted to Herbert Spinden and Archie Phinney for collecting and publishing other versions of the Nez Perce myths that have been essential for conducting this analysis. The accurate translations of Haruo Aoki have been indispensable in this and any future interpretations of Nez Perce myths. We also thank the University of California Press for permission to reprint material from Aoki and Walker (*Nez Perce Oral Narratives*, 1989) and Columbia University Press for granting permission to reprint material from Phinney (*Nez Perce Texts*, 1934). Translations have been lightly edited to improve clarity, and the most appropriate versions have been used where multiple versions are available.

For their assistance in funding this project, we thank the National Science Foundation; Dr. Barbara Voorhies, chair of the University of Colorado Department of Anthropology, and Dr. Evelyn Hu-DeHart, director of the University of Colorado Center for Studies of Ethnicity and Race in America. Marc Seahmer's illustrations add an exciting dimension to the text.

▼▼▼▼▼

PREFACE TO THE
PAPERBACK EDITION

ORIGINALLY ENTITLED *Blood of the Monster: The Nez Perce Coyote Cycle,* this book was conceived primarily as a collection of stories rather than a study of the theoretical controversies surrounding how anthropologists interpret myth. Our goal here is to provide a straightforward, descriptive presentation of the character of Coyote in the context of his interaction with other characters in Nez Perce mythology.

Our personal familiarity with the Nez Perce Coyote character began in the late 1950s. Raconteurs were still numerous at that time, and we discovered that the Coyote tales were best known by such elders as Racehorse Charlie Wilson, Corbett Lawyer, Albert Moore, Sam Slickpoo, Charlie White, Richard Half-moon, Joe Blackeagle, Linus Walker, Sam Watters, Elizabeth Wilson, and others. We discovered that the character of Coyote was a central figure within a cluster of closely interconnected tales. These Coyote tales form what we have termed a cycle, in the literary sense used by scholars when referring to all of the tales or stories surrounding a hero or mythic figure. Examples would include the myth cycle of tales surrounding the semimythic or mythic figures of Charlemagne or Renard and the Fox from Europe.

In presenting this Nez Perce literary cycle, we have tried to avoid the distortions created by structural-functional, symbolic, psychoanalytic, or postmodernist interpretations imposed on American Indian mythology by various scholars. Attempts to interpret Nez Perce myths from such perspectives have clouded or even eliminated the views of the Nez Perce people, whose concerns are central in our presentation. Our hope is that the character of Coyote, his motives, and his interactions with other mythic characters will be understood as the Nez Perce understand them. To this end we have attempted to present their views faithfully and with the clarity and directness they deserve. This permits the educated reader to appreciate the myths without having to struggle through the theoretical issues under debate in academic circles.

In the course of preparing this preface we have benefited from advice and various types of constructive criticism offered by both tribal and academic colleagues. Generally speaking, they have found our presentation clear and uncomplicated by theory but have tended not to favor our focus on only one character of the myths, the Coyote. Linguists have suggested that our presentation does not explore the nuances and subtleties of style evident among the raconteurs from whom we obtained the tales. Some reviewers believe that we have overlooked the deeper symbolism they detect in the myths, while other colleagues would prefer a more structural-functional analysis. We would certainly welcome these types of analyses, which our presentation makes possible. We have been informed by the Nez Perce that there is virtue in the relative simplicity of our presentation, quite unlike the confusion they sometimes feel when reviewing other more theoretical presentations.

We should remind the reader that while the character of Coyote is widespread in American Indian mythologies, his expression may vary substantially from one tribe to another—for example, the trickster-transformer figure of Coyote in one tribe's mythology is not necessarily the Coyote of Nez Perce mythology. It must also be stressed that little connection exists between the myths and Nez Perce social or cultural reality. In a very real sense they are part of a separate mythic reality, in which many of the normal cultural and existential rules and principles do not operate. It is a world separate from the ordinary day-to-day existence of the Nez Perce, one in which the miraculous, magical, forbidden, and impossible become real, whether in the actions of Coyote or in the actions of his fellow mythic characters.

▼▼▼▼▼

INTRODUCTION

In 1962, fewer than two hundred Nez Perce were fluent in their language. By 1994, fewer than thirty spoke their language fluently. Thus the Nez Perce oral tradition, which is responsible for preservation of the myths of these people, is rapidly disappearing. In order to preserve at least a portion of this tradition, we have assembled the largest collection of those myths that concern Coyote—the most complex character in Nez Perce mythology.

The activities of the characters, the imparted values, and the physical culture described in these myths allude mainly to Nez Perce culture of aboriginal times. In aboriginal times, the Nez Perce occupied approximately 13 million acres located in what is now north–central Idaho, southeastern Washington, and northeastern Oregon. Nez Perce territory included the Clearwater and portions of the Salmon River and Snake River drainages. This area has many mountains, rivers, and deep canyons that provided a wide variety of resources and protection from invaders. The river valleys also provided grazing areas and protection from extreme cold in winter. Traditional food plants included camas bulbs, bitterroot, wild carrot, wild onion, several varieties of berries, sunflower seed, pine nuts, moss, and bark. Food animals included salmon and other fish, elk, deer, moose, mountain goats and sheep, bear, small game, and birds. The Nez Perce seasonally migrated throughout their territory in order to take advantage of various resources. Additional resources were acquired on expeditions to what is now southern Idaho, eastern Oregon and Washington, down the Columbia River, and even into the northern Great Plains for buffalo. Mobility was greatly enhanced after the adoption of the horse, and the Nez Perce became greatly renowned for their large herds and selective breeding.

The aboriginal Nez Perce lived primarily in small settlements of thirty to two hundred individuals. These villages were politically unified into bands that, in turn, were organized into composite bands. This pattern of political organization was largely the result of the location of the villages along streams and tributary systems. Villages were identified with the smaller feeder streams, bands with the larger tributaries, and composite bands with larger rivers. A typical village was made up of several related extended families usually led by one headman (generally the eldest able man, occasionally a shaman) whose powers were sharply limited by village elders who elected him. The headman's duties were to demonstrate exemplary behavior, act as spokesman for the village, mediate intravillage disputes, and attend to the general welfare of village members. Women did not speak in most council proceedings but normally influenced their male relatives to achieve their goals. The elected band leader was usually the leader of the largest village in the group and was often assisted by prominent warriors. Composite band councils were composed of band leaders but tended to be led by prominent warriors who elected a temporary leader. This type of organization facilitated large operations such as buffalo hunting ventures into the Great Plains. The head chief system in which the entire tribe was represented by a permanent leader was a product of later treaties and the reservation system that emerged after A.D. 1840.

Most older relatives took part in training children. Nez Perce children developed close ties with grandparents who typically cared for them after weaning. In contrast to a more formal relationship maintained with their parents, children could joke with and tease grandparents whom they tended to regard as equals. A grandfather would usually direct a boy's first attempts at hunting, fishing, sweatbathing, and horse riding; a grandmother would usually direct a girl's first root digging or berry picking. Grandparents also spent many hours recounting myths, which were a primary means of educating the young. Siblings and cousins were regarded as brothers and sisters, and aunts and uncles were called by terms also used for father and mother. By the age of six, boys and girls were making substantial contributions to family subsistence. At adolescence, children of both sexes were sent out to seek tutelary spirits in vision quests.

Marriages were arranged by family heads, and childhood betrothals were common. Families would decide if the couple were compatible in terms of personality, relative wealth, and social prestige. Marriage between known relatives, even distant cousins, was forbidden. Marriage of more than one son into a family was common. Sororal polygyny, or a man marrying two or more sisters, was not uncommon. The levirate and sororate (the option to marry the eldest brother of the groom or a sister of the bride in the event of their death) were also observed. Couples lived with the parents from whom they could expect to gain the most, usually those of the groom.

The traditional Nez Perce believed that humans and natural objects had souls, without which they ceased to exist. Tutelary spirits differ from souls in that they are acquired during life and are rarely lost. Heaven and hell were concepts brought by Christian missionaries, but there were earlier conceptions of an afterlife. Shamans were people who demonstrated particularly strong supernatural powers during medicine dances and in healing, and they performed various ceremonial services in the community.

Nez Perce culture has undergone rapid transformation since first contact with Euroamericans, but Nez Perce myths are quite conservative and reveal few new materials. For example, although horses played a large role in shaping Nez Perce life after about A.D. 1700, horses do not appear as characters in the narratives, are rarely mentioned, and even then appear only as minor details. The values associated with the behavior and activities of mythical characters in particular contexts as well as the physical culture described in the narratives allude with few exceptions* to traditional Nez Perce culture of the prehorse era. Nez Perce myths do not directly or systematically reflect traditional Nez Perce culture in a typical structural–functional manner. Instead, the myths form a semi-independent sector of Nez Perce culture and depict a distinct reality whose construction is based on its own rules, some of which are revealed in our following interpretation. In our view, Nez Perce mythology is not necessarily a function or an outgrowth of any other sector of Nez Perce culture. Likewise, it has survived largely unchanged despite massive changes in other sections of Nez Perce culture.

Like myths from other cultures, Nez Perce myths impart basic values and beliefs and provide moral instruction. They help explain the creation of the world and its inhabitants, the origin of rituals and customs, and the meaning of birth, death, and other natural occurrences. Myths are mechanisms for educating children, for stimulating social interaction and cohesion, and for amusement. Nez Perce myths were traditionally recounted by elders during winter. They are inhabited by a cast of characters that include animals, plants, rocks, rivers, celestial bodies, and other figures who behaved like humans in a precultural era before humans were created. These characters share much in common with the tutelary spirits that Nez Perce individuals traditionally acquired during vision quests. Tutelary spirits could confer special powers and abilities to those who observed proper rituals and taboos, or they could cause misfortune and death to those who violated taboos. The Nez Perce believe that although the animals became mute after humans arrived, they could still reveal their full power to humans in visions and dreams. The behavior of animal characters in myths also instructed children in proper behavior and taught them practical lessons, such as the habits of animals, the location of food and other resources, how to use implements and tools, and the geography of their territory. Some

---

*Exceptions include a flintlock gun, smallpox, horses, white people and black people, but these remain insufficient to contradict our assertion that the myth corpus is overwhelmingly conservative and reflects pre-contact culture.

explain the origins of animals, environmental features, customs, and so forth. Others emphasize the positive or negative outcomes of various types of behavior, reinforcing the prized values of honesty, justice, bravery, generosity, self–discipline, and self–reliance.

Narratives that include Coyote make up more than half of the entire existing corpus of Nez Perce myths, reflecting the importance the Nez Perce assign to Coyote. Because Coyote created them, they consider themselves to be the children of Coyote—*Iceyé´yenm mamáyac.** There are many other mythical characters inhabiting the world in which Coyote's adventures take place (see Table 1), but he is the most complex in Nez Perce mythology. Few other characters manifest a survival capacity equal to his. He represents and expresses many of the most basic human drives: lust for power, hunger for food, and unrestrained desire for sexual gratification. These drives motivate his actions in most of the myths in which he is a principal actor. His methods for satisfying these drives often include deception, evasion, trickery, and disguise. His actions are often destructive and disruptive of the social life of his mythical associates, yet he seems to be aware that his activities may benefit the human beings whom he is soon to create.

Coyote and the other mythical actors are a prehuman combination of animal, human, and superhuman qualities. We should not expect their behavior to be entirely human, and we should not assume that these actors directly reflect traditional Nez Perce culture. Coyote acts largely on his immediate urges and impulses and is only marginally social in the human sense, which helps to explain his amoral actions that conflict sharply with traditional Nez Perce behavior. It is also worthwhile to note several other things about Nez Perce Coyote. He is not a god in the Euroamerican sense; he is not a hero in the sense used by Joseph Campbell; he is not a creator in the sense of Jehovah; and he is not merely a picaresque figure. The term trickster–transformer, often applied to Coyote, also omits several important aspects of his character, because he is not only the perpetrator of tricks but also the victim of tricks perpetrated on him by others. His role as a transformer has been exaggerated, especially in view of his motives, which are self–centered.

What follows is a comprehensive collection of Nez Perce Coyote myths with an interpretive section illustrating Coyote's character based on his relationships with other mythic characters. Readers who wish to review the texts in the Nez Perce orthography are encouraged to consult the original publications. The former title of this volume refers to the narrative "Coyote and Monster," which ends with Coyote creating the Nez Perce and other tribes from the parts of the slain monster. We present "Coyote and Monster" first, because it shows the importance of Coyote in Nez Perce cosmology; however, it could have been presented last because the other myths occur in the time before human beings are created.

---

*Our writing of Nez Perce words does not always conform with the method employed by linguists.

Table 1: Principal Characters in the Nez Perce Coyote Cycle

Air People	Elder Brother	Pinion Bird
Bald Eagle	Elk	Porcupine
Bat	Excrement Children	Prairie Chicken
Black Bear	Fir People	Raccoon
Black Brush Pheasant	Fish Hawk	Racer Snake
Blackfeet	Flathead	Rattlesnake
Black–tailed Buck	Flint Man	Raven
Blindworm	Fox	Robin
Bluejay	Frog	Rock
Blue Racer Snake	Goat	Salmon
Bobcat	Golden Eagle	Sea Monster
Bobolink	Goose	Shadow People
Brown Bear	Gopher	Sioux
Buffalo	Grasshopper	Skulls
Butterfly	Grizzly Bear	Snowshoe Rabbit
Cannibal	Hummingbird	Spiders
Cayuse	Jackrabbit	Sun
Chinook salmon	Killer Baby	Sunflower
Cicéqi	Land People	Swallow
Cixcixícim	Lynx	Swan
Coeur d'Alene	Magpie	Turtle
Coldweather People	Marten	Wasco People
Cougar	Meadowlark	Warmweather People
Cow Elk	Mistoyno	Water Woman
Crane	Monster	Wayaćaynwá·yaćayn
Crawfish	Moon	Weasel
Cricket	Mosquito	White Bull
Crow	Mountain Goat	White Duck
Curlew	Mountain Sheep	White Mountain
Cut–Out–of–Belly Boy	Mouse	Rabbit
Death Spirit	Muskrat	White–tailed Buck
Deer Tick	Mussel–Shell Woman	Wolf
Disobedient Boy	Night Owl	Women at the
Duck	Otter	Headwaters
Duck Man	Owl	Woodpecker
Eagle	Pend d'Oreilles	Worm
Elbow Baby	Pine Squirrel	Worm People

Prepared by Deward E. Walker Jr.

The Nez Perce Homeland and Their Neighbors

▼▼▼▼▼

PART ONE

COYOTE MYTHS

Coyote severs Monster's heart with his flint knife.

COYOTE AND MONSTERS

1

COYOTE AND MONSTER

COYOTE WAS BUILDING a fish-ladder by tearing down the waterfall at Celilo, so that salmon could go upstream for the people to catch. He was busily engaged at this when someone shouted to him, "Why are you bothering with that? All the people are gone; the monster has done them in." "Well," said Coyote to himself "then I'll stop doing this, because I was doing it for the people, and now I'll go along too." From there he went along upstream, by the way of the Salmon River country. Going along he stepped on the leg of a meadowlark and broke it. The meadowlark in a temper shouted, "*Lima', lima', lima'.* What chance do you have of finding the people the way you are going along!" Coyote then asked, "My aunt! Please tell me about it. Afterward I will make you a leg of brushwood." So the meadowlark told him, "All the people have already been swallowed by the monster." Coyote then replied, "Yes, that is where I, too, am going."

From there he traveled on. Along the way he took a good bath, saying to himself, "Lest I make myself repulsive to his taste," and then he dressed himself all up: "Lest he will vomit me up or spit me out." Then he tied himself with [very long ropes] to three mountains. From there he came along up and over ridges. Suddenly, behold, he saw a great head. He quickly hid himself in the grass and gazed at it. Never before in his life had he seen anything like it; never such a large thing—away off somewhere melting into the horizon was its gigantic body.

Coyote shouted to him, "Oh Monster, we are going to inhale each other!" The big eyes of the monster roved, looking all over for Coyote but did not find him because Coyote's body was painted with clay to achieve a perfect protective coloring in the grass. Coyote had on his back a pack consisting of five stone knives, some pure pitch, and a flint fire-making set. Presently Coyote shook the grass to and fro and shouted again, "Monster! We are going to inhale each

(Recited by *Wàyi'làtpu*; originally published in Phinney, 1934. See also "Iltswewitsix, The Kamiah Monster" in Spinden, 1908.)

other." Suddenly the monster saw the swaying grass and replied, "Oh you Coyote, you swallow me first then; you inhale first." So Coyote tried. Powerfully and noisily he drew in his breath, but the great monster just swayed and quivered. Then Coyote said, "Now you inhale me, for you have already swallowed all the people, so swallow me too lest I become lonely."

The monster inhaled like a mighty wind, which carried Coyote along just like that; but as Coyote went he left in his wake great camas roots and great serviceberries, saying, "Here the people will find them and will be glad, for only a short time away is the coming of the human race." He almost got caught on one of the ropes, but he quickly cut it with his knife.

Thus he dashed right into the monster's mouth. From there he walked down the throat of the monster. Along the way he saw bones scattered about and he thought to himself, "It is to be seen that many people have been dying." As he went along he saw some boys and he said to them, "Where is his heart? Come along and show me!" Then, as they were all going along, the bear rushed out furiously at him. "So!" Coyote said to him, "You make yourself ferocious only to me," and he kicked the bear on the nose. As they continued, the rattlesnake bristled at him in fury, "So! Only toward me you are vicious—we are nothing but dung." Then he kicked the rattlesnake on the head and flattened it. Going on he met the brown bear who greeted him, "I see he [the monster] selected you for the last. So! I'd like to see you save your people [derogatory diatribe]."

All along the people hailed Coyote and stopped him. He told the boys, "Pick up some wood." His erstwhile friend Fox hailed him from the side, "Such a dangerous fellow [the monster], what are you going to do to him?" "So!" replied Coyote. "You too hurry along and look for wood."

Presently Coyote arrived at the heart and he cut off slabs of fat and threw them to the people. "Imagine you being hungry under such conditions! Grease your mouths with this." And Coyote started a fire with his flint and shortly smoke appeared from the monster's nose, ears, eyes, and anus. The monster then said, "Oh you, Coyote, that's why I was afraid of you. Oh you, Coyote, let me cast you out." And Coyote replied, "Yes, and later let it be said, 'He who was cast out is officiating in the distribution of salmon.'" "Well then, go out through the nose." Coyote replied, "And will not they say the same?" And the monster said, "Well then, go out through the ears," to which Coyote replied, "And let it be said, 'Here is ear-wax officiating in the distribution of food.'" "*Hn, hn, hn!* Oh you, Coyote! This is why I feared you; then go out through the anus." And Coyote replied, "And let people say, 'Feces are officiating in the distribution of food.'" His fire was still burning near the heart and the monster began to writhe in pain. Coyote began cutting away on the heart, and very shortly he broke the stone knife. Immediately he took another and in a short time this one also broke and Coyote said to all the people, "Gather up all the bones and carry them to the eyes, ears, mouth, and anus; pile them up and when he falls dead kick all the bones outside." Then with another knife he began cutting away at the heart. The third knife he broke and the fourth, leaving only one. He told the people, "All right, get yourselves ready because as soon as he falls dead each one will go out of the opening most convenient. Take the old women and old men close to the openings so that they may get out easily."

The heart hung by only a very small piece of muscle and Coyote was cutting away on it with his last stone knife. The monster's heart was still barely hanging when Coyote's last knife broke; Coyote threw himself on the heart and hung on, just barely tearing it loose with his hands. In his death convulsions the monster opened all the openings of his body and the people kicked the bones outside and went out. Coyote, too, went out. The monster fell dead and the anus began to close. But the muskrat was still inside. Just as the anus closed he squeezed out, barely getting his body through. But alas! his tail was caught; he pulled and it was bare when he pulled it out; all the tail hair had been peeled right off. Coyote scolded him, "Now what were you doing; you had to think up something to do at the last moment. You're always behind in everything."

Then he told the people, "Gather up all the bones and arrange them well." They did this, whereupon Coyote added, "Now we are going to carve the monster." Coyote then smeared blood on his hands, sprinkled this blood on the bones, and suddenly there came to life again all those who had died while inside the monster. They carved the great monster and Coyote began dealing out portions of the body to various parts of the country all over the land: toward the sunrise, toward the sunset, toward the warmth, toward the cold, and by that act destining and forenaming the various peoples—Coeur d'Alene, Cayuse, Pend Oreilles, Flathead, Blackfeet, Crow, Sioux, and all the others. He consumed the entire body of the monster in this distribution to various lands far and wide. Nothing more remained of the great monster.

Fox came up and said to Coyote, "What is the meaning of this, Coyote? You have distributed all of the body to faraway lands but have given yourself nothing for this immediate locality." "Well," snorted Coyote, "and did you tell me that before? Why didn't you tell me that a while ago before it was too late? I was engrossed to the exclusion of thinking. You should have told me that in the first place." And he turned to the people and said, "Bring me some water with which to wash my hands." They brought him water and he washed his hands and now with the bloody washwater he sprinkled the local regions saying, "You may be little people but you will be powerful. Even though you will be little people because I have deprived you, nevertheless you will be very, very, manly. Only a short time away is the coming of the human race."

"You will have lots of blood and blood soup."

2

KILLER MOSQUITO

THERE ONCE LIVED five mosquito brothers and their grandmother. They used to wander around, sucking the blood out of people and killing them. They were killers. The people were troubled. "How can we do it, how can we kill them all?" One of them suggested, "Let's make a strong lodging."

And that's what they did. They invited the mosquitoes to that place. "You will have lots of blood and blood soup," and the mosquitoes all came. They ate the soup and got filled up. The youngest was suspicious: "Something is up," and he tried to find out. "There is one opening, which is just large enough for me to get out." So he didn't eat much, and when the people set fire to the place, he got out and flew away. "One got away!" the people yelled, "The youngest got away!" The rest of the brothers and the grandmother were burned.

From the mud bath, the youngest heard something and said, "My brothers are exploding." He counted four explosions, and the last sound was the grandmother, who made a hissing noise: Just "*chisss*"! "Oh! My grandmother exploded." He hid himself at the mud bath. The people looked for him and found him hiding there, but they did not go in after him for he would suck their blood. They poked at him with twigs, but Mosquito dampened the twigs with some red paint that he had. He smeared the bush with it in several places. They said, "We have killed him." Then they left, and he told himself, "There is no reason for me to stay here."

He made a raft and went downriver on it. He sang as he went, "This is my grandmother's wandering place. This is where my grandmother spent her days, where she wandered around." He cried as he went. Then the people knew that the mosquito boy was coming down on the raft. They called out, "Mosquito! Drift ashore! Here you'll have biscuit roots, mush, and other things." He answered them, "Those are the very things that cause my diarrhea." Then one

---

(Recited by Watters; originally published in Aoki and Walker, 1989. See also "Mosquito and Coyote" in Phinney, 1934.)

of the people said, "Why tell him that? Mosquitoes never eat such things. Just tell him to come ashore for some blood soup." "Oh yes!" he said in Flathead, and then he pulled himself ashore. He came in, and the blood soup was set before him.

The people had prepared sharp grass, and they put it on either side of the aisle. If he were to run out that way, the rye grass would cut him up. When Mosquito had had plenty to eat, he got up and got ready, and he flew away in that direction. He looked ahead, "That's where I'm going out through." Just before he went through, the point of the rye grass split his belly—poof! Making a humming sound, he flew on to the mountains. Coyote hollered after him, "You will never be a killer again. People will say that mosquitoes are all around the mountains or meadows. They will be afraid of you. You will cling to them. That's the way you will spend your days. You will never be killers again. You'll never kill all the people."

From then on, mosquitoes have been found throughout the mountains—or else, if they are around the rivers first, then they go off to the mountains. Since then that is the way they have lived.

3

COYOTE DEFEATS
THE SUN

ONCE UPON A TIME, when Coyote was wandering around, he came upon a tribe of gophers. The gophers were all baking camas, carrying them under their armpits. They sensed that someone was around, and so they all ran into the house. Coyote waited outside for a long time, and finally he caught one of the gophers.

With an arrowhead that he had, Coyote cut out eye slits on both sides of Gopher's face. Suddenly Gopher's eyes blinked, and he was able to see. He shouted to his friends, "You come too! He made eyes for me!" "What? Eyes?" they asked, bewildered. "I can see lots of things," he tried to explain. Still, they could not understand what he meant, and the confused questioning continued for a long time. Finally Coyote made eyes for each of them, and afterward he taught them how to bake camas properly. They cooked them the way he had told them, and afterward they ate lots and lots, rejoicing over the food. After they had finished eating, Coyote told them all that his great desire was to get to where the sun was.

By and by Coyote got married to five sisters in the gopher tribe. He ordered his brides to make a road for him underground so that he could get to the sun. He directed them to make air holes every so often from the passage for him to breathe through. Finally it was finished, and Coyote set off on his journey, taking with him his dog X̲at'xat'ílac. Coyote fastened arrowheads all over the dog's body. He knew that Sun also had a pet grizzly bear-dog. Also, Sun's father was living with him. Whenever Sun would bring back his kill, the father would bite off its genitals and eat them raw.

Coyote finally arrived at the place where Sun was living. He found Sun lying in wait for his victims, with his back to Coyote. Coyote approached him,

---

(Recited by Watters; originally published in Aoki and Walker, 1989. See also "The Sun and the Moon" in Spinden, 1917.)

"You first, brother," Coyote offered, *"then I'll drink too."*

"Brother!" he exclaimed, startling Sun. "Brother, you're in the wrong place. You'll never catch anything here! Your father and my father used to sit over there, where the fire was, to wait for their victims."

Coyote took Sun to the place he had described. "Here it is, right here. Look—there they go." Coyote had previously planned to have his excrement children travel along that road.

"They'll pass you by that way. Here's the place where we used to build fires. They used these things to build the fires, and arrowheads and other things are here." Coyote started digging, and he dug up lots of things.

"Sure enough!" Sun exclaimed, surprised. He couldn't imagine how those things could have been dug up or how they got there, since he had been there all the time, from the beginning of time.

Just then Coyote suggested that they go on a chase. As they went along Coyote used his magic to make a spring with water purified by gravel. "Here is a spring!" shouted Coyote when they came upon it. It looked good, and Coyote suggested that they have a drink.

"You first, brother," Coyote offered, "then I'll drink too."

Sun was about to put down his club, but Coyote told him, "No, wait, brother! The way our fathers did this was to hold the club for each other."

So Coyote held the club, and just as Sun was stooping down to take a drink, Coyote clubbed him again and again until finally Sun was dead. He made a rumbling sound, "*Hulululu*," as he died.

Coyote went back and told his friend Fox that he had killed Sun. Then he carried Sun home, and he changed into Sun's clothes. Again he used his magic to transform himself into the image of Sun.

Then Coyote, disguised as Sun, carried Sun back to Sun's father's house. As usual, the first thing the father did was to cut the genitals off the victim and eat them raw.

"Pah! That was sort of bitter!" Sun's father complained.

Then they both went into the house to go to bed. There, lying around in a circle, were the skulls of former victims. The old man and Sun had killed many.

Coyote lay uneasily in bed, on his back, waiting until the old man began to snore. Finally he did, and at that point Coyote made up his mind to leave. He got ready and left, and he walked until daybreak. At that time Coyote thought that he must have come a long way, and he decided to go to sleep.

Meanwhile, just at daybreak, Sun's father stepped outside to urinate. Right there, in front of him, was Coyote, still disguised as Sun.

"Why would my son be sleeping here at the dancing ground?" he wondered. "Young man," he said to his son, "I feel death around here."

This same thing occurred the next night, and the next, and the next, for five nights." I don't think I'll ever get out of here," despaired Coyote. Each night he traveled till daybreak, went to sleep, and woke up to find himself in front of the door. Then Coyote came up with a plan. He decided to cut the old man's head off while he was asleep. And that's just what he did. When he got through cutting the head off, Coyote exclaimed, "They will say this about you [Sun], 'This is the daytime sun.' The sun will be traveling and will not kill anyone any more."

Then Coyote said, "I'll return to my old form as Coyote. This old man will become the night-time sun [moon], and no longer will he do anything to anybody, nor will he eat anything raw again. The humans will be coming soon." That's all.

4

COYOTE AND FLINT

ONCE UPON A TIME Coyote and Fox were living there, and Coyote had five children, all boys. The Flint tribe was also living around there. Coyote used to leave in the springtime for the north, returning after his spring stay.

Flint Man was the kind who would kill anything that annoyed him or got in his way. Nothing could do him any harm. That's how he was. When Coyote left for the north, leaving his children behind, Flint Man killed all of Coyote's children, leaving Coyote alone in the world. Fox did have one daughter, however, who was married.

When Fox was returning to the south, he met this Flint Man. He gave Fox some flint out of which Fox made an arrowhead. Fox gave that arrowhead to his son-in-law, who put it in a secret place. Whenever the son-in-law would kill a deer with it, Fox would rush over immediately to the bloody wound because the precious arrowhead was there. After some time, Coyote became suspicious of what Fox was doing. "I wonder why he's doing that," Coyote mused. "Something's fishy!"

So Coyote planned to wait and see what this was all about. Soon the son-in-law came in with his kill, and Coyote made a mad dash for it before Fox could get there. Coyote grabbed the meat, and in spite of Fox's protests that the meat was his, Coyote told him, "This is my kind of meat! Do you think you're the only one who has a right to eat this bloody part? I want it too!"

Fox kept on trying to get the meat from Coyote, but he could not get it. Coyote kept pushing him away, shouting, "Get away! Get out of here!" Finally Fox gave up, and Coyote cooked the meat and began eating it. All of a sudden he bit into something hard.

"What's this?" he exclaimed, and he took it out. It was the arrowhead. He turned angrily to Fox, saying, "So! The person who gave you this is the one who's caused me to be alone in the world. Why didn't you tell me that he'd been here!"

(Recited by Watters; originally published in Aoki and Walker, 1989.)

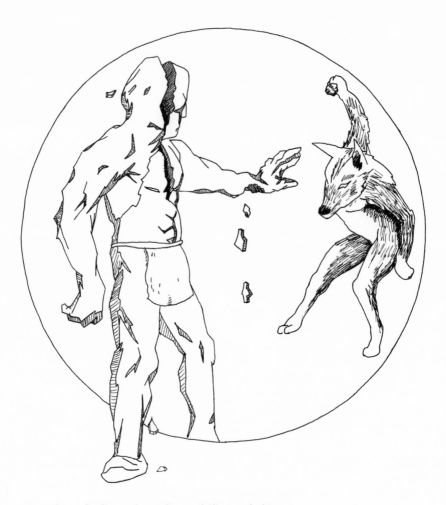

Coyote began hurling rocks at Flint, and Flint cracked in two.

Coyote stormed at Fox, "When did he pass by here? Tell me exactly when, what month?" Fox told Coyote when the Flint Man had been there. Coyote, upon hearing this, quickly told his wife to make him some moccasins and get him ready. He was about to depart, and he asked Fox the direction that Flint Man had taken.

"He went that way," Fox answered. "There's the trail." So Coyote followed the tracks and went that way. The trail finally led him right across the Snake River, and there was Flint. Coyote caught up with him and he followed Flint over several ridges, some distance behind him. Coyote slouched down low and crawled after Flint, standing up occasionally for an instant. Flint sensed something, and he called out to Coyote, "Coyote! What are you skulking about, stooping down like that for? Stand up! Let's fight, come on!" Flint repeated this several times as he went along, Coyote still crouching behind. Finally, Flint thought to himself, "I guess there's nothing around here after all."

Flint was afraid of Coyote because he had killed all of Coyote's children and he was sure that Coyote would try to take revenge on him. Coyote picked up some rocks and put them inside his shirt under the belt.

Flint, however, made a crown of straw, covered himself with grass, and lay on his stomach. He thought to himself, "Coyote will be going through here somewhere." When Coyote did pass over there, Flint stood up and again called out, "Coyote! Stand up! Come here and fight! Why are you stooping down?"

Coyote held back without getting up, and he lay still. After this had happened several times, Flint thought again that Coyote must not be around after all. So Flint started to go over the ridge, and as he was passing close by to where Coyote lay, Coyote suddenly jumped up. He began hurling his rocks at Flint, hitting Flint so hard that finally he split him open, and Flint cracked in two.

Coyote was going around in a circle, and Flint himself was turning too. Coyote kept splitting him up that way. Finally Flint gave up, and he thought, "It's no use." Coyote threw himself at Flint harder, finally splitting Flint in two. Flint fell back dead, and Coyote gave a war cry.

Meanwhile Coyote's friend Fox was in the house and, hearing the noise, cried out, "Now my friend Coyote made that noise. He has killed him." Those nearby told Fox, "How do you know? Whichever of the two made the noise, he did the killing."

From there Coyote packed up his killing, which he had cracked, and in places where the pack was rotten it felt different. Coyote noticed the rotten places and he threw out what was rotten. He threw out a little as he went along.

This is why you come across such pieces of flint along the way [near Huntington, Oregon]. This is how it is to be explained. It was thrown there by Coyote. And that's how Coyote revenged himself and killed the Flint Man.

Magpie told Coyote, "Run and get a hold of that white feather. Pull it down and you will kill them."

5

COYOTE AND
HUMMINGBIRD

COYOTE WENT UPRIVER. He was always wandering around, and he went upriver. Then suddenly he heard, "Whoever is going upriver, let us kill one another." Coyote said, "What?" Then again, "Whoever is going upriver, let us kill one another." Coyote said, "Yes. I wonder who he is."

Then something surprised him and hit him on the head—it was a hummingbird. It quickly killed him and he dropped dead. It picked him up and threw him into the river, and he drifted down one bend and a half, and then he drifted ashore. There Magpie was flying around. "Oh, there's Coyote. What has happened to the poor thing?" He landed near him and started to peck at his eyes. Coyote woke up, "Ah ahaah ah . . . Oh, you disturbed me. I was just helping some girls get across the headwaters. I was helping a chief's daughter get across in a canoe. You disturbed me."

Then Magpie said, "Oh! Who were you helping across where? That hummingbird upriver killed you. The hummingbirds live up on the hill, and they have a white feather hanging from a tree there, high up. That's their heart. Now you will go upriver, and again they will say twice, 'Whoever is going upriver, let's kill each other.' As soon as they say it the second time, you answer, 'Ho!' and go up as fast as you can, speeding up to where the white thing shines. Meanwhile Hummingbird will be dashing down. You will rush as fast as you can. Run and get a hold of that white feather. Pull it down and you will kill them. That's their heart." Then Coyote said, "That's what I already thought. That's just what I thought I would do." Magpie said, "You never did think anything like that. Go on. You just do it right; otherwise they will kill you again."

And Coyote went upriver again. Then he heard them: "Whoever goes upriver, let's kill one another." "Ho!" he said, and he sped up and ran. The

(Recited by Wilson; originally published in Aoki and Walker, 1989. See also "Coyote and Humming Bird" in Phinney, 1934.)

hummingbirds were there, and they said, "Oh! Coyote has come back!" Coyote was almost to the feather. Then he quickly grabbed it and broke it, and they fell on their backs. He had killed the hummingbirds. That is one job that Coyote worked on. That's all.

▼▼▼▼▼

6

KILLER BUTTERFLY

ONCE AGAIN I will tell a short story about Butterfly. Coyote went upriver. He saw and heard something as he went, and he turned around. There Butterfly was opening and closing herself. "Oh, what's that?" Then he went toward her, and there was Butterfly, a good-looking Indian girl, and she flirted and giggled. Coyote was taken in by her, and then she put her arms around him and suddenly closed in on him with her legs. Even though he struggled, she killed him.

When Butterfly realized who she had killed, she said, "Oh, it's just Coyote." Then she dragged him and threw him into the river, and he drifted down one bend and a half. Magpie, who was flying upriver, said, "Oh, poor Coyote has drifted down there. I wonder what happened." He flew down and started to peck at Coyote's eye. Coyote spoke, "You awakened me while I was helping girls across at the head of the waters." "Why? where? what?" Magpie said to him. "It was Butterfly who killed you upriver there. She is nothing more than a killer—that Butterfly. It's impossible to kill her. She kills whoever passes by there and goes down. She kills all of them. Don't go there again." "That's what I thought. I knew that all along," Coyote replied.

Then Coyote went upriver, and he hit his hip. His children jumped out and started to play. He said to them, "Come on, come back in," but he blocked the youngest out. He asked him, "Son, what shall I do? Tell me." And the youngest said to him, "She is a killer. If you don't follow my advice, she will kill you again. Go to her there, hug her and make love. Then push back what she used to trap you with. Push them back—way back. That's the only way you can kill her. That's what you should do." "That's what I already had in mind," Coyote said.

Then Coyote went upriver. He was prepared when he saw her there. She was opening and closing, and he went to her. The girl flirted and giggled. Then

(Recited by Wilson; originally published in Aoki and Walker, 1989. See also "Coyote and Butterfly" in Phinney, 1934.)

When Butterfly realized who she had killed, she said, "Oh, it's just Coyote," and she threw him into the river.

Coyote hugged her, and just when she was about to trap him with her legs, Coyote grabbed them and pushed them backward. Then poor Butterfly dropped dead. Coyote said, "People are coming soon. You will not be a danger to them, Butterfly. You will be flying around and will be harmless from now on. You will not be dangerous." That's all I told.

▼▼▼▼▼

7

MUSSEL-SHELL KILLERS

COYOTE WENT UPRIVER. I am going to tell the story the way my ancestors used to tell it, even though some of the words are not proper for polite hearing. Nevertheless, I am going to tell it that way.

Coyote went upriver. Suddenly he heard someone calling him. "I wonder where she is." "Come and sleep with me," she said. "What is she saying?" Coyote went down to the water where Mussel-Shell Woman was opening and shutting it. Coyote was taken in. Mussel-Shell Woman grabbed him. No matter how much Coyote cried, it was no use. Mussel-Shell just squeezed tighter. Thus Coyote was squeezed to death.

"Oh, it's nobody, just Coyote," Mussel-Shell Woman said. Then she threw him in the water, and Coyote drifted down one bend and a half. Then he drifted ashore. Magpie was flying by there. "Oh! That's Coyote. Why is he lying ashore there? It's just like him." Then Magpie flew down to him and started to peck at Coyote's eye fat. He woke Coyote up. Coyote said to him, "You are disturbing me. I was helping girls across at the head of creeks, and you spoiled it for me." "There isn't anyone anywhere. Just upriver from here, a Mussel-Shell killed you," Magpie said. "Don't pay any attention to her and keep going. Pass by and keep going."

In this way Coyote continued upriver. He hit his hip, and his excrement children ran out. They started to play, but Coyote said to them, "Come in, come in." He asked the youngest, "What shall I do?" The youngest answered, "She is just a killer from long ago. Don't pay any attention to her. Just keep going, and she will give up. You will be able to go on." Then he went back in.

Soon Coyote heard, "You there! Come this way and sleep with me." Coyote didn't pay any attention to her. Nevertheless, she caught up with him, as Coyote was passing by.

(Recited by Wilson; originally published in Aoki and Walker, 1989. See also Watters's "Warmweather and Coldweather" in the same volume and "Coyote's Wars" in Spinden, 1917.)

Then he heard something splash, and it splashed and stuck to his face. He grabbed it and threw it away, and he heard a splash again. He grabbed the thing, saying, "Now, I'm going to eat it. What is this thing?" Then he roasted it and ate it. Suddenly all his teeth fell out. He became thirsty, and when he drank, his teeth suddenly fell out. I am connecting this to the story I told about the five goose brothers and their sister. The brothers told their sister, "Whoever comes, he will be your husband." To that story I am adding this. That's all.

▼▼▼▼▼

8

KILLER BABY

COYOTE WENT UPRIVER. He was busy doing nothing. He was just going upriver when he heard a baby cry. Then he quickly turned around and went downriver from there. "Oh, a cute child is sitting there. What are you doing? Where is your mother? What? how? . . ." But the child just cried. Coyote went up to him and said, "Let me carry you on my back. Let's look for your mother." Coyote sat down, and he picked up the child. He walked on for a while, and the child tightened his grip on Coyote. Even though Coyote cried, "Stop, stop, stop," the child didn't, and Coyote dropped dead. Coyote swished his tail as he dropped dead.

Then the child picked him up, "Oh, it's just Coyote." He dragged him down to the water. Coyote drifted down one bend and a half and floated ashore there. Magpie came upon him. "Look what happened to Coyote. He never does things right." He flew down toward him and started to peck at Coyote's eye. "I will eat eye fat." Then Coyote awakened and said, "You are bothering me. I was at the head of the rivers. I was helping some girls get across." "What?" said Magpie. "A killer child killed you upriver. Don't ever listen to him again." Then Coyote said, "That's just what I thought."

Coyote hit his hip, and his children ran out. The youngest, Cicéqi, said, "Do this. Don't ever listen to the child, even though he will cry soon. Blink your eyes at him and pass on. Keep going until you are safe. If you stop there again, then he will kill you." "Yes, now go back in for good," Coyote said. Then Coyote went upriver, and again he heard a child crying as he went. "Oh, such bothersome crying," Coyote said. "I'm not going to listen to it." Then he walked on, and he didn't listen to it as he went on upriver. Thus he saved himself. The child would kill all those who passed by there. He was a killer. That's all.

(Recited by Wilson; originally published in Aoki and Walker, 1989. See also Watters's "Warmweather and Coldweather" in the same volume.)

9

FROG AND COYOTE

THERE WAS A FROG WIDOW who was maltreated and became angry. So she went up the river to the source and sat over the fountain-head, so that the entire river went dry. There was no water except in some deep holes. The people had not missed her; but Coyote thought something like this must have happened to make the river go dry. He went upstream because he knew the place where the water had been stopped. As he traveled up the dry bed, he made five rafts and placed them about five bends of the river apart.

At the head of the river he saw a lodge. He was nearly dead of thirst when he arrived, so he entered the lodge. Inside he saw a bucket made of the horn of a mountain sheep and it was filled with water; and he said to the woman, "Pass that water to me; I have drunk a great deal of water along the river today, still I am very dry." So he drank up all the water.

Coyote lay down on the opposite side of the lodge from the woman and covered his head with his blanket. But he had an eye hole in the blanket; and he saw her rise, take the empty bucket, and dip up water from where she had been sitting. After this, Coyote arose and went out.

Near that place he spat upon some tule rushes and told them to give war whoops after he had re-entered the lodge. So he went again into the lodge, and soon there was a great noise of war whoops. He said out loud to himself, "I thought I heard something when I was outside." But for all his strategy, the frog widow would not budge from where she sat. So Coyote seized her by the arm and jerked her up. Then the water came out. When the water was running freely, he threw the woman into the stream, saying, "This is the way you will always be: whenever high water comes, it will always carry frogs down the river."

Coyote then started downstream, running as fast as he could. When he reached the place of the first raft, he found it had broken adrift. So he ran on

(Originally published in Spinden, 1917.)

When the water was running freely, he threw the woman into the stream.

to the next one and found it also adrift; and the third the same, and the fourth. He reached the fifth, however, just as it was breaking loose, and managed to jump aboard. Then he went down the river on the raft. This is how Coyote recovered the water from Frog.

▼▼▼▼▼

10

FROG AND BLUEJAY

Frog had a smooth pole set in the ground, and with it she had devised a means of killing off all the birds. A race would be run up the pole, and whoever got to the top first would cut off the other one's head. The pole leaned a little; and Frog would get on the upper side and make the opponent get on the underside. Thus, Frog continued to win races for a long time and managed to kill off many birds.

Coyote was in the camp. He became afraid that Frog was going to kill off all the birds. So Coyote gave a big feast and invited everyone to attend. He wanted the people to work out a plan to get the best of Frog, but everyone was afraid to run a race against Frog. After a scheme had been devised, Bluejay undertook the job; and Coyote made a speech, calling everybody to the pole and announcing that there was to be a race between Frog and Bluejay.

Little Frog became uneasy and feared that Bluejay was going to win and then kill her. So when they were half-way to the top, Frog tried to kick Bluejay off the pole. When they were nearly to the top, Bluejay used his wings and flew the rest of the way. He got to the top first. When Frog got to the top, Bluejay kicked her, and she fell to the ground and was killed. Ever since that race there have been no feathers on the side of Bluejay's face because Frog had torn them all off when she tried to knock Bluejay from the pole.

After the race was over, Coyote made a speech, saying, "Hereafter, there will be frogs on the earth, but they will never hurt anyone. People will hear the frogs singing, and then they will know that warm weather is coming."

(Originally published in Spinden, 1917.)

▼▼▼▼▼

11

CANNIBAL

THE PEOPLE were living all over but they often gathered together. It was their custom to go hunting every morning. And when they brought home meat, they distributed it to each other, to everyone. Nobody went hungry. There were five brothers. The oldest had a wife. The other four were single. All five went hunting together.

One day they went out to hunt. The oldest shot a deer high up in the mountains. The wounded deer ran down the hill. The man chased it. It came to the canyon and he butchered it there. He cut himself. Blood came out, and perhaps with some smearing of his own blood, he ate that meat. He tasted his own blood, and then somehow his own blood made him change. It made him think differently. It tasted different and better than the other meat. He searched around for this different meat. He found blood running and thought, "This must be it," and he cut himself and ate his meat. Saying, "This is it," he ate. Then he ate himself clean down to the bones. Finally he became only bones. Though he had started to butcher the deer, he just let it lie there.

In the evening the people returned from the hunt, and the younger brother said, "Our oldest brother is missing. He has not come back. Make an announcement now." Then the camp crier went around on foot. "Oldest brother is missing. Somehow he got lost. Tomorrow early in the morning, we will go and look for him. All of you get ready."

The next morning everyone got ready, including the four remaining brothers. They went up the ridge to where they had hunted. They hollered around the ridges. The oldest one had eaten himself, and the next older brother was looking for his oldest brother. The second brother was the one who had seen his oldest brother last. He shouted everywhere, "Older brother, older brother." Then the oldest said, "Ho," from the canyon below. "Older brother!" "Ho, come here below, younger brother," he said. Then the second brother went down. Quickly he thought, "I wonder how my brother is." He met him, and his

(Recited by Wilson; originally published in Aoki and Walker, 1989.)

brother was all bloody. Even though the younger brother wheeled around and ran, the oldest brother was too fast. The oldest brother caught up with him in a little while. He had made a rope of intestines, and he caught up with him and lassoed his leg. Then he dragged his brother there and killed him. He ate him and piled up the leftover bones.

Now the second brother failed to return, and again they made an an-nouncement. "The brother failed to return. Tomorrow the third brother will go look for the second. He will climb up and look for him." Early in the morn-ing the boy woke up. Then he went on uphill in the same way. "Older brother! Older brother!" He was hollering. Then the oldest answered, "Ho, younger brother, come here. I am down here." "Thanks, my older brother. I found him." Then he ran fast. In the same way he met him and saw that he was all bones. His heart was clearly hanging out. He was quite ugly to look at. The boy wheeled around quickly, but even though he ran, the oldest brother lassoed him with the rope of intestines. He caught him easily. Then he dragged him and took him home. There again he killed his younger brother—his second younger brother.

When the second younger brother failed to return, the people said, "Some-thing is happening. Another brother is now missing. I wonder if they are tak-ing care of one another. The fourth will go look for him tomorrow. He will go by himself. No one will follow." Thus the third brother went out alone. He went early in the morning. He left there, saying, "I will find all my brothers and see what they are doing. Perhaps they got in an accident and are caring for each other." Then he went up the ridges, and he went over to the mountains. He hollered around the ridge, "Older brother, older brother." "Ho, here we are. Come to us." Then the poor boy ran down. In the same way they met there, and the oldest brother took a rope of intestines. Even though the boy ran, he lassoed him and caught him securely. Then he took him home, and he killed him in the same way. He ate from his bones, and then he piled up the brother's bones.

When the fourth brother failed to come home, the people asked, "What is happening? Maybe they are working on something. Now the youngest will go tomorrow early in the morning." "Somehow I will find them." The boy went in the morning. Before dawn he went on up the ridges. He went up and broke Meadowlark's leg. "Oh!" he said, "I broke your leg, Aunt. Can you tell me what happened to my older brothers? I am looking for them? Do you know any-thing, Aunt Meadowlark? I will make a hardwood leg for you, and your leg will heal. Tell me everything."

"Yes," said Meadowlark. "Your oldest brother first went hunting and killed a deer there. The wounded deer went down below and he chased it. He butchered it there. He tasted his own blood, and it made him crazy somehow. Finally he ate himself to the bones, and he is horrible looking. Then your older brothers went. First, he answered when they shouted, and then they went down. Then your oldest brother lassoed them with a rope of intestines. With that he lassoed them and ate them all to bones. Now just bones are piled there. Your oldest brother did this to all of them. No one is there now. Your oldest brother is quite horrible looking. He has eaten himself. His beating heart is visible. He is quite vicious, quick, and strong. I am telling you that there is a high mountaintop where there is flint. Make many sharp pieces. Tie flint all over so that there are very sharp points on both sides of your legs. When he lassoes you, run fast so that the flint will cut up the intestines." "Thank you." Then he made a leg for Meadowlark. He repaired the leg, and the poor one left. Then he made many sharp pieces of flint. He tied them all over on his legs. Then he went. He thought, "My oldest brother is vicious, and my older brothers are now gone."

The youngest brother went up the ridges to look for his older brothers. When he came, there he hollered, "Older brothers, older brothers." "Ho, here we are below," the oldest answered. "Come on down here. Here we are." Slowly the youngest one went down. He did not run down as his older brothers had. He was watching out, thinking, "Maybe in a little while I will still be alive or maybe my oldest brother will kill me." He walked slowly. Then he met him, "My oldest brother is so ugly looking." The oldest brother took a rope of intestines, and even though the youngest wheeled around quickly and ran, the oldest brother caught up with him. He felt the rope trapping him. He went as fast as he could, but the rope almost made him fall. He gave strength to his legs and ran on up. He tore the rope into pieces. Oldest brother shouted after him, "You escaped, youngest brother. You got away." The youngest brother used all his strength, and he ran on up.

He came back and told the people, "I found my oldest brother. He has eaten himself. He is ugly and scary to look at. He has killed all his younger brothers. He is very vicious and may come here. He will kill us all."

Then Coyote made an announcement. "Tomorrow we will go east. The youngest brother found out that his oldest brother has eaten himself, and he is horrible to look at. If we stay here, he will kill us all." "Ho," they said.

Then it became dawn and they took down each of their tepees and got themselves ready. They came to the wife of the oldest brother and said, "Now we are going." She had a small child who was only just sitting up. They said, "Now we are going. Your husband is surely vicious." "No," she told them, "I am staying. I will wait for him. My child and I will be here. We won't go from here. He will come to us somehow. We will wait here." They gave up trying to convince her and all of them moved downriver. Only the woman's tepee was left. There she and the child spent their days alone.

One day, she heard him coming when it was almost midday. "Oh, what did I hear?" and she listened. Then she heard, "I wonder if Fir People's maidens will hear me. He killed and ate his brothers. *Hi hi hi* [his bones were making noise]. I wonder if Fir People's maidens will hear. Oh, he killed and ate his brothers. *Hi hi hi*," and his wife became scared. She looked out and saw him coming. He was ugly to look at. She came in and sat down, holding the child in her arms.

In a little while, he looked in and came in and sat down. Blood was flowing, and his heart was visible. "Oh, where is the child? Give it to me now." Then she was scared, and she handed the poor baby to her husband. "Just one swallow," he sang. He said, "You are just enough for a swallow. I will eat you in one swallow." The woman was scared. She said, "Hand it over for a little while. It is dirty. Let me go and clean it. Let me have it for a little while." There was a big wooden spoon lying near the doorway. She picked it up quickly as she went. Then she took the child down. She thrashed the willows there and spat on them. She told them, "When he calls me, you answer him, 'Ho ho,' Willows." "All right," they said. Then she took the wooden spoon to the river. "Become a canoe!" The spoon turned into a big canoe. She got into the canoe. She took the child and pushed herself away from the shore. She went downstream in the canoe and went out into the main stream.

Meanwhile, Cannibal [lit. Fir Person] had become impatient. "Quick, where are you? Come!" He heard the willows saying, "Ho ho." He thought, "They must still be there." When they failed to come, he called out again, "Come quickly." "Ho," the willows answered. Then the husband thought, "That doesn't quite sound like my wife." So he ran out. No one was around. "Oh, where did she go?" Then he went around shouting, and he saw the willows and realized that the willows had said, "Ho." He took a huge stick, and he beat the poor willows. He beat them to shreds. Then he went on up. Then he thought, "Now I am going after them."

Meanwhile the woman had gone downstream in the canoe until she came to the rest of the band, and she told them, "He is quite ferocious. Soon he will come after us. We barely escaped." Then Coyote made a plan. "I wonder how we can be ready for him." The young crane was not very big. He said to them, "Carry me to Magpie Bend and dig a hole there and bury me so that my knees will be sticking out just this much. Cover me with dirt." "All right." Then they carried him and made a hole just long enough to put Crane down in it. They left his knees sticking out when they covered him. There was a hole that he could breathe through by turning his head. He remained covered there for quite some time.

Then the people heard the oldest brother from afar, and Crane heard him coming too. "I wonder where Fir People's maidens are. Oh, he killed and ate his brothers. *Hi hi hi,*" [the bones were making noise while he moved]. I wonder if Fir-People's maidens will hear. Oh, he killed and ate his brothers. *Hi hi hi.*" Again there was the sound of dry bones. Crane was afraid. He almost jumped and ran away, but he lay still. Then he heard him coming closer, and Crane felt him sitting down, "Oh, my brother. What happened?" Cannibal felt Crane. He was still looking for a knife. Then Crane took out his legs and kicked him down over the cliff. All the bones of Cannibal fell down with him. Crane followed him with his eyes. The bones scattered and killed Cannibal, and Crane went home. He told the people, "Now he is gone." Crane told the people how Cannibal met his death. People used to live here on the land across from where you go around Magpie Bend. Near Nikise there is a cliff where Crane kicked Cannibal down. That's all.

At first Coyote thought, "He will never kill me."

▼▼▼▼▼

12

BLINDWORM KILLER

Coyote went upriver. He was just wandering; he was relaxing and wandering around. Then he came upon a tepee, and inside somebody was making noise. He heard: "One stick, two sticks, three sticks, four sticks, five sticks . . ." and on to the tenth. That is what the voice said. "My, what could it be?" Coyote said. He peeked in and an old man was counting these long things, a little longer than the bone sticks used in the gambling game. He was counting them and putting them down.

"Oh, wonderful!" said Coyote, and he grabbed one, and again the old one counted. One stick, two sticks, three sticks, four . . . ," he counted. "Oh, only nine sticks, not ten sticks. Why?" He looked for the missing one. Then he counted again and again Coyote took one. He counted, "One stick, two sticks, . . . Oh, now two sticks are missing! What happened?" And he looked for the missing sticks. He thought, "How [did I lose two sticks?]" And then he thought, "There is someone here," and Coyote saw him put the sticks down. The old man took out a parfleche, and out of it he took a rope and laced up the tepee door very tightly, so that nothing could run out.

"How wonderful," thought Coyote. "What is he doing?" Again he saw him pulling out another parfleche, and he took a big club out of it. "What is he doing?" thought Coyote. "How marvelous." Then the blindworm started hitting the ground: *Kux kux.* Coyote was dodging, *trrr,* he made himself brave. He was showing his bravery by jumping. He was hard to catch. "Nothing will touch me, *trrr,*" he said, and the worm went on hitting. He could hear Coyote over that way. At first Coyote thought, "He will never kill me." But finally he got tired. He could hardly move, and then the old man hit Coyote's leg, and then again, and Coyote dropped dead. And then the old man felt Coyote and said, "Oh, it was just Coyote." And he dragged him to the river and threw him in.

(Recited by Wilson; originally published in Aoki and Walker, 1989. See also "The Log Worm" in Spinden, 1908.)

Coyote drifted down one bend and a half, and then he drifted ashore. Magpie was flying around, and he saw him, "Oh, poor Coyote, what happened?" He came down and pecked on his eye: *Kaw kaw.* Coyote muttered, "Eh, oh, oh? You woke me. I was helping some girls across, upriver there, and you spoiled it. You're no good. I was helping them across at the head of the river." Then Magpie said, "Oh? Where was that? It was a blindworm that killed you upriver. Now you do this, and do it right this time."

Before he went on, Coyote hit his hip and his children ran out. Then they told him what to do. "When he counts the sticks, you should have some pitch ready, or something like that. Then you should grab his sticks and run outside. And he will count them again as before and notice a stick is missing. Then you take the second one. He will lace up the door securely with rawhide rope as before. And when you hear him going *kux kux,* jump around outside saying, *trrr.* He'll keep pounding, thinking, 'He's still inside.' Finally, while he's doing that, you set fire to his tepee. Even if he cries to get out, you already have a stick, and you poke him back in with that. In this way you can kill him." "That's what I thought," Coyote said, and then the children ran back in.

Then Coyote went upriver. And then he heard, as he went, "One stick, two sticks, three sticks," all the way to ten. Coyote came in and grabbed one; he took one, and he went outside. Then the worm counted. "Now again one is missing. Someone is here." Then he put his sticks down and pulled out a parfleche. He took out rawhide rope and laced up the door. And he pulled out another parfleche and took out a war club. And he moved around hitting: *kux kux.* Now Coyote went *trrr trrr* outside, and poor blindworm kept hitting. Then Coyote set fire to the tepee, and it burned up.

Then Coyote said, "All this time you have been killing many of the legendary people. Now human beings will come soon, and you will have no power. You will be just something that grows in rotten tree stumps. You will be nothing." That's all.

13

COYOTE BREAKS
THE FISH DAM
AT CELILO

THEY LIVED in an encampment between the Salmon River and where the Snake River goes up. This place is known as Joseph Plains. There Coyote and others lived and wandered around.

At first there were Coyote and his wife and their son. Their son had two wives, one white and the other black. The white one was a duck, and the black one was a cricket. Duck had no children, but Cricket had a son.

Then Coyote deliberated, "I am going to get rid of my son." One morning he asked his son to accompany him. "Let's go and catch eaglets. We'll climb where the eagles have their nest."

And that's what they did. They came to the foot of a tree. They looked, thinking, "There are eaglets up there." Now before the son climbed up, he took off his clothes and set them down. Then he started up and said, "Don't look up after me, Father!" The young man climbed, and Coyote judged when he would just be reaching the nest, and then he snapped his eyes up at him—or, in our language, it is also, "He looked up." So the nest shot farther up. The son told his father, "You looked up." "I just slipped accidentally, son," Coyote said. And his son climbed on up. Thus finally he was way up, and it was not easy for

---

(Recited by Watters; originally published in Aoki and Walker, 1989. For versions of various segments of this narrative, see Wilson's "The Five Swallows and Coyote" and "How Coyote Got Rid of His Son" in the same volume; "Coyote His Son He Caused To Be Lost" and "Coyote and His Anus" in Phinney, 1934; "How Salmon Got Over the Falls" and "Coyote and Salmon" in Spinden, 1908.)

Coyote came to the dam and tore it loose here and there.

him to talk to his father. Coyote looked up after him, and his son went on into the clouds. He disappeared, but his clothes were left behind.

Coyote put on his son's clothes, and he transformed himself by saying, "Let me look exactly like my son." Then he started home, calling and crying for his father: "My father has disappeared." He arrived home, crying, to the place they were living. The female duck was his daughter-in-law, and he came to her. At that time the word *huyqúyx* was not used yet—just "duck that is white." [In today's Nez Perce, *huyqúyx* means white male duck.] That's where he went. Duck did not recognize him, but the other wife, Cricket, did. She started crying for her husband. Coyote scolded her, "You're bringing bad luck. Here I am, your husband." This is the way they spent their days for some time.

Meanwhile, Coyote's son went up through the fourth and fifth clouds, and finally he came upon some old men, each making hemp rope. They dropped their work and, taking up war clubs, said, "Brrr, why is it so cold? You made us cold. Who are you? What are you doing?" They were eager to kill him, but he told them, "Grandfathers, I am your grandson." And they answered, "We have no grandsons anywhere, except Coyote's son, whom his father caused to be lost." Then he told them, "I am that one," and they believed that it was he. They said to him, "Grandson, we are suffering because our legs are sore from making rope, and our hemp is running out." He said to them, "If I ever get back down, I will send some grease back up to you some way." Then they promised him, "Now you will go back," and they told him what had happened. "Your father went to his white daughter-in-law, and he is living with her there. The people are having a hard time. They haven't killed any game."

When they had finished telling him about that, they said, "We're going to bundle you up, and then we're going to lower you down. You'll bump into something five times. The first time you will roll around five times. Then you will keep falling. Again you will bump into something. Then you will do the same thing again, up to the fifth time. But the sixth time, if you roll around for a long time and nothing happens, then untie yourself. Pull hard on this and you will be able to untie yourself."

That's what the son did. First, bump, and then he rolled. Again there was an opening. Then he did it the second time, third time, fourth, fifth, and then the sixth time. Nothing else happened. Finally he took hold of that thing and pulled it, and it loosened everything. He loosened it and he looked around, and there was a food cache, which the old men had placed there. Then he took some grease and fat and he wrapped up a lot of it. He ran around with it, saying, "Now it's moving. Now it's ready." And they pulled it up.

When he was through with this task, he tracked his father's trail thinking, "They [Coyote and the others] went that way. This is it, this is their trail." Then he found a place where they had made a camp. In one of the places they had occupied, he found his son's little bow and arrows, which young Coyote was fond of. "This is my son's," he said. He picked it up and took it.

He kept looking for them where he used to hunt. In the past, the son of Coyote would plan the hunts while the people were gathering at their campsites. He would kick wood, and *puff!* the fire would come up and start burning. The men would warm themselves there before hunting. Then he would give them hunting orders: "You go that way, you go this way, and you people that way." This is the way he would direct them, and they would kill game.

Coyote did the same thing: He kicked the log, but it just went *pshh,* and no fire started. The people thought there was something strange about him; they thought he was a different person [pretending to be Coyote's son]. Then Coyote told the people, "I used to think that magic was my own possession, but it belonged to my father, and he has taken all that away from me." And so they had to do without, and they were hungry, hungry for meat. Then Coyote told them, "Build a long tent." He went back and forth singing along the aisle; he made a wish, and so forth. But again they were about to move from that place.

As they left the camp, Coyote's son caught up with them. His wife was behind the others, carrying her child and whatever possessions she had. Her husband caught up with Cricket. She was crying; she was chanting—sort of singing and crying at the same time. "My husband, Cricket; my husband, Cricket; *ahahahahahaha* [meaning obscure]." That's what the widow Cricket was crying out, and that's how she was when he caught up with her. She was dragging a rawhide rope.

Then Coyote's son showed the bow and arrows to the child, and the child saw him and said, "Daddy, the bow." Cricket touched her son with her arm and hand without looking back. "Child, your father is nowhere. You are sad. You are renewing the sorrow." After a short while the child would say the same thing again. Finally Coyote's son stepped on the rawhide rope that she was dragging. She tried and tried to drag it, thinking, "I wonder what's holding it," and then she saw that her husband was very near. She said, "Oh, you have come back." She was happy and thankful.

Coyote's son told her, "You shall make a lodging a little way from camp and hide me out of sight there. Women will be coming home with grass for the flooring. Talk to the one carrying the most grass, saying, 'You don't even try to help this orphan who's freezing. You don't even feel sorry for him. You should give him a little of that bedding.'"

The woman carrying grass was approached, and she answered, "Oh, she is right." And that's what they did. Already the people knew that that one [Coyote] was not the son of Coyote but Coyote himself, so they shared so much each [for Coyote's son]. Finally a fine bed was made, and she built a nice tepee over it. She built a fire there. The same thing happened when the people returned from the hunt. She said, "Why not share a little piece to help the orphan child? "Why don't you give him some meat?" All those that had killed anything little by little gave some for him. She cooked it for her husband and for the child, and then they ate.

Before, Cricket would cry, but now she had stopped. And the people suspected. "Why is Cricket quiet now and then? Let's go see." When they approached, she would resume crying. She hid her husband and then would cry again. Just she and her child would be sitting there. Mosquito told the people, "Now I'm going," and he flew out of the smoke hole. He flew high up and looked in through her [Cricket's] smoke hole. There she was loving her husband. Immediately, Mosquito shouted, "Coyote's son has returned from his hard trip." That's how he yelled and he kept yelling as he ran, "Coyote's son has returned!"

Coyote was still dancing the length of the aisle. His friend Fox told him, "Hush, they're saying something," but Coyote had heard them already and knew that his son was back, and he told them, "It's just that the boys have roasted a piece of shoulder, and because of that they must be saying they have roasted some shoulder meat. That's all they're saying." At last they heard it clearly: "Coyote's son is back from his hard trip. That son is back now!"

Then Coyote quickly picked up a piece of charcoal and smeared his face with it. Coyote said, "I must have changed places with my son while I was climbing. Instead, my son picked up and went. He must have been me instead. We must have changed places while we were climbing. I thought I was the one who went, but my son must have gone up." Then White Duck was embarrassed; she realized: "Oh, I have been living with my father-in-law." She rushed out and quickly seized a bone spoon. Then she made a nose out of the spoon and swam out into the mainstream and kept on going. She became a male duck, and she came to be called *huyqúyx* from that time.

Next day Coyote's son and the people went hunting. The people were happy and they came. When Coyote's son kicked a log, sure enough, *puff!*, it started to burn. Then they warmed themselves at the fire. That evening Coyote's son gathered the boys and told them, "You follow those tracks. There is a black-tailed buck. It's already butchered there." With red clay he painted its intestines, the deer's intestines, and he made a rope for Coyote with them. That was the way he was going to get even with his father. Coyote's son said to Coyote, "You take these boys over there." Then he told the boys, "Don't wait for him when the rope breaks. Just leave him there." Then he told Coyote, "This is your grandson's rope." When they were going after the meat, he said to Coyote, "This was your grandson's rope; take it along." Coyote said, "I might break it, son." His son answered, "No, that's what it is for [tying up bundles of meat]."

Then they took the rope and left. They found the meat. Each of the boys carried just a little of it. Coyote said, "I myself am going to carry this backbone." He arranged the backbone the best he could and carried it on his back. Then they went on. But in a little while the rope broke. Coyote tied the broken ends together. He managed to join them, but in a little while the rope broke again in another place. Finally, he became tired of this, and at the same time he became thirsty. Then he heard the rumbling of river water nearby. He let the backbone slide down, and he named the place by saying, "This place will be called Backbone Ridge." And this very place is known as Backbone Ridge to this day.

Coyote ran down, and he took a drink at the river. He said, "Let me cool myself in the water," and he swam. "I will swim down the river" and he swam down the swift river. Then he said, "Oh, what fun! I will go down there." And he continued to swim on down. Then he came ashore. At the place where he got out of the water, mosquitoes swarmed on him, so he named that place by saying, "This will be Mosquito Place." A while later, he came out of the water again and said, "Oh, this is a nice sunny slope. They will call this place Sunny Slope." In this way he gave a name to each place as he went.

Finally he swam down to the place of the Wasco People. There he heard a waterfall. "Oh, waterfall." So he came out of the water and went to see the falls from there. There he saw five girls swimming. He went back upstream. He transformed himself by saying, "Let me be on a raft laced up in a Flathead-type baby board, and let me drift down like that on the little raft." Then he drifted down, crying as he went, "Wah! Wah!" The girls heard him and thought that some people had drowned and their child had drifted down, that all of them perhaps were drowned and only this baby was left to float down. They swam over to it, and the oldest girl said, "Whoever catches the baby first gets to keep it." And this is what they did.

Coyote heard them, and he signaled the oldest girl by raising his eyebrows, indicating, "You beat the others over here." And that is what she did. The oldest girl was the first to get to the baby, and then the youngest knew who he was. She asked her older sisters, "Why are you making a baby out of Coyote?" The baby started hanging his lips as though he were about to cry, and he looked sad. The older sisters said, "You are hurting your nephew's feelings." They treated him as her nephew. Then they took him home, and there they fed him whatever would make him grow. He was quite smart, and soon he was crawling around. He was growing up fast. He asked his mother about things, saying, "What is this?" and "What is that?" and he would laugh about it. He asked about face, eye, and so on, about everything about the body, and then he would be in hysterics.

Then the sisters took him digging for yellow bell bulbs. While they were digging, he spilled the water on purpose. Then he said to his mother, "Water! Water! Oh! I am tired. Who will go and get some water for me?" The youngest sister said, "Why don't you make him go down?" The mother pointed and said, "There, there is a river flowing over there. Now you go!" And he started to crawl in that direction. When he was out of sight, he ran and when he was back in their sight, he crawled again. Then he looked back to see if he was still in their sight. The oldest sister said to them, "Look at your nephew! He is getting there," and the youngest answered, "Surely, because he is Coyote." Coyote came to the fish dam and tore it loose in several places. When he finished tearing it, he shouted, "Mothers! Our waterfalls have broken down!" Then the youngest said, "Didn't I tell you that he was Coyote?" And the sisters ran down.

Coyote took a spoon and covered his head with it. The sisters hit him and beat his head—*kayi'* [sound of hitting]. The youngest was still coming, looking for a stick as she went. Then she shouted, "Why are you hitting his head?" Coyote thought, "Oh my! This is scary. Now she is going to break my legs." The youngest shouted, "Hit the legs!" Coyote jumped up, threw off the spoon, and ran as fast as he could [lit. "broke his legs": an idiomatic expression meaning "ran as fast as possible"] up the hill. Then sitting high up, Coyote yelled to the sisters, "What made you think that the baby drifted down from someplace? You have deprived all the people of salmon and fish for such a long time by keeping them from going upstream. Now the people will be happy to get the salmon. Now salmon will go straight upriver and spawn, and the people will have salmon to eat." Then he told them, "If you girls have babies, you should give them such-and-such names if they are boys and such-and-such names if they are girls. Only the youngest of you kept me away, so she may not have a baby." Then Coyote left the sisters. This is how Celilo [Oregon] originated, where the Wasco people are today. Because Coyote tore down the fish dams, salmon could come upriver and spawn.

From there Coyote went upriver. As he was traveling, he became hungry. He came up the Columbia, but instead of following the mainstream, he came up the Touchet River [in Washington]. There he saw salmon going by. They were going upstream. Coyote asked them as he sat down, "Why is it that not even one of you swims out to the shore?" He said, sitting by the water, "Come out of the water this way! I saved your life." Then the salmon said to each other, "He is right about that. He has given us these good streams to go up. You swim out to him." And so one Chinook salmon swam out to the shore. Coyote had a blanket named anus. Coyote wrapped up the salmon with the blanket, but the salmon tore it up and went back into the river. Coyote said, "What now?" and went further upstream, sort of hungry, saying, "It got away from me."

Then Coyote broke Meadowlark's leg. Coyote said, "Aunt, tell me what I can do to keep hold of the salmon." And Meadowlark said, "You'll never succeed by wrapping it up. Just say the same thing again." Then Coyote made a new leg for Meadowlark, and he placed a grinding basket around her neck. And Meadowlark said to Coyote, "When you say that again, you should have a stick ready to hit the salmon this time. When a salmon comes out, hit it." Coyote answered, "Hmm, I knew it all along. You are only telling me what I already knew." Again he shouted in the same way, "Swim out to me. I saved you." The salmon looked at each other, saying, "Who is willing to be caught?" And a salmon swam out to him, saying, "This time I will." Just as it came to the shore, Coyote hit it with a club. He cut the sides of the salmon off and roasted each one on a stick; then he went to sleep. That is why the place is now called Touchet [*tú·se* means roast]. And Coyote slept while the salmon meat cooked.

About that time several four-footed animal boys came around. They were hunting for birds and other things. They were looking for eggs. They came to Coyote and they asked, "Shall we take this salmon out of the fire, old man?" Coyote answered, "N . . ." in his sleep. "He says, 'All right,'" said the boys, and they ate the roasted salmon all up.

Then one of the young wolves cut out Coyote's rectum. He cooked it right next to the fire and spit on the charcoal to dampen it. Coyote's rectum kept on cooking while Coyote slept. When he woke up, there were only empty roasting sticks and footprints. Coyote said, "Oh, my grandsons must have gone through here. Why didn't they talk to me? They left so little of the intestines for me." So he ate it; he cut it as he ate. A bird said to him, "You are eating your own rectum." "Oh?" Coyote said. "Once they buried an old woman alive here; she must be the one who is talking." But finally the boy who roasted Coyote's rectum became uneasy and ordered an ant to go to the opening in Coyote where his rectum used to be. Coyote felt something; he felt that place and found it empty. He said, "Oh, he was telling the truth." So he took what was left and put it back in.

From there Coyote went upriver. He went to find those who had played the trick on him by stealing his salmon and cooking his rectum. "They are sleeping. They must have roasted all the eggs," Coyote thought. Then Coyote ate up all the eggs and put things like sand and dirt back into the empty eggshells. Coyote painted the face of a young fox with egg yolk. He wrinkled up the noses and mouths of the wolves. That is the way he made them. He painted them with charcoal and other things. When the animal boys woke up, they came up from below to a place where they chased Coyote around. Coyote was making fun of them from up above. They chased Coyote, and they wore him out by chasing him. Then Coyote transformed himself by saying, "Now let me be a Flathead man shooting grouse, wearing a blanket diagonally." And then he was aiming at a grouse. Coyote's tracks came running right up to where this man was shooting a grouse. The animal boys came to him and asked, "Didn't Coyote come this way?" But he just told them, "*ʔoˑtá*" [the Flathead word for no]. The boys said to each other, "What is he, anyway?" Then they went away. Thus Coyote escaped. And he ran from them in the opposite direction.

Coyote went upriver farther. He went on up and came upon a rock. "Oh, a rock is lodged here." Then he urinated on it. Coyote went upriver from there; then the rock caught up with him. Coyote saw it coming: "Now the rock is after me." And the rock chased him around there. Coyote ran up the hill, thinking it would roll back. But no, the rock kept rolling up. Even though Coyote said, "Break! My legs, carry me fast!" and "Let me be safe," it was useless. The rock caught up with him, ran over him, and killed him. Rock said, "Oh, it was just Coyote. No wonder he was so ornery." Then Rock threw Coyote into the water.

Coyote floated down one bend and a half, and then he floated ashore. Magpie was flying upriver with his wings gleaming. "Oh, there he is. I wonder what killed him. Perhaps he has some eyebrow fat." So Magpie flew down to him and looked for Coyote's eyebrow fat. Then Coyote was awakened by Magpie's pecking. "You woke me up at a wrong time." Then Magpie said, "Grey cataract is flying around." Coyote said, "Oh, you woke me up at a wrong time, I was helping some women cross at the head of the waters." Then Magpie answered, "Where at the head of the waters did you help women get across? There is no such thing. A killer upriver killed you."

From there Coyote went upstream and hit his hip. His excrement children ran out. They fought each other, while Coyote dried himself well. Then he told the children, "Come! You can poke out each other's eyes." That is what they did; then they went back in. But Coyote blocked his youngest child and said, "Tell me how I can kill Rock." The youngest said, "When are you going to keep us from getting wet? Do the same thing [to Rock] as before. First you should prepare pitch; and so on, then take it to the bush and set fire to the bush from all sides. It will burn. This is the only way you can kill him. He will burn and when he does, he will explode. That is the only way you can kill Rock, the killer." And that is what Coyote did. When everything exploded, the bush burned up. Then Coyote named the place by saying, "Let this be known as Shale-Rock Mountain." And that is the way it is called to this day.

From there Coyote went farther. He continued up somewhere near the head of the waters. Then he came upon a good crossing place, a place to jump over, and he jumped over. Something touched him as he went. He turned around, saying, "Oh, what fun." Then he jumped back across and he felt something again. He did this several times, then finally it hit him. When it hit Coyote, it said, "Oh, it was just Coyote." Then it knocked Coyote downriver.

Coyote floated down one bend and a half and drifted ashore. Again Magpie came to him. In the same way as before, Magpie was flying upriver. When Magpie came to Coyote, he said, "Maybe you have some eyebrow fat, my friend." He pecked to look for it and woke up Coyote. Coyote said, "You woke me up. A gray cataract is flying. I was helping women to cross the headwaters." Magpie replied, "Where are those women you were helping to cross the headwaters? There is the killer, White-tailed Buck. From the beginning, he was the one who hit you and killed you."

Then Coyote left that place, went upstream, hit his hip, and his excrement children ran out. Then Coyote built a fire and dried himself. Now he was completely dry. He called his children, saying, "Now, come! You might pierce your eyes." But the youngest had already lost one eye. They ran on in, but when they were all in, Coyote blocked the youngest one, saying, "Tell me!" The youngest told him as before, "You are always making us chilly in the water. That one was known as White-tailed Buck, the killer. He is the one who hit you with his horns as you went by. He sits there always and he hits anyone who comes and jumps across there. That is what he does to people." Then the youngest said, "Get a weapon. When you jump across, spear backward at the same time. This is the only way you can kill him, and there is no other way."

And that is what Coyote did. He got ready with a weapon, and he speared backward when he jumped across. He aimed at the forehead and hit it with the weapon. White-Tailed Buck fell into the water. Coyote dragged him out, butchered him, and made dried meat. Then he said, "Now human beings are coming soon, and you cannot go on being killers. You will be just for killing. They will make dried or fresh meat out of you. They will eat you. That will make people happy." In this way Coyote put a spell on them. From then it came to be that white-tailed bucks were for eating.

Finally, from there Coyote went out of the woods to Buffalo Country [Montana]. There he caught up with the others. This is the end of this story. That's all.

▼▼▼▼▼

14

COYOTE AND
WHITE-TAILED BUCK

WHEN THE DIFFERENT KINDS of deer were created, so was White-tailed Buck. Coyote used to see him sitting. Nothing disturbed him, even when Coyote came over and tried to scare him by shouting in various ways. He was just peaceful and sat chewing his cud. For a long time Coyote studied the matter, wondering, "How can he become more alert? He is too indifferent. Anyone, even a woman, could club him to death." Coyote continued to think.

Then he had an idea. "Maybe this will do it," and he pointed his genitals at White-tailed Buck's nose, almost touching it. Buck got the scent and gave a warning snort. After that, whenever Coyote showed up, Buck snorted. "There, you reacted in the right way," Coyote said. "That's what will make you wary. Only a man who prepares himself, taking a sweat bath and cleansing himself, will be able to kill you. But not those who do not bathe. You were just too complacent, so much so that even women could kill you. That's the way you were. But this is the way you will be from now on."

From that time on, White-tailed bucks became difficult to approach. Only those who are prepared properly have a chance to kill them.

(Recited by Watters; originally published in Aoki and Walker, 1989.)

From that time on, White-tailed bucks became difficult to approach.

15

HOW COYOTE MADE
DIFFERENT PEOPLE

ONCE UPON A TIME Coyote deliberated for a long time. "Now I am going to create the human race," he said. And he built a fire and mixed the ingredients. He made a mold in human form, with feet, arms, legs, and all those human features—head, eyes, mouth. He completed the mold, put it in the oven, and stoked the fire. But he was too impatient and took it out while it was still just white. He wasn't satisfied with this and threw it across the ocean. That became the white people.

Because it wasn't right the first time, he made another and decided to bake this one longer. And that's what he did. When he put the mold in this time, he waited too long and it became black, just totally black and burned. "This isn't quite good enough, too black," he thought. And he discarded it toward the south. That's why the black people are from there.

Coyote tried a third time, and this time he took greater care. He put it in, and then he deliberated and watched carefully for just the right time—neither too long nor too short, but right in the middle. He opened the oven and took it out, and there it was baked just fine, and he was completely satisfied. He said, "Yes, these will be the People hence." And that's how Indians got their name. That is the reason they were put here. The Indians never came from any other place. They are Coyote's creation. That's all.

(Recited by Watters; originally published in Aoki and Walker, 1989.)

"Now I am going to create the human race."

▼▼▼▼▼

16

COYOTE SHOOTS
COW ELK

ONCE UPON A TIME Coyote was living in an encampment somewhere upriver near Ahsaka. One day the food ran out, and Coyote decided that he would go hunting. He slipped on snowshoes and was off.

As he was going along he came upon Cow Elk, and Coyote shot her and wounded her. Cow Elk took off along the tops of the hills, with Coyote close behind her. They crossed over the upper part of Potlatch Creek, and Coyote followed her along the breaks of the hills that came together. Just above the place called Yahtoyn, Cow Elk landed at the bottom of the hill and crossed on over it. "Oh," she exclaimed, "Coyote is after me on his snowshoes."

They came to a place where there was no snow, and so Coyote took off his snowshoes, and to this day they lie there just where Coyote took them off. He went on tracking her, coming over the side hills, across the creeks. In this manner he went on chasing her across the creeks down the river.

All at once Cow Elk dropped dead, with her head down into the snow. At that place you can see the ears of Cow Elk where she lay for a while. The place that Cow Elk died was on the other side of the river. To this day they say that Cow Elk slid down headfirst between here and where Hatway Creek goes up.

(Recited by Watters; originally published in Aoki and Walker, 1989.)

Cow Elk took off along the tops of the hills, with Coyote close behind her.

17

HOW THE SALMON FOUND OUT THAT THEY SHOULDN'T GO UP POTLATCH CREEK

COYOTE WAS SITTING on the top of a hill. He saw that the salmon were starting to swim upstream, after he had completed the destruction of the falls at Wasco.

From there Coyote came up. Coyote saw them pass as he went up the first tributary, which was the Snake River. It goes up that way to the Snake River, and its water is clear. Then Coyote saw from there that they were going up the Clearwater River to spawn. He saw that the run was going upstream to Potlatch Creek, and he remembered that there was no gravel where chinook salmon could spawn at the headwaters of the creek.

He hollered after the salmon, "You are going up where there are only split rocks. From where you are now, go right over to the big clear river."

And they did so. Some of them were going up to *Tamsó'ypa* [one mile up from the mouth of Potlatch Creek], and from there they jumped over to the Clearwater River, where the saddle is. By now some of them were way up near the mouth of the stream and just below that. There they heard the other salmon say, "We are going up this kind of stream" [the Clearwater River]." Then they jumped over to Eagle Point, where the saddle is.

From then on chinook salmon never went up Potlatch Creek, for its headwaters are only split rocks. That's all.

(Recited by Watters; originally published in Aoki and Walker, 1989.)

"From where you are now, go right over to the big clear river."

▼▼▼▼▼

18

WORM PENIS

Coyote was wandering around, and all at once he heard trees falling. He wondered where they were. Then he went from where he was toward the sound, saying, "I wonder what he is doing." He came upon a person who was moving quickly from one tree to another. He was cutting, *chop, chop, chop,* and a tree would fall, *whoosh!*

Coyote was envious of his cutting tool. "My! It's wonderful," he said. "I would take this to the fish trap and use it to cut trees for the fish dam. I wonder if he would exchange it with me?" Coyote said to him, "Friend, let us trade." The man answered, "It's a nuisance. It just takes you around the timber. That's how it is, but if you want it . . ." Coyote said, "Yes, I want it. I'll take it up to the fish trap." The man said, "All right, I agree."

Coyote started cutting with his agate knife, but it broke, and Coyote started cutting with another one. Then he cut through it and they made their exchange. The first thing Coyote did was to run with it. The man said, "I was lucky that he exchanged for it. It's been a nuisance." Then he left for an unknown place.

Then Coyote started using the worm here and there. At first he just laughed, "Ha ha." When he cut trees down, he would laugh. Thi-i-i-i-s is the way he went on, and now he ran out of the trees; he was led out of the timber by it. There was nothing anywhere; there were no trees anywhere. The worm got to Coyote's groin, and it kept biting. Now Coyote thought, "My! How disgusting! I wonder where that person went." But he was nowhere to be found. Right then and there the worm chewed him to death, and there he lay with his tail wagging, *swish, swish, swish.*

The worm, who was from rotten pine, never became compatible as Coyote's private parts. Coyote was the first one to cut with the implement.

(Recited by Watters; originally published in Aoki and Walker, 1989.)

Coyote started using the worm to cut down trees.

▼▼▼▼▼

19

COLD AND WARM
BROTHERS WRESTLE

THERE ONCE LIVED the Warm People, who were on one side of the river, and on the opposite side were the Cold People. The Cold People had five sons and one daughter, the same as the Warm People, who had five sons and one daughter, and a daughter-in-law, the oldest son's wife. The eldest son had a wife.

Coyote came to the Coldweather People first. They did not have much of anything to eat. Then Coyote crossed the river. He came to the Warmweather People, who were living it up there; they had meat and fish and everything to eat. That's the way they lived.

Now Coyote started to plan. He told the Cold People, "They are easy to throw and put down in wrestling. You will wrestle, and the winner will cut off his opponent's head." For a long time they did not agree to do this. Finally they said, "Yes, if they agree," and they got ready.

The Coldweather People had icicles that they spilled over the area where they wrestled, which gave them a firm foothold. And the Warmweather People had sturgeon fat, which they used for the same reason, to get a firm foothold. The Warmweathers were in too much of a hurry; they were the first to spread their stuff out. So the Coldweathers (having put their ice on top) were the first to throw their opponents down, with the understanding that the winner would cut his opponent's head off. In each case a Coldweather killed his opponent.

The old man, his wife, and their daughter were left, and from that day the Coldweathers had control over the three. Whenever the Warmweather old man and his wife fished, anything they caught, the Coldweathers would take away.

Coyote ate well there, where he was spending his days. He watched the Warmweathers all the time when they fished. He would say to the Coldweathers,

(Recited by Watters; originally published in Aoki and Walker, 1989.)

Coyote told the Cold People, "You will wrestle, and the winner will cut off his opponent's head."

"Now they've caught it for us and you go after it." And then they would chase after them in a boat, catch up with them, and take the fish away. Thus they spent all their days.

The oldest son of Warmweather had a wife, and when they were killed and wiped out, this woman went back to where she was from. There she gave birth to a baby boy. When the boy grew up, he would ask his mother, "Why do I have no father? All those that I play around with have fathers. I have none." For a long time she didn't tell him why. Finally she told him. "Yes, my son, this is what they did to your father and your uncles. They threw them all down in wrestling. For that reason I left and came home, and you were born here. Your grandfather, grandmother, and aunt are still there. They are living in the same place to this day, and they are ruled by the Coldweathers. The only thing they have to eat is what they can catch, what they can fish out. Your grandfather is old now, and he cannot go hunting, he cannot shoot deer or anything, because he is so old."

The young man cleaned himself and bathed. Then he got ready by pulling up trees, first small ones, and finally big ones. Then he told his mother, "I am ready now. I am going over for revenge now that I know what happened." After she had told him about what happened, he went up to the mountaintop, and from there he looked over and down. Then he saw the smoke of his grandparents and aunt's house. He lay on his stomach and cried, and his tears ran down. To this day there is a loose rock that looks as though something is running down it. That is where the tears of the Warmweather youth flowed down.

It was dark about the time that he arrived at his grandfather's and grandmother's. He introduced himself, "I am he." The grandparents were happy to see him. They told him, "Yes, this is how they have a hold on us. We fish, and then they take our catch away from us. Now and then we catch fish. Coyote is always on the watch for us. He spends his days on the Cold side." The young man told them, "Yes, Grandfather and Grandmother, I will get revenge. My aunt, I will get revenge. Now make lots of fish grease." This they did from what they had saved. When they went fishing, he told them, "I am going to lie on my back in the canoe. When they row after you and they are close, tell me. Then we will get away from them."

And that's just what they did. They caught fish and took them out. Then Coyote saw them, saying, "Now they have some fish; you go get it." And the Coldweathers went after them in a canoe, and they just about caught up with them. They called out, "Give it to us. You cannot run away. What are you running away for? You will never get away from us. Give it up, give it to us, and quick. That is ours." Now they were very close. Then the youth doubled his knees up. When he stretched the boat started up fast, and it almost went out of the water. "You'll never escape," they said, and they kept rowing after them.

Now they were getting very close again, and the youth did the same thing. The canoe went clear out of the water. The young man stood up. He ran his hand under the gills of a sturgeon, and with his little finger he carried it out to the shore. The Coldweathers saw him going, and they gave up hope and went back. They told Coyote, "Well! That young boy has come." "I will go back and find out," said Coyote, and he crossed the river. He came to the old man, who said, "This is my oldest son's boy. He has grown this big."

Then Coyote cried, "Oh, my nephew! Oh, my nephew! You resemble him. You have come to get revenge. Give them what they deserve, revenge." The boy said, "I will see." Then Coyote said to the Coldweathers, "He came back to the Warmweathers. The eldest son of that old man had a son, who was born over there, and he's that big. It is easy, he is alone. In a little while you will wipe out the whole bunch." Then Coyote went back across. "They say, 'We will wrestle again.'" "Yes," the boy said, "if you say so, I'm ready for it. I'll get even."

And that's what they did. They set a date. And the boy talked to his grandmother and aunt; he instructed his grandparents thoroughly, "Don't be in a rush when we meet. When they've spread ice, you cover it with fish grease. There I'll have sure footing and I'll put them down." That's what they did. Nothing happened at first, and the Coldweather girl began to worry, so she thoughtlessly poured ice first. Then the Warmweathers threw fish grease over it. Right then the youth threw the oldest one down, and the old man cut off his head. Now the second time around, the girl again got worried and poured ice down, and the old man spread the fish grease over it. Again the youth threw his opponent down. Thus, all five of them were killed. The old man and his wife and daughter ran away.

Then Coyote said, "I'm going to take that Coldweather girl as a spoil." He chased her upstream, and she took off her clothes and threw them away as she ran. She ran into the water and stood in the middle. At that spot there used to be a rock standing up out of the water, but now it is not there any more. It was flooded over when they made the dam and made the lake. Coyote gave up. He could not chase after her into the river, for it was too cold for him. He said, "Then you will just be a rock. People will see you and say, 'That's the Coldweather girl; Winter's daughter is standing in the water.'" She answered, "In the same way they will see that there is Coyote stooping over my dress."

From that day on, it came to pass that when the warm weather comes, freezing people melt away because the Warmweather People conquered the Coldweather People.

20

HOW THE ANIMALS
GOT THEIR NAMES

THERE ONCE LIVED lots of people. They had a chief, and he announced, "One day we'll have a big dinner and eat." And that's what they did. Soon it was the day, and lots of them came—fish, birds, and four-footed animals—they all came. The chief had two or three or more sitting where he was. They spread the food. They put something long down. They brought lots of food of all kinds there, and they cooked it in different ways.

When all these people had eaten, all the four-footed animals came forward one at a time. They were named by their movements and looks. They were named thus: White-tailed Buck, Black-tailed Buck, Elk, and so on through all the hooved animals. Then the unhooved animals came to be named: Wolf, Cougar, Grizzly Bear, Brown Bear, and so on. Whatever their habits were, by those they received their name. Then the birds came, and they received their names according to their appearances. That's the way their names were given to them; the name was theirs to keep—such as Prairie Chicken, according to his cry. For this reason he was named Prairie Chicken. Grouse was named according to his song or tune. Robin and others were named in this way, too.

Soon Bluejay came, but his name had not yet been decided. Bluejay told them he wanted the name Eagle. But they told him, "That name is already taken. That's not for you. You look too small and slender. You can't fly up into the air, way up in the sky, to all those places. You are too weak." Then he went back and told his grandmother what they said. She gave him a name, and he took that name back to the council, but they rejected it: "That name is already taken," This went on for a long time.

Finally the chief said, "These are the judges. We name you according to your habits. Fly up to the branch and sing a song." When Bluejay flew up to the

(Recited by Watters; originally published in Aoki and Walker, 1989.)

branch from the ground, he sang, "*Quyé's quyé's quyé's.*" "All right," Coyote said, "that's your name. You shall be known by that name."

They were all given names according to the looks and habits of each of them. That is the way their names and songs began. Similarly I have told about *ti·ptí·pnu* and others, such as Cottontail and Jackrabbit—for Jackrabbit was a fast runner. Snowshoe Rabbit was next in line, whose coat turns white in winter and changes back to its color during summer. In this way, different animals—fish, birds, and everything that one finds—received many different names. They were told, "This will be your name according to your behavior and habits." These were all studied, and they were named accordingly. That's all.

21

HOW COYOTE BROUGHT
THE BUFFALO

COYOTE WAS SOMEWHERE around the Snake River. He decided to go to the Buffalo Country, and he started out. He took the trail through the Bannock Country. He went from there to where there are hot springs. He finally came to the country where the buffalo were, and he found lots of people living there. He stayed for a while, but not too long because he became restless. He thought of things that he should be doing, and he went this way and that. He left the encampment, and he wandered all alone.

Coyote went over the hill; there were many buffalo grazing, and they were content. He watched them for a while. He thought the buffalo were too far from the West to be hunted. "Now I am going to take them," he thought, and he rounded them up. He started taking them through the Bannock Country, using the same route he had before. He came to a place whose Indian name I forgot. But it's a place where a stream, an outlet of *q̓oyxciníma* [Weiser River], runs into a river. From there he hunted over the ridge. He went over the mountain; in this way he brought them, going out of the timber where the Wasco People are, then further downriver [above Vancouver]. That's where he landed, and he spent many nights.

When he brought the buffalo above the falls [Celilo Falls], he stayed with them one night. It had taken many days to come from the Buffalo Country, and that's where he brought them. Coyote planned to take this whole herd of buffalo way over near the ocean. But he left them there, and he went on to the places where he wanted to take them. He couldn't find a good place anywhere where they could stay and grow. There were too many trees. He knew that these buffalo were used to the plains. He couldn't find such a place or their kind of food. There wasn't any food for them anywhere. He couldn't do anything and

(Recited by Watters; originally published in Aoki and Walker, 1989.)

"The people will see these buffalo sitting around here. They will remain as rocks."

he was undecided. He couldn't find any place where the buffalo could live and grow.

So Coyote came back and found them still sitting around, waiting and resting, for they had a long trip to make, and he could not take them back. "I have failed in my plans," he said. "Now it will be this way. The people will see these buffalo sitting around here. They will remain as rocks." And he left them that way; he left them at that place, and they remain there as rocks. That's all.

. . . he cut his eyes out and juggled them several times.

‪▼▼▼▼▼‬

22

HOW COYOTE
LOST HIS EYES

ONCE UPON A TIME when Coyote was wandering around crossing over a ridge, he came upon a man dancing on only one leg. The other leg he carried over his shoulder. Coyote was astonished to see such a thing, and he marveled greatly at it. Then Coyote went over the ridge and cutting off one of his own legs, he also began to dance. Then he heard someone singing as he danced.

The first man had a feeling that there was someone else dancing, and when he spotted Coyote he promptly cut off Coyote's other leg and threw him into the river.

Coyote floated down the river one bend and a half. There Magpie was flying up the river with his wings gleaming in the sun. "Oh, there is Coyote floating around. I wonder if he has some eye fat." Magpie landed on Coyote and began pecking his eye fat. This awoke Coyote and he stormed angrily at Magpie, "Damn it! Your pecking woke me up just as I was helping the women cross the river!" "You weren't taking any women across the river," Magpie retorted. "You were killed here by the old-time killer."

With that Coyote proceeded upstream and hit his hip, and his excrement children came out. As he was drying himself, the children began fighting with each other, and Coyote told them, "Look out, you will poke out each other's eyes," and he told them to go back in. But he blocked out the youngest, Cicéqi, and asked him, "How can I revenge myself?"

Cicéqi replied, "There is an old-time killer who dances around and always kills, and he is Grasshopper. Whatever he does he always takes off his leg and puts it back again. You should go there then and cut his other leg off."

And that is what Coyote did, and he killed Grasshopper. Then Coyote said, "Ah! No longer will they say that he is a killer. People are coming soon, and the

---

(Recited by Watters; originally published in Aoki and Walker, 1989. For versions related to various segments of this narrative, see Wilson's "How Coyote Lost His Eyes" in the same volume; "Coyote and Curlew" in Phinney, 1934; "Up a Creek" and "Katstainomiots or Elbow Baby" in Spinden, 1908.)

human beings will say, 'This is Grasshopper, who lost his legs, and will creep around.' You won't kill anyone."

From there Coyote went on over another ridge. All of a sudden he came upon a man who was juggling his eyes. The man would throw them up, shouting, "My eyes fit!" and they would come right back into their sockets. Coyote was amazed to see such a thing, and he started doing it too. He went over the ridge, and he cut his eyes out and juggled them several times.

Then the other one had a feeling that someone was imitating and mocking him. "So! It's Coyote who is doing it!" he stormed. He took a stick and hooked one of Coyote's eyes away. Coyote hollered for his eye to come back, but to no avail. Coyote thought to himself, "Maybe it's waiting for the other eye." So he threw the other one up, and the man hooked this one also.

So Coyote became blind and hollow-eyed. He groped around till he came to a pile of rocks. "Oh! Excuse me for scattering your biscuit roots around, Grandchildren," he apologized. "Oh, never mind, we're just a pile of rocks," answered the rocks.

Coyote stumbled into some brush. "Oh! Forgive me for breaking up your house," he apologized again. The brushes answered; "We're just old brushes here!"

In this way Coyote groped his way around until finally he became hungry. He felt around for some food, but there was nothing. He rested for a while to cool off. As he did so he heard a bird singing. "Empty eyes, empty eyes," the bird mocked.

"Oh!" mourned Coyote, "that makes me long for the place where I heard that song before." He named the place where he had heard the bird. "You're making me so lonesome. Come closer and say it."

The bird got closer. "Say it here, right beside me," Coyote coaxed it. The Curlew Bird did, and instantly Coyote grabbed the bird and yanked its eyes out. He threw the eyes into his own sockets, and into Curlew's eyes he threw some thickened clots of blood. That's why the bird's eyes are red.

Coyote could see again with Curlew's eyes, even though they were small. He could search for things again, and he ate whatever he could find. He traveled around this way for a while, until he heard Owl hooting. "That owl has bigger eyes," thought Coyote. He went up to Owl and said, "Ah, how I long for the days! I remember once when we were camping, I heard the hooting of an owl. You make me feel so lonesome. Come closer and hoot again."

So Owl did just that, getting closer and closer at Coyote's urging. When he was close enough, Coyote caught him, yanked his eyes out, and put Curlew's eyes into Owl's sockets, with Owl's eyes in his own. Suddenly he saw a little better, and he moved on.

As he went along he began hearing the sound of someone pounding. He went into the place where the sound was coming from, and there was an old woman, named Mistoyno, pounding. "Where are they?" asked Coyote. "Oh, the grandchildren? They have gone to a party where lots of people are having fun playing with Coyote's eyes. When they come back, they'll eat this." She was pounding sunflower biscuits, mixing the grease in as she did so. She gave some of the biscuits to Coyote, and when he finished eating he made up his mind to kill her. He clubbed her to death and she collapsed in his arms.

Careful not to get any blood on his clothes, he put on the old woman's clothes. After transforming himself into the image of the old woman, he hid her body away. Then he ate up all the biscuits she had been pounding for the children, so he had to make some more. While he was pounding more biscuits, he heard the sound of children returning. He quickly lay with his face down, moaning and groaning. "Grandma! What happened?" the children cried. "Oh, it pains me where he shot me," Coyote moaned. "It's the wound I got when I was shot in the war in the old days, the pain comes back to me now! I couldn't pound more for you."

"Oh, never mind, we'll do it ourselves," the children offered. "You just rest, Grandma, and lie with your face down." They told him, "The people at the dance said, 'You come now.'" "Carry me over there, Grandchildren," Coyote asked. They carried him over.

When morning came, everyone was off again to the party that had been going on the night before. Throngs of people came, all having a great time dancing with Coyote's eyes. The oldest granddaughter carried Coyote along to the party. Coyote asked her to lower him a little. She did so, and Coyote took advantage of the position to copulate with her. The girl felt something strange and put him down. The girls took turns carrying Coyote. The same thing occurred with all three of them. But when it came to the youngest one, she told the others, "This is Coyote! I wouldn't carry him for anything!"

Finally they got to where all the festivities were going on. Lots of people were dancing with Coyote's eyes. Suddenly Coyote burst out, "Let me do it too, Grandchildren! Let me dance with the eyes!" They handed him the eyes and he danced back and forth with them. Then he spied an open door, through which he dashed out. "Heavens!" the girls exclaimed. "I wonder why he took the eyes away." Coyote was perched high up above the crowd, and he told them, "Ha! You thought that I was Mistoyno, the old lady, dancing here. I got my eyesight back from you. I also copulated with all the girls, except the youngest, who rejected me. I don't know if she'll have a baby or not, but you should name these children who will be born."

This is how Coyote got his eyes back.

Frog said, "My husband, where am I to sit?" and Sun told her, "Here, on my eye."

▼▼▼▼▼

23

THE SUN
AND THE MOON

THE SUN HAD TWO WIVES, Frog and another woman. At that time, the Sun moved across the sky so very hot that the people were nearly killed by the heat. They did not like this state of affairs. For that reason Coyote called a council of all the people; he knew Sun did not love Frog and would not invite her to come, so he begged her to come to the council and obey what Sun told her to do.

So she went and stood at the door, and said, "My husband, where am I to sit?" and he told her, "Here, on my eye." Then she advanced a few steps and jumped up to his eye; and the people tried to pull her off, but could not. And Coyote told the Sun, "You are acting badly for a chief"; and Coyote decided that Sun should become the night sun [Moon], and that the Moon should become the Sun. So the irregular one is now the Moon, and the frog is seen over his eye.

(Originally published in Spinden, 1917.)

24

COYOTE AND WINTER

HAVE A WAR

Yaunyaiye said to Coyote, "You cannot do anything to me." Then Coyote answered, "You are good for nothing; I could kill you if I wanted to." They were both angry, so they agreed to make war. They named three months for endurance to see who was the best man. Then Coyote said to Yaunyaiye, "Let us have war for five months." They agreed on the terms of the battle, but nobody knew how Coyote planned to kill Yaunyaiye. Coyote collected all the winter food he could. He took the fat off the bear and all other animals. Both arranged to be ready when the time came.

Yaunyaiye came to Coyote and said, "When you are ready, we will have the war." Then Coyote answered, "Let us begin now." In the middle of the night Coyote woke up and went out. He saw snow over everything. He had made his house poles out of large trees, perhaps two feet in diameter. It snowed the entire first month. The snow reached a long way up the side of the house. It snowed till about the middle of the second month. The snow almost covered the house then. After Coyote had lived through four months, Yaunyaiye began to give up. Coyote endured the siege and killed Yaunyaiye. Then Coyote came out of his house and went down to the river. He saw ice chunks floating down and it was crying. Coyote picked up a stone and hit it.

(Originally published in Spinden, 1908.)

▼▼▼▼▼

25

COYOTE AND BULL

Coyote was going along upstream, hungry as usual. He came upon a big, fat buffalo bull. Coyote said to him, "Friend, I am hungry. Is it possible for you to change me into a bull just like you, so that I, too, could become fat and sleek?" Bull heeded him not the least. He only wandered away grazing and not a word would he reply to Coyote. Coyote was insistent. He said again and again, "I wish that I, too, were a bull so that I could get fat."

Finally Bull got tired of hearing this and said to him, "Coyote! You are inveterately foolhardy in the things you do; you could never do what I might ask of you. You are becoming a great bother." Coyote replied, "No, friend, I will do exactly what you tell me to do. Here I see you fat and sleek. Here is much grass and you live well, while, you see, I am painfully hungry. I will do just anything you tell me." Bull then said to him, "Then go over there and lie down." Coyote accordingly went and lay down. "Absolutely do not flee; do not move when I dash at you. You must, absolutely, remain still and I will heave you upward with my horns." "Yes, friend, why should I flee?" replied Coyote as he lay down.

Bull went off to the side and there he incited himself to terrific anger. He tore up the turf; he threw dirt upward; he bellowed and breathed clouds of vapor from his nostrils. He became terribly angry and then he dashed upon Coyote. But Coyote had been glancing at Bull and had seen him become so terrible. He saw Bull come at him and he jumped quickly aside. "Now that is what I spoke of—that you would run away," Bull said to him. "Let me try again, just once more," Coyote said. "I will not move next time." But Bull went away even though Coyote beseeched him weepingly.

Coyote followed, tearfully entreating him, "Once more, just once more; I will not run away again." Bull said to him at last, "You are most bothersome to me. Now I will try you once more and if you move, do not beg me any more, for I will heed you never again. We are trying for the last time." Coyote placed himself on the designated spot again and Bull went aside, as before, to become

(Recited by *Wáyi'látpu*, originally published in Phinney, 1934.)

79

Bull threw Coyote high into the air with his horns.

terribly angry. Now he dashed at Coyote. This time Coyote steeled himself and Bull threw him high into the air with his horns. Coyote fell and suddenly became a buffalo bull. He stood up and began to graze. He could see all kinds of things and eat them. Finally he parted from the other bull, which had wandered off somewhere feeding.

Soon another coyote met him and recognized him as erst Coyote. "Oh, friend, how is it, friend, that you have become like that? I am terribly hungry; I wish that you would make me like that, too." Coyote-Bull only looked at him sullenly and walked away to feed, unmindful of what the other said. The coyote insisted, "Friend, make a bull of me, too. I fare piteously and you are very fat."

Coyote-Bull then spoke to him, "You are very bothersome. You would never do those things that I would ask." "Yes, friend, I will follow out absolutely every word you say. Try me." "You have been a nuisance to me," Coyote-Bull said to him; "but place yourself there and I will dash upon you angrily and toss you into the air with my horns. You, absolutely, are not to move. If you run away, do not tearfully entreat me for another chance." The coyote placed himself there while Bull made himself angry. He bellowed and pawed the ground. He imitated in every way the movements that he had seen the other bull do. Then Bull dashed upon the coyote, and *oh!* he picked him up and hurled him upward with his horns. The coyote fell—*thud!* To the ground he fell, but still a coyote. At that very same moment Bull, too, changed back into a coyote. Suddenly they were standing there—both coyotes.

They stormed and they scolded each other: "You! You have caused me to change back into a coyote. There I was a bull living happily and you caused me to change back into a coyote." "Ha, you imitator! You thought you could make me into a bull too as the other one did to you." And one chased the other up the valley. The coyotes chased each other. Then Coyote lost interest. "I was acting silly! I thought I had become a bull." He went along up the valley from there, unmindful of all that had happened.

Elk knew that Coyote was hungry and wanted meat. He said, "Let me cook meat for you."

▼▼▼▼▼

26

COYOTE VISITS ELK

AND FISH HAWK

I AM GOING TO TELL another short story. Coyote was living with his wife, Mouse. They had a child named Cicéqi. And Coyote said, "Now let's go visit the elk family; Elk and his wife are living there." Then he left and came to them. Elk knew that Coyote was hungry and wanted meat. He said, "Let me cook meat for you." "Yes, all right." Then Elk went to his wife and cut off his wife's sleeve. He boiled the sleeve, since he had some hot rocks ready. He quickly boiled the sleeve of the dress of that woman.

Coyote wondered, "What's up?" When it was cooked, Elk took it out. Sure enough, Coyote saw good meat with fat. Then poor Coyote ate it. Elk said, "Now let me give you camas for dessert." Then he went outside. Coyote saw Elk bringing something out. He peeked around after him, saying, "What?" Elk defecated and stuck something up his anus and brought it out, saying, "Wonderfully delicious camas." Then Coyote was happy, and he took them home. Coyote said to Elk, "You come visit me too." "Yes, I will come to see you," Elk said. Coyote then brought the camas and a little meat to his wife.

Sometime later Elk went to see Coyote. Poor Coyote and his wife were living miserably. Coyote acted bravely, saying, "Come on in; now let us serve you something." Elk thought, "What will Coyote do [for food]?" Coyote took an agate knife and cut the sleeve of his poor wife, Mouse, and cooked it. When Coyote took the sleeve out, it was the same old dress—there wasn't any meat. Elk felt very sorry for Coyote. Then Coyote went outside and stuck a stick up his anus, but nothing came out. Elk felt sorry for him. Elk thought, "Poor thing, he cooked her dress, but nothing came from it. He is copying what I did."

Elk went back home again, and Coyote said, "Now I am going to see Fish Hawk." He went as a guest. Fish Hawk was happy, saying, "Oh, we're glad to see

(Recited by Wilson; originally published in Aoki and Walker, 1989. See also "Coyote and His Guests" in Phinney, 1934.)

you, Coyote. Surely you came to see us." "Yes," said Coyote. They [Fish Hawks] knew that Coyote was always hungry. Fish Hawk went out and brought in lots of fish, which he quickly cooked. There was a pile of them. When Coyote finished eating, he brought home all the fish that was left. Coyote said, "You can visit me too." "Yes, I will sometime." Then Coyote went home. And many days passed.

One day Fish Hawk came. "It's good to see you," Coyote said, and he ran and climbed a tree. The river was running. There was a hole in the ice. Coyote said, "Let me stick a twig in there to catch fish." But poor Coyote fell in on his head by mistake. He had missed his mark on the ice, hit his head, and killed himself; but he recovered soon. Fish Hawk felt sorry for him. He knew what Coyote had done. Fish Hawk said, "Wait here, Coyote. I will go catch some fish." Then Fish Hawk went, and Coyote saw him high in a tree. Fish Hawk was away for quite a while. Then he came back. He had caught and brought back fish on a forked twig. Coyote said, "Thank you." Thus I have told the story of how poor Coyote hit his head. That's all.

▼▼▼▼▼

27

HOW PORCUPINE
WENT TO THE PLAINS

ONCE UPON A TIME Porcupine planned a trip to the Buffalo Country. He packed up about half a sack of sunflower cake and was on his way. He came upon some buffalo droppings and asked the droppings, "How old are you?" "Twenty years," the droppings replied. Porcupine trotted off and began to sing, "I am traveling, Porcupine traveling," over and over. Soon he became tired, but he went on singing, although more slowly. He came upon some more buffalo droppings after he had crossed a ridge. He asked again, "How old are you?" and this time the dung answered that it was fifteen years old. He knew he was getting closer, and he went on singing as before.

About noon, he decided to eat a sunflower cake. He went on, and whenever he found some dung, he would ask its age and be told "such-and-such many years." He passed over the divide, and the dung he found there was only ten years old. He was getting closer. Then he found some that was only five years old. He went on traveling slowly, and again he slowed down in his singing, eating away as he went.

Finally he found some three-year-old dung, then two, and soon one-year-old dung. "Now I'm catching up with them," he thought. He began to travel faster. Soon he came to dung that was only one day old.

Then he came to a wide river, and he looked across. There, on the other side, the buffalo were sitting. There was no way for Porcupine to cross the river, so he shouted across to them, "Wade over to me!" And the buffalo began talking among themselves: "He's caught up with us! Who will wade over to him?" One of them shouted to Porcupine, "Shall it be me?"

Porcupine answered in the Flathead language (he was half Flathead), saying, "No! Not you!" There was a calfless buffalo sitting at the upriver end of the group, and Porcupine said to himself, "I wish she would wade over to me."

(Recited by Watters; originally published in Aoki and Walker, 1989. See also Wilson's "Porcupine and Buffalo" in the same volume, and "Porcupine and Coyote" in Phinney, 1934.)

Coyote said to Porcupine, "Heartless friend. Throw down something, just anything. Even the ribs!"

The buffalo kept asking Porcupine, "This one? This one?" But he refused them all. Then came the turn of the one sitting upriver at the edge of the group. "This one?" they asked, pointing to her. "Yes" (in Flathead), Porcupine answered. "Ah," they said, "he wants you to ford over!" Then she lifted up her head, shook herself, and waded across. She came ashore to him, and she told him, "Sit here on the back of my head in the middle."

"But," Porcupine said, "when the water gets into your ears, you'll shake your head and I'll fall off into the river." "Then get onto my back," she replied. "The water will be running over your back, and I'll drown," Porcupine said. "Then I'll wrap you around me with my tail," she suggested. "But," Porcupine protested, "you'll stick your tail out and I'll fall into the water." Finally she said, "Then come right inside me, and stay there." "Yes, that's it!" Porcupine agreed, and he went into the big buffalo. She waded across. As he felt her coming out of water, he pulled out his biggest quill and pierced her heart with it. She began running, but soon she dropped over—dead.

Porcupine [emerged and stood over her] where she lay, and he realized with chagrin that he had forgotten to bring his knife. So he tried making some sharp edges out of a stone, but none of them turned out to be sharp enough. He began to hum, "I wish I had something to butcher my big cow with . . ."

Nearby a coyote was roaming about. He overheard Porcupine humming, and he tried to hear his words. He was finally able to make them out, and he went up to Porcupine asking, "What are you saying?" "Nothing," answered Porcupine. "No, I heard you," said the coyote. "And this is what you were saying . . . ," and he began to hum Porcupine's song. "Well, where is it?" Coyote asked Porcupine.

Porcupine took Coyote to where the huge cow was lying. Coyote said, "Now we'll jump over it, and whoever goes over without touching will have the buffalo." And so they did, and it was Coyote who got over it, while Porcupine, even though he took a running start, just bumped into it. "Now it's mine," said Coyote.

But later he suggested, "Let's urinate over it—over the ridge of the buffalo's body." And so they did. Coyote's urine landed far beyond, but Porcupine's landed right there. "You're no good," said Coyote, "you're getting it all wet and ruining it."

Porcupine pleaded: "Give me just some part of the meat." "No! That's my favorite," Coyote answered. Then he butchered the cow completely. "Give me just the head then," Porcupine asked again. "No! It's all mine," said Coyote. "I won it from you." Then he hit his hip, and his excrement children ran out. He stopped the youngest one and said to him, "You stay here." So the children ran back in, except for the youngest, whom Coyote kept out. He told him, "You keep watch here while I go and get your mother." Then Coyote clubbed Porcupine.

Coyote walked off, leaving Porcupine lying with his bristles sticking up straight. After Coyote had gone some distance, Porcupine arose, but Coyote's youngest child began shouting, "He's coming to, Daddy!" So Coyote returned and hit Porcupine again. Just at that moment Eagle was circling above, and he felt sorry for Porcupine.

Porcupine remained prostrate until Coyote was out of sight. Then he arose, and Eagle came down to him. Eagle clubbed Cicéqi, Coyote's youngest son, to death, and then he said to Porcupine, "I'll move your things to a higher place." And so he moved the meat to some shelters he had made in a tree. They propped Cicéqi up, and they let him bite a piece of fat.

Just then Coyote and his bunch returned, making a lot of noise. Coyote said to his children, "Where could he have hauled the meat?" Coyote wondered. He tried to track the meat, but it was nowhere to be found. Just as he was about to give up, he saw it. "Oh!" he exclaimed, "They are up on the pine tree!"

He said to Porcupine, "Heartless friend! Throw down something, just anything. Even the ribs!" "It's my favorite," replied Porcupine. "Everything is." "Not even the head?" pleaded Coyote. "Throw it down to me." "All right, I'll throw it down," replied Porcupine, "but it might get ruined when it lands, so put your heads together and I'll throw it down to you."

So they put their heads together, and at that point Porcupine killed them all. Little Cicéqi was saved for some reason. The head missed him, but it killed all the rest. Porcupine took Cicéqi up and fed him. Porcupine forced him to eat and he ate too much, and his stomach became upset. Porcupine said to him, "We'll have a stink around here!" He ordered Cicéqi to climb up the big limb and defecate there. So Cicéqi began climbing up. But coyotes never climb trees, and Cicéqi became uneasy about climbing. He stopped midway and then he fell to the ground.

Porcupine had gotten them all.

▼▼▼▼▼

28

COYOTE'S TRIP
TO THE EAST

COYOTE DECIDED, "Now I'm going to the Buffalo Country; I'm going to where there are plains. I'm going after buffalo. I'll drive them over here, and we'll have buffalo for our own." He went fa-a-ar away for many days. Finally he got to the Buffalo Country. He went over the mountains and came out of the timber. He kept walking, and finally he walked up to a buffalo bull.

There the buffalo sat—he was pitiful, skinny, and he had sores all over his body. His eyes were closed. "What happened?" Coyote asked, and he saw that the buffalo was very sick and ailing. Now Coyote played a trick on him and urinated on him; he urinated on his sores. Buffalo said, "Oh, Coyote, you're going too far." He got angry and stood up. Coyote ran and said, "No, my friend," and he turned around toward him. "No, I will make you horns, the very best. I will help you whenever you are in need." Buffalo replied, "Coyote, you're piling misery on misery for me. A young bull has taken all my cows. I fought with him, and as you see he defeated me. He almost killed me. Both my horns are broken, and look at my sores. And you poke fun at me in this sad state." "No, my friend," Coyote said. "I'll make you good horns and I'll help you. We'll kill the bull who defeated you."

Then Buffalo said, "All right, Coyote," and Coyote made horns; he made very good and sharp ones out of a syringa tree. He made each one for him, and then he said, "You just rest, and then we'll go." The old bull got better, and he looked for the young bull. "They were there, somewhere; he took them over there." Then the old bull and Coyote followed. The sick one bellowed, and the young bull heard them, and the old bull saw the young one coming. They met, and they fought. Coyote was there to help. They dashed at each other ferociously all day. And then, with his sharp horns, the old bull tore off the skin of his adversary.

(Recited by Wilson; originally published in Aoki and Walker, 1989. See also "Coyote in the Buffalo Country" in Spinden, 1917.)

Coyote said, "I'll make you good horns and I'll help you. We'll kill the bull who defeated you."

Then Coyote made himself brave. He took bow and arrow and shot as the young bull went by, and soon the young bull was stretched out dead. (Oh, yes. Before this the old bull for whom Coyote had made the horns said, "Now, Coyote, you help me." Before Coyote would agree to help him, Buffalo had said, "If we defeat him, then I will give you thirty buffalo cows to take home.") Then he said, "Now that we've finished this business, you take the thirty cows. Take good care of them. When you go into the mountains, go slowly and let them rest. Don't for any reason scare them. Take them gently and treat them well, and take them across to the other side of the mountains. These buffalo will grow bigger there." Coyote said, "All right, I'll do as you say."

Then Coyote followed them. The buffalo left and they rested; they ate grass, drank water, and sat down. And each time when night came, they would find a resting place. And there they slept, sitting on their haunches, while Coyote slept bunched up under a tree. They kept going, maybe for five nights; and then, they were in the mountains. They stopped there for the night. When the buffalo were sleeping, Coyote started thinking. He got up during the night and looked them over: Which one was the best? He touched them, and they got scared, these buffalo, and they stood up and dashed back home to the Buffalo Country. Then Coyote gave up, and he came back home alone. He had lost the buffalo. If only he'd followed the instructions of that bull who said, "Take them. Don't scare them for any reason." Poor Coyote came home empty-handed.

Coyote said, "I will eat the same amount as you. You have left me out. You are quite heartless."

29

COYOTE AND FOX

THERE ONCE LIVED Coyote and his friend Fox. Coyote went around catching mice and picking wild roseberries. He would bring them to his friend and toss them over to him, saying, "You eat too." And Fox would pick them up and eat them. They ate, and that's all the food they had.

Then Fox saw that their pitch was running out. He knew where there was a big fallen log for getting pitch, so he went down there and chopped. He kept throwing the pitch in back of him, until he thought he had chopped enough. Then he looked back, and there was a pile of dried Chinook salmon. He carried this home and put it in a cellar that he made under his bed. And he ate some and left some for the future.

Just then Coyote came in with wild mice and roseberries, saying, "This is for you." But because he was filled up on meat, Fox picked up only the roseberries. The mice that Coyote had caught scattered around and ran away, Coyote said, "My hard work is unappreciated. You are letting my catch run away."

When they went to bed, Coyote thought to himself, "Why is he not hungry?" Then he heard sounds as if Fox were eating. What is he eating? Coyote wondered. He dashed over to him, saying, "What are you eating?" There Fox was, eating Chinook salmon. Fox threw [some salmon] over. Coyote said, "I will eat the same amount as you. You have left me out. You are quite heartless."

When they were through eating, Coyote asked him, "Where did you get it? Who gave it to you? Where did you get it?" Although Coyote kept asking him, Fox simply answered, "You don't do things right." Finally Fox told Coyote, "I

(Recited by Watters; originally published in Aoki and Walker, 1989. See also Wilson's "Coyote's Troubles" and "Coyote, Fox, and the Wild Carrots" in the same volume; "Coyote and Fox" in Phinney, 1934; and "Coyote and Fox Get Food" in Spinden, 1917.)

went down from here and chopped pitch, and I threw it backward. I thought I'd carry that much home. And then there was a pile of salmon, and I brought that home."

"Hm," Coyote said. "If you can, I am certainly able to chop a whole lot too. I can do anything and I am strong." And that's what he did. Next morning Coyote started chopping, and he chopped plenty, and when he looked back, there was a pile of dried Chinook salmon. "Hm, I will have lunch," he said, and he ate it all up. "I'm going to chop and chop again," said Coyote, and he threw it backward. Then he thought, "Now there's plenty." He looked back, but there was only a pile of pitch.

He brought the pitch home, and he grumblingly came upon Fox, to whom he said, "You're always lying on your back, and you never worry about pitch. I brought pitch home." "There must be something wrong with the way you did it," said Fox. And thus they spent their time, with Coyote just looking for ants and mice and looking for roseberries to bring home.

One day Fox was sitting outside in the shade, and all of a sudden he sang, "We wish we had something, my friend and I, five packs, thump, thump." Just as he stopped singing, there landed five packs, thump, thump. Oh! They were different kinds of dried meat, tallow, and so forth. Then he hauled them inside, and there again he made a cache. And as before, Coyote suspected that Fox was eating something. Again he ran over to him at night. The meat was packed away in a parfleche. And Coyote pushed his friend Fox aside, saying, "Let me eat just as much. You are always heartless, leaving me out, while I go and gather berries and bring home mice to you."

Again, the next morning he asked, "Where did you get it? And how?" Fox said, "I was just sitting out here and that's what happened. I sang, 'I wish we could hear something, my friend and I, the sound of five packs falling, thump, thump.'" "Hm," thought Coyote, "I will somehow get more than this tomorrow." That morning he also sat and called out, "We wish we could hear five packs, thump, thump." All of a sudden they landed. And this is the way they spent their days. Every other day they would call, Coyote more often than Fox. They lived quite well.

Coyote wondered what it was that gave the packs to them. He watched and waited. The instant that he saw it, he called after it, "A ponytail, a ponytail went over." From then on, even if they repeated the words, nothing happened, nothing happened anywhere. Fox said, "You goofed it again!" and Coyote answered, "Oh! I just called after him like this." And then some more time passed.

Fox was wandering around one day, and he came upon a couple of people who were taking a sweatbath. He came up to a man who was sweating, and he was with a young boy who was rolling and playing with a toy of fat. Fox got a quick bite out of it. The boy said, "Father! This old man is eating my plaything." Then the father told his son, "Tell him, my son, that he may go to our home and help himself to our food." The boy told him, and Fox went from there to their house. Oh! There were all different kinds of meat drying, and there were also various kinds of meat and fat stacked all around. He helped himself, and he cooked and ate until he was quite full.

Then the father and the son came home, and Fox said, "Yes, I ate." The father said, "That is yours, just as much as you can carry, just as much a load as you can stand." Then the old man gave him all that, and Fox took it home. He did the same thing: He hid it, thinking to himself that Coyote didn't do things right and for that reason shouldn't be in on Fox's secret. Just as before Coyote found the food. "How and where did you get it? How?" Coyote said. Fox said, "I just came upon a man, and he gave it to me. I did as he told me. He gave me the meat, which I brought home. He told me to take as much as I could lift."

Coyote said, "Hm, if you can bring that much, I can bring more." Then he went in the direction Fox had told him until he came to them. There was a man sweating in a mudbath, and there was a boy playing with some tallow and rolling it. Coyote bit a piece of it off. "An old man is bothering me," said the boy, whereupon the father said, "Tell him to go to our home where he can cook himself food." The little boy told him, and Coyote went. There he lay on his back, saying, "I, a chief, will not cook for myself or serve myself. I will wait until they do it for me." Then he lay on his back.

When the old man and his son came, they prepared their own food. Then they got through eating and went to bed without saying anything to Coyote. They thought he had already eaten. Coyote got angry and lost his temper. "How could he think that I, a chief, would prepare my own food?" But they had gone to bed. "The fire sparks are landing on you," he said, but even though he kept telling them this, they were just quiet and relaxed. He figured to himself, "There is a lot of meat hanging here, so this is where my friend and I will move in."

Now Coyote went to the old man and cut off his head. He cut off the heads of both father and son, and they dropped dead. At that moment all the meat hanging and all the personal property that was there and all the floor matting and so forth ran away, and only the drying racks remained, greased up. So Coyote took a lick. "Oh!" said Coyote, and at that moment [Fox's] fawn-skin blanket and other things suddenly got up and ran away. Fox thought to himself, "Now Coyote must have done something wrong again." Coyote came back empty-handed. Fox said, "What happened?" and Coyote answered, "I cut off the heads of the father and son, just like that and then everything that they had ran off."

Coyote lost his luck with food. From then on he never found anything because he threw away favors that were given to him.

Sometime after that, Fox was wandering around the shoreline, and he happened to stick his tail in the water. When he lifted it up, it felt heavy. "Now what?" he thought. "I just dropped my tail in the water." When he took it out, there were wild carrots wrapped around his tail, and he took them home. Coyote asked him, "Where did you get them?" Then Fox and his friend ate the wild carrots. Then Fox told Coyote, "You are not reliable. I am not going to tell you." Then Coyote demanded, "Where did you get them?" Fox answered, "I just stuck my tail in the water; I did it unintentionally. Then I brought these wild carrots out."

"Well, I am able and versatile too," said Coyote. And that's what Coyote did. He stuck his tail in the water, and he felt the weight and brought it out. Wild carrots were sticking to his tail. Then he ate. "I will have lunch now. Then I will get a lot more for sure." Then he stuck his tail in again, and the weight dragged him down. He tried to grab the twigs along the shore, but to no avail. He was dragged down and taken farther into the deep. Ice had formed on his tail. There were no wild carrots anywhere.

Coyote had thrown away his good fortune again, and that's why you can't pull out wild carrots anymore nowadays. That's all.

▼▼▼▼▼

30

COYOTE AND FOX
PRETEND TO BE WOMEN

COYOTE AND FOX were short of food, and Coyote said, "Let us plan to get married to some man!" Fox answered, "But how can we marry men when we are men ourselves?" Coyote said, "That is easy enough! We will just put on women's clothes, and the rest will only be smooth talking." So Fox agreed that it was a fine plan to marry someone that way. They dressed up in women's dresses and went to see two young unmarried wolves. They told these wolf brothers that their parents had sent them out to try and find good husbands. Then the wolves agreed to marry them.

Then with smooth talking Coyote told the wolves, "For five days you cannot really marry us, but instead must give us food to take home to our parents." The wolf brothers believed what Coyote said, because they did not recognize him in that disguise. So for five days Coyote and Fox pretended to take a supply of food home to their parents. At the end of this time Coyote did not know how to get out of the difficulty. On the evening of the sixth day, he said to Fox, "Be ready all the time, we shall leave for home tonight." Now the wolves had two sisters who were dwelling near their brothers' camp. After dark Coyote went to the house of the girls; and when one of them went outside, he seized the other and violated her. This girl made a great cry; and when Fox heard the cry, he jumped up and ran off. Coyote ran away also, and the wolves never caught him.

(Originally published as "Coyote and Fox" in Spinden, 1917.)

▼▼▼▼▼

31

FOX AND COYOTE

AS SHAMANS

SEVERAL PERSONS WERE SUFFERING from swellings of the body, and they sent for Fox to treat them and make the swelling go away. When these persons were nearly well, Coyote asked Fox for permission to help in the curing. So Fox let Coyote act as shaman, and the patients grew worse again. This happened several times. Fox would make them better, and Coyote would interfere and make them worse. By and by the sick ones ordered Fox to tell Coyote not to help because he was not a good medicine man.

(Originally published in Spinden, 1917.)

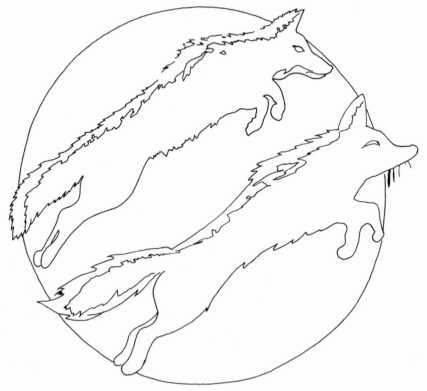

When the race was about half over, Coyote gave out, and Fox was left to finish.

▼▼▼▼▼

32

COYOTE AND FOX
RUN RACES

THE MOUNTAIN SHEEP, the elk, the black-tailed deer, the white-tailed buck, and the mountain goat outran all other animals. The wager was that those who were beaten should lose their heads. These five animals always won. Now Coyote and Fox happened to come to that place; and Coyote said to Fox, "Partner, we shall also race them; we two against those five." They made a challenge and arranged a race with five black-tailed deer. So they ran a long way, crossing gulches and hills; but when the race was about half over, Coyote gave out, and Fox was left to finish. Pretty soon the five black-tailed deer gave out also, and so Fox won the race. Then the five black-tailed deer were beheaded in a gulch, and Coyote and Fox devoured the bodies and rested. After this, Coyote and Fox ran races with each of the other four kinds of animals. They won all the races and killed the defeated runners.

No other animals dared to run with Coyote and Fox. Soon, however, these two got fat from eating too much meat. Then Jackrabbit, White Mountain Rabbit, Bald Eagle, Golden Eagle, and Magpie decided to challenge them. Coyote said to Fox, "We have beaten all the good runners; let us beat these as well!" The race was a long one as before; and Coyote gave out, and every one on the other side gave out but Magpie. Magpie was behind Fox when they came to a steep hill at the end of the course. Then Magpie swooped down and won the race.

Coyote said to the victors, "You are fine runners, and have beaten us fairly. Just let me get a drink of water, and then you may cut off my head." So they told him to get a drink and come back. Now down at the creek there were some children playing, and they saw Coyote take off his clothes and crawl into

(Originally published in Spinden, 1917.)

the water and under a root. A boy cried out, "Here is Coyote! Come on! He is crawling under the root!" They all pulled him out and took him where Fox was, and then they beheaded both. It did Coyote no good to hide after he had lost.

33

THE FIVE GRIZZLY BEAR SISTERS AND THE FIVE WOODPECKER BROTHERS

THERE LIVED LOTS OF PEOPLE at a certain place and among them were five Woodpecker brothers. (Also, some distance away, there lived the Grizzly Bear sisters.) These brothers were greatly respected by the people. One day Coyote made a plan, and he went to tell the woodpeckers about it.

Coyote came to the woodpeckers' place, and he made them a proposition. "Here is what you'll do . . ." He announced to the Woodpecker brothers and to the people in general, "Let's go hunting for grizzly bears!" Coyote knew how he would be repaid for organizing this project.

The people followed Coyote and were off to the hunt. Coyote went to the grizzly bears and told them, "They're really going to give it to you with this arrowhead, but actually it's only made out of stick. It really couldn't even make a hole in anything, let alone a grizzly bear!"

The grizzly bears, taken in by Coyote's hoax, went along with it—the oldest first. The hunters shouted, "There's a grizzly bear running downstream!" The oldest woodpecker rushed to catch up with her, and not long after he caught her, she tore his head right off. She thought to herself, "This red head is so pretty to look at," and she started to run away with it. Her sister, seeing this, envied the sister having that pretty head. Coyote told them, "You all will have your chance to have one of these." At this the next oldest grizzly bear proceeded to do the very same thing to the next oldest woodpecker, and so for the

(Recited by Watters; originally published in Aoki and Walker, 1989)

Young Woodpecker makes an arrowhead from Grandfather Rattlesnake's teeth.

third pair. Then there were only two more left. When the fourth one was killed, the youngest suddenly found himself all alone and he said to Coyote, "Not tomorrow or the day after, but some time, I'll get revenge on you for this!"

So when the youngest woodpecker had a chance, he went to see his paternal grandfather, who was a pine squirrel. When he explained to his grandfather the reason he had come, his grandfather said to him, "Come, Grandson, I'm going to make some shoes for you." And so he did, and with those shoes the young woodpecker could climb up anything very quickly, and nothing could catch up with him. Those were the kind of shoes that his grandfather gave him.

After seeing his grandfather, the young woodpecker went on to another person, who was a rattlesnake. When he got there, he said to the rattlesnake, "Grandpa, I've come because the grizzly bears have killed us all and I'm left all alone. They haven't seen the last of me. I'll fight them again, but I need something to kill those grizzly bears with."

"All right, Grandson," said Rattlesnake, "I'll give you something." Rattlesnake pulled out his own teeth and said, "Do it with this flint and fasten it together with arrows."

The young woodpecker took it home, and he made the arrowhead as his grandfather had instructed. Whenever a piece would chip off, lots of small little birds that were around picked up the little pieces. These little birds were in sympathy with the young woodpecker. From these chipped pieces the birds also made arrowheads by fastening them together.

Then the time came to go out hunting for the grizzly bears. "You go that way! Right along that way! You'll catch them and kill them over there!" shouted the leader to the various members of the hunting party. When they thus dispersed, some people began shouting, "The grizzly bears are going downstream!"

Then the little birds joined in. They shot the grizzly bears and stung them. The grizzly bears ran downstream, shouting, "It burns, it burns!" Some shouted, "Those arrows really work!" One of the grizzly bears felt the arrowhead sting her before she saw it coming. Then she saw Woodpecker. "There he is, waiting for me," she said, and she ran straight at him. He shot her dead.

Then Coyote began cutting up the meat of the grizzly bear, and he took it home to bake. There he would distribute it to all the people. But he decided to give the grizzly bears a little more than their share. "Here's your baked meat," he said to them. Only four of the grizzly bears were left.

Then someone (Woodpecker) grabbed the meat back from Grizzly Bear and killed her. He said, "Now she'll not harm [make a slave of] anyone again." Then he said to the other birds, "Tomorrow you'll get your revenge on the next one." In this way the Woodpeckers killed the Grizzly Bears until only one was left.

The rest were done away with. That's the way it happened to those Grizzly Bears, who had always got the best of people.

This is what resulted from the woodpecker's grandfather giving him the shoes with which he could run up anywhere easily, and from the rattlesnake teeth, given by his other grandfather, with which he could kill something quickly.

After that time the woodpecker became harder and harder to find, and now he is seen only in the mountains. He went to spend his days in the mountains after all this had happened. And in the same way, the one remaining grizzly bear escaped to the mountains.

With the little birds' assistance Woodpecker defeated them. Coyote had almost killed all of the woodpecker brothers; if he had, there might not be any woodpeckers alive today.

▼▼▼▼▼

34

HOW THE GRIZZLY BEAR
SISTERS WERE FOOLED

Lots of people were living at a certain place, and some distance away from there the Grizzly Bear sisters made everyone uneasy and anxious because they would kill anyone who passed by their place. Everyone was upset over it.

The Grizzly Bear sisters wanted very much to marry a certain young man who lived at the people's place. When the people found out that the bears wanted this boy, they all got together and made a plan. They said, "We will make a plan." (I forgot which one did the planning, maybe Owl or someone.) When they were ready they said, "We will do it this way. We will build a strong house, a long house. Then we will tell the Grizzly Bear sisters, 'Just the five of you dance around here, and you go around five times. Then our young man will look you over.'" Their custom was, if a man selects the oldest sister [as a wife], all the sisters have him as a husband.

So Coyote went to the Grizzly Bear sisters, narrowly escaping getting killed by them. He told them, "This is why I've come—the Chief's son is planning to look the five of you over at a dance you'll do. You are to go around five times, and if he selects the oldest one when he looks you over, all of you will have him for your husband."

The oldest one had a baby, but the other sisters were childless. That's the way they were. The sisters agreed with Coyote's proposition. "Yes, we'll do it," they agreed. Then Coyote told them, "Go there in the evening and dance in a single file. Go around five times, and he will look you over and make his selection."

So the Grizzly Bear sisters got ready, and when it came time they went to do as had been planned. The people had the fire prepared for the occasion. When they got there, Coyote said to them, "Now all of you cover your heads with

<hr>

(Recited by Watters; originally published in Aoki and Walker, 1989.)

The grizzly bear sisters made everyone uneasy and anxious because they would kill anyone who passed by their place.

veils, so that no one can see your faces. In that way he will select one of you."
So that's the way they came to the ceremony.

As the sisters were dancing in single file, the people all slipped out of the
house, including Coyote, who kept on jabbering as he slipped out. The people
were outside, encircling the house, and they joined in with the sisters' singing
while they were dancing. The sisters moved in single file, the oldest one leading in front with her baby.

The people outside set the fire, and it started burning. The baby screamed,
"Ouch! It burns!" The oldest sister admonished the baby, "Be quiet! Be quiet!
Your stepfather [uncle] can hear you!"

They were alone in the house like this for some time. Suddenly the youngest
sister had a feeling that there was no one else inside the house. She had a feeling that the people were outside somewhere, talking and singing.

The youngest sister quickly pulled her veil off and cried, "So! He's not giving us anything anyway! That young man isn't going to select us! They've set
us on fire!" The girls ran about madly, but the house was solid and tight as
drum, so they couldn't escape. The house continued to burn.

And so the people got rid of the Grizzly Bears, who had always killed anyone who came by and made the people so uneasy. From that time on they
never bothered anyone again.

Grizzly Bear packed up her things, got ready, and went to Black Bear's house to claim her husband.

▼▼▼▼▼

35

DON'T CRACK
THE BONES

ONCE UPON A TIME Coyote was living with his son. The son had a wife, Black Bear. Coyote's son often used to go hunting, bringing his catch home on his back. At such times he would warn his wife, "Don't ever break the bones of these animals!"

But one day the wife felt that it was really a shame to waste the bones that were piled up in the house. "My!" she thought, "I wonder why he forbids me to break these bones—I could make broth with them." So that's what she did. She proceeded to break the bones, but all at once a piece of one of the bones fell away as she was cracking them, and it flew out through the chimney. It flew over to the house where Grizzly Bear woman was living.

She saw the piece of bone come flying into her place and, taking this as a sign, said to herself, "Well! My sister [Black Bear] has caused me to become the wife of her husband." She packed up her things, got ready, and went to Black Bear's house to claim her husband. She went there and just moved right in.

"What in the world are you doing here?" cried Black Bear, alarmed. "Why, you've caused me to become your husband's wife," answered Grizzly Bear. "Now we've both got him as a husband." There seemed to be nothing that could be done about the predicament.

When her husband came home and saw what had happened, he reproached his wife. "You see? This is why I forbade you to break bones—I said to you, 'Don't do that!' "

And so they began to spend their days together, the three of them. One morning one of the wives would get up and make breakfast, and the next morning it would be the other wife's turn. When Coyote awoke in the morning, he saw the fire burning, and he clearly saw Black Bear cooking the food they would eat.

(Recited by Watters; originally published in Aoki and Walker, 1989.)

However, on the morning when it was Grizzly Bear's turn to cook breakfast, she would wake up and the food would already be there, all prepared. She called everyone to breakfast. "Come on and eat, breakfast is ready!" she called, and everyone came to eat. This is how it went day after day.

By and by Coyote began to wonder about Grizzly Bear. "I wonder when she makes the food? How does she prepare it? When I wake up in the morning the food is already there in its place."

One morning he plainly saw Black Bear getting up, taking roots, meat, salmon, and so on and preparing them for breakfast. She cooked all of it and the people ate. But since he never saw Grizzly Bear do this, he kept wondering, "When does she make her food, and how does she do it?"

So one night Coyote decided to stay awake all night. Toward morning, he heard something—Grizzly Bear was making some kind of noise. Coyote heard the sound of voracious eating, "Gobble, gobble," and he looked and saw her eating all the food. After she had eaten all the various kinds of food, she picked up her dishes and took them away outside. She was gone for some time, but after a while she came back with the food all prepared!

Coyote was even more perplexed to know how she prepared the food. So the next time, Coyote decided to follow her outside. What he saw was this: Grizzly Bear put the containers and dishes underneath a log that was suspended [under a tree] in the air. She ate up all the food as before and then proceeded to defecate into the containers. Then the excrement suddenly turned into different kinds of food, such as cooked salmon. That was how the food was prepared, and that was what she took home. "So!" exclaimed Coyote, "That's what she did!"

And so the next time that Black Bear prepared breakfast, Coyote shouted to the people, "Come on, people, now we'll eat real food!" But when it was Grizzly Bear's turn, he would tell them, "Come on, now we'll eat the excrement—oops! I mean, we'll eat the food—I always get my words mixed up!"

Then Coyote went to the Worm People, and he said to them, "You gnaw this log with your teeth, so that when Grizzly Bear sits on it, it will break."

Grizzly Bear came, as usual, to that log, and she placed the containers beneath it and sat on the log above the containers, defecating into them as she moved little by little across the log. The worms had gnawed the log almost all the way through, and as a result, when she was in the process of making her food, and when she had defecated for the second time over the log, it broke and she fell backward. "Oh!" she exclaimed in alarm, "this has never happened before—the log must be weak." She got suspicious, and she thought to herself, "This must be Coyote's doing!" Then she saw the worms. "Oh, the worms have chewed it!"

So she was able to take home only a little food. She cleaned herself quite thoroughly, and then she brought the food in. Coyote edged forward a little from where he was sitting, and he took a sniff. "I smell excrement," said Coyote. "Where is that smell coming from—who is it?" Upon hearing this, Grizzly Bear went out and cleaned herself again. She came back in, and as she came in, Coyote again smelled her and exclaimed, "Who smells of excrement?" This made Grizzly Bear really angry, and she dashed out, slamming the door behind her. She stayed outside, furious. "Now see what you've caused, Coyote!" she stormed to herself.

When Coyote saw how mad she was getting, he and everyone else escaped by turning themselves into something different. Fox, who was also there, wondered, "What shall I turn into?" and he made himself become a piece of half-charred wood. All that could be seen of him was a burned stump lying there. Coyote turned himself into a door, but unfortunately when Grizzly Bear came running back into the house she slammed the door, and Coyote screamed, "Ouch!" Then she accidentally stepped on the piece of wood, causing it [Fox] to groan in pain. "Oh, this must be Fox!" exclaimed Grizzly Bear. "He never used to say anything against me; he never used to hate me." She passed him by, but she went about killing all the rest of them. She went up to whatever they had turned into, saying, "Here you are!" and then she would tear them to pieces.

But still she hadn't found Coyote, and she wondered where he was. She started to dash out of the house, but as she was doing so, she got the feeling that he was around there somewhere. "Ah, here you are!" she screamed, forcefully tearing the door off. Coyote pleaded, "No, daughter-in-law, no, don't," but his pleadings were to no avail and she tore him apart too, killing him. She had defeated them all, and finally she was ready to take on the last one—Black Bear.

But before Grizzly Bear and Black Bear met, Black Bear greased herself with fat, becoming sleek and shiny. Thus, although Grizzly Bear tried to grab her, Black Bear could slip out of her grasp. From then on Grizzly and Black Bear fought jealously, but Black Bear got the best of Grizzly Bear because she could not be caught by virtue of her slippery fur. That's how Grizzly Bear was finally put down. That's all.

Then Grizzly Bear opened his mouth. Coyote threw the hot rocks in.

▼▼▼▼▼

36

HOW COYOTE KILLED
THE GRIZZLY BEARS

Once again I am going to tell a story. There were many people living. A girl who was playing with something got a bone stuck in her foot. The bone was sticking out of her foot. She was laid up in bed, and no one could cure her. Even though they tried, no one succeeded. It just swelled up, and she cried and cried. Then the people left the tepee, and they left her in it. She was alone there. She moaned pitifully; she was moaning there all alone.

Coyote was wandering by, and he saw the tepee. "What's that? I will go and see what it is." As he approached, he heard the girl moaning and crying. He went into the tepee, saying, "What are you doing?" and the girl said, "I have a splinter in my foot; a bone is sticking out, and the people have left me. They just gave up and left for good. I am quite sick now, and I have given up." He said to her, "Let me try. I will fix it." Coyote said, "Stick your foot out," and she stuck her legs out. Coyote grabbed that bone with his mouth, and it came out. Pus and black blood came out quickly, and Coyote cleaned it all for her thoroughly and bound it up with buckskin, and she stopped moaning. She had no pain, but still she couldn't walk. Then Coyote made a cane for her, and she started walking well. Coyote said, "Now we will follow the people. We will track them and catch up with them. They must be living somewhere. We will go." And they went.

They got ready, and then they traveled for a long time. They came to a plateau. Coyote looked out from there, saying, "There they are—below. There are tepees all over. We have caught up with them." Then they went down. Coyote asked them, "Where is my aunt, Mouse?" The people answered, "She is in that ugly tepee there."

(Recited by Wilson; originally published in Aoki and Walker, 1989. See also "Coyote Bears He Killed" and "Coyote the Expeditioner" in Phinney, 1934; and "Grizzly Bear and Coyote" in Spinden, 1917.)

So they went to the tepee. The people followed them in, noticing that Coyote was escorting a good-looking girl. The people said, "Oh, surely that girl must have recovered." Coyote, leaning on his back, made the pretty girl sit down, and he rested his head on her. He was singing happily. He was showing off. Some of the young men disliked him. They brought in Frog. The young men took the good-looking girl away from behind Coyote and made Frog sit there instead of the girl. Coyote was carried away with his singing. Then he turned around, "Let me take a look at the girl." But only Frog was sitting there, blinking. They [the young men] had taken the girl away. Coyote became angry at poor Frog, and he grabbed her and threw her out.

Then Coyote began to make a plan. The people had said to Coyote, "The grizzly bears are ruling us. They seem to be living below, and they rule over everything." So Coyote made a plan. "Now you are going to challenge them." And he said to Cicéqi, "Go to their head chief and ask him to give you their most valuable deer-hoof bell." Cicéqi went. "No," said Grizzly Bear. "I won't give this to anyone. But I will give you something else." "No," Coyote said. "I just want the deer-hoof bell." Now Grizzly Bear was mad at Coyote. "We are going to kill Coyote by all means." But Coyote knew this, so he got ready ahead of the grizzly bears.

Coyote heated up some round rocks. He took a lot of grease and put it on them. Then he arranged a contest. "Now let's go," and the oldest grizzly bear went. Coyote saw him from up high, and he met the grizzly bear. The grizzly bear came growling quite angrily. Coyote said to Grizzly Bear, "There, now older brother, let me throw this grease into your mouth. When you eat me, you may upset your stomach because of my fur." Then Grizzly Bear opened his mouth. Coyote threw the hot rocks in. Grizzly Bear fell over backward and he rolled down. He was burning all over inside, and he moaned. His band of people said, "Go to your mud bath. Go." He went that way and threw himself around, but nothing helped him at all. "To the bear's back-resting place, go!" So he went there, but he dropped dead.

Then younger brother got mad and jumped up. "Surely, I am going to get you. Nothing is going to stop me. I am going to tear you up, Coyote." But Coyote was prepared. He was ready. Coyote met Grizzly Bear, and again he said, "Older brother, just let me do this; then we can continue." He picked up rocks; Grizzly Bear opened his mouth, and Coyote threw them in. In the same way, Grizzly Bear rolled over, suffering. The people said, "Go to the bear-wallow." Even though he went there, it didn't help him. "To the bear's back-resting place, go." Though he went, it did no good.

Now the third brother grizzly bear went up in the same way. Coyote told him, "Younger brother, open your mouth. Let me throw this in so your stomach won't be upset by my hair." Then Grizzly Bear opened his mouth, and Coyote threw the rocks in. In the same way, Grizzly Bear rolled backward in pain. "Go to the bear-wallow," the people said, and even though he threw himself around, it didn't help. "Go to the bears' back-rest." Even though he went there, it didn't help him, and he too dropped dead.

And still another got angry in the same way. "Now surely I am going to get you, Coyote." He got even madder as he went. Once again Coyote said, "Younger brother, now let me throw this in." Then Grizzly Bear opened his mouth and Coyote threw the rocks in, and like the others Grizzly Bear rolled over biting himself. He too went to the bear-wallow and to the bears' back-rest, but nothing would relieve the pain. Then he dropped dead.

Then the youngest came, and although he was courageous, Coyote killed him too. In the same way, he said, "Younger brother, open your mouth." The youngest opened his mouth, and Coyote threw in red hot rocks. Grizzly Bear threw himself around. Then all the grizzly bears were scared. "Now Coyote has slaughtered our chiefs." That's what Coyote did to them. Then Coyote felt like a chief. "Now I'm a chief. I will take away all the houses from the grizzly bears." That's what he did to them, and he moved in there. He took his Aunt Mouse along and Cicéqi. There they lived. That's one thing that Coyote accomplished. That's all.

Coyote started shooting Grizzly Bear until he finally fell over dead.

▼▼▼▼▼

37

COYOTE KILLS
GRIZZLY BEAR'S SONS

ONCE UPON A TIME lots of people were living at a certain place, and Coyote was the chief of them. He had five sons. Then Grizzly Bear's sons caused Coyote's sons to be killed, and Coyote was left alone in the world. He made a plan to get revenge on Grizzly Bear for it. Here is what he did.

He gathered together the people, and he told them, "Now we're going hunting." He instructed each of them in hunting. Coyote's son-in-law, Bobcat, was there also. Coyote ordered them, "You go that way. There you will kill all of Grizzly Bear's sons. They'll be going that way."

Then Coyote went to Grizzly Bear's sons, and he told them, "Now you go that way to the Place Resembling Aiming. There you will see something [a rock] that looks just like a rock aiming a bow and arrow. That's why the stone that looks that way is called the Place Resembling Aiming." So they went that way, advancing upstream. Coyote was on this side, and old man Grizzly Bear himself was on the other side. Behind the grizzly bears followed Pinion Bird.

When they arrived there, the oldest one stopped. "It looks just like a real person," he said, "but it certainly doesn't look like a rock. But we were told by our uncle [Coyote] that it is just a rock in the form of a person aiming." They went on.

Just then, Bobcat [who was actually the rock] pulled out his longest whisker and in his aiming position, shot it, killing all the bears. Pinion Bird tried to move aside so that the arrow would miss him, but it tore off his hip. Pinion Bird turned back and began hollering, "*Pak, pak,* Coyote has caused all of Grizzly Bear's sons to be killed."

Grizzly Bear, on the other side, stopped and listened. "What are they saying?" Grizzly Bear asked. "Oh, never mind," said Coyote nervously, "they're just

(Recited by Watters; originally published in Aoki and Walker, 1989. See also "Bears and Coyote" in Phinney, 1934.)

saying that there's a wounded animal running down the stream, and you'd better be prepared for it." Coyote thus deceived Grizzly Bear about what was really going on, but finally, amid Coyote's frantic chatter, Grizzly Bear said, "Shut up!" and he listened, finally hearing plainly what Pinion Bird was saying. Just then Grizzly Bear tipped his quiver over and it hit Coyote's forehead, tearing it off—but it did not kill Coyote. Coyote ran away, pursued by Grizzly Bear.

As he ran, Coyote said, "Let my legs be broken [let them go fast]." Now Coyote was scared of Grizzly Bear. "Or else," Coyote continued, "let me be a rock that rolls as on the frozen ground." Bear was gaining on Coyote. Coyote had used up all his strength and was completely exhausted. Grizzly Bear was still gaining. Just then, Coyote transformed himself. He said, "Let me be a lodging, just any old one. Let there be lots of pounded root there, and let there be an old man full of sores and with boils all over him, sick in bed. Let there be a stream running with deep river bottom, and let there be just a small bridge over it."

Grizzly Bear was still tracking Coyote, and he came across the lodging. He said, "Yes, that's your trail, Coyote. Even if you are changed into the worst thing, I'll bite you, that's for sure!" Grizzly Bear forced the door open and ran in. But when Grizzly Bear saw the old man [Coyote], he became ill at the sight of the pus-filled sores. Bear asked the old man, "Did Coyote pass by here?" "I don't know," the old man answered. "I just heard footsteps on the bridge."

Again Coyote used his magic: "Let there be tracks running across the bridge." And so there were. Grizzly Bear thought that Coyote must have crossed the bridge. The old man said to Grizzly Bear, "Allow me to hold the bridge for you. It's very unstable, and it tips a lot."

Grizzly Bear started out onto the bridge slowly, while Coyote was holding it steady. Just as he was almost to the middle, Coyote tipped the bridge over, causing Grizzly Bear to fall off and plunge to the bottom. Coyote let loose with a powerful war cry, and suddenly he removed the scab on his forehead to show Bear. "You see," Coyote said, "you almost killed me. There's the sore, right here." Then Coyote started shooting Grizzly Bear until he finally fell over dead. Then he commanded the things that he had transformed to return to their old forms, and Coyote too was changed back into his old self. He butchered the corpse of Grizzly Bear, and he took it home.

So this is how Coyote revenged himself on Grizzly Bear and killed him. Grizzly Bear had caused all of Coyote's sons to be killed, and, in turn, Grizzly Bear had all his sons killed by Coyote, and then Coyote himself killed the old man Grizzly Bear.

38

COYOTE AND THE
SHADOW PEOPLE

COYOTE AND HIS WIFE were living together. His wife became ill. She died. Then Coyote became very, very lonely. He did nothing but weep for his wife. The death spirit came to him and said, "Coyote, do you pine for your wife?" "Yes, friend, I long for her most painfully," replied Coyote. "I could take you to the place where your wife has gone, but I tell you, you must do everything just exactly as I say; not once are you to disregard my commands and do something else." "Yes," replied Coyote, "yes, friend, and what would I do? I will do everything you say." The ghost told him, "Yes. Now let us go." Coyote added, "Yes, let us be on our way."

They went. The spirit said to Coyote again, "You must do whatever I say. Do not disobey." "Yes, yes, friend. I have been pining so deeply and why should I not heed you?" Coyote could not see the spirit clearly. He appeared to be only a shadow. They started out and went along over a plain. "Oh, there are many horses; it looks like a roundup," exclaimed the ghost. "Yes," replied Coyote, though he really saw none. "Yes, there are many horses."

They had arrived near the place of the dead. The ghost knew that Coyote could see nothing, but he said, "Oh look, such quantities of serviceberries! Let us pick some to eat. Now when you see me reach up, you too will reach up and when I bend the limb down you too will pull your hands down. "Yes," Coyote said to him, "I'll do just as you tell me." The ghost reached up and bent the branch down and Coyote did the same. Although he could see no berries he imitated the ghost in putting his hand to and from his mouth in the manner

(Recited by *Wàyi'làtpu*, originally published in Phinney, 1934.)

The spirit said, "Your wife will be with you, but you must never, never touch her."

of eating. Thus they picked and ate berries. Coyote watched him carefully and imitated every action. When the ghost would put his hand into his mouth, Coyote did the same. "Such good serviceberries these are," commented the ghost. "Yes, friend, it is good that we have found them," agreed Coyote. "Now, let us go."

And they went on. "We are about to arrive," the ghost told him. "There is a long, very, very long lodge. Your wife is there somewhere. Just wait and let me ask someone." In a little while, the ghost returned and said to Coyote, "Yes, they have told me where your wife is. We are coming to a door through which we will enter. You will do in every way exactly what you see me do. I will take hold of the door flap, raise it up, and, bending low, will enter. Then you too will take hold of the door flap and do the same." They proceeded to enter in this manner.

It happened that Coyote's wife was sitting right near the entrance. The ghost said to Coyote, "Sit here beside your wife." They both sat. The ghost added, "Your wife is going now to prepare food for us." Coyote could see nothing, except that he was sitting on an open prairie with nothing in sight; yet he could feel the presence of the shadow. "Now she has prepared our food. Let us eat." The ghost reached down and then brought his hand to his mouth. Coyote could see nothing but the prairie dust. They ate. Coyote imitated all the movements of his companion.

When they had finished and the woman had apparently put the food away, the ghost said to Coyote, "You stay here. I must go around to see some people." He went out, but he returned soon. "Here conditions are different from those you have in the land of the living. When it gets dark here it has dawned in your land and when it dawns for us it is growing dark for you." It began to grow dark and Coyote seemed to hear people whispering, talking in faint tones, all around him. Then darkness set in. Oh, Coyote saw many fires in a longhouse. He saw that he was in a very, very large lodge, and there were many fires burning. He saw various people. They seemed to have shadow-like forms, but he was able to recognize different persons. He saw his wife sitting by his side. He was overjoyed and he joyfully greeted all his old friends who had died long ago. How happy he was! He marched down the aisles between the fires, going here and there, and he talked with the people. He did this throughout the night. Now he could see the doorway through which his friend and he had entered.

At last it began to dawn and his friend came to him and said, "Coyote, our night is falling and in a little while you will not see us. But you must stay right here. Do not go anywhere at all. Stay right here and then in the evening you will see all these people again." "Yes, friend. Where could I possibly go? I will spend the day here." The dawn came and Coyote found himself alone sitting in the middle of a prairie. He spent the day there, just dying from the heat, parching from the heat, thirsting from the heat. Coyote stayed there several days. He would suffer through the day but always at night he would make merry in the great lodge.

One day his ghost friend came to him and said, "Tomorrow you will go home. You will take your wife with you." "Yes, friend, but I like it here so much. I am having a good time and I should like to remain here." "Yes," the ghost replied, "nevertheless, you will go tomorrow, and you must guard against your inclination to do foolish things. Do not yield to any queer notions. I will advise you now what you are to do. There are five mountains. You will travel for five days. Your wife will be with you but you must never, never touch her. Do not let any strange impulses possess you. You may talk to her but never touch her. Only after you have crossed and descended from the fifth mountain, you may do whatever you like." "Yes, friend," replied Coyote.

When dawn came again, Coyote and his wife started. At first it seemed to him as if he were going alone, yet he was dimly aware of his wife's presence as she walked behind. They crossed one mountain and, now, Coyote could feel more definitely the presence of his wife; like a shadow she seemed. They went on and crossed the second mountain. They camped at night at the foot of each mountain. They had a little conical lodge, which they would set up each night. Coyote's wife would sit on one side of the fire and he on the other. Her form appeared clearer and clearer. The death spirit, who had sent them, now began to count the days and to figure the distance Coyote and his wife had covered. "I hope that he will do everything right and take his wife through to the world beyond," he kept saying to himself.

Coyote and his wife were spending their last night, their fourth camping; on the next day, she would again assume fully the character of a living person. They were camping for the last time and Coyote could see her very clearly as if she were a real person who sat opposite him. He could see her face and body very clearly, but he only looked and dared not touch her. But suddenly a joyous impulse seized him; the joy of having his wife again overwhelmed him. He jumped to his feet and rushed over to embrace her. His wife cried out, "Stop! Stop! Coyote! Do not touch me. Stop!" Her warning had no effect. Coyote rushed over to his wife and just as he touched her body she vanished. She disappeared—returned to the shadowland.

When the death spirit learned of Coyote's folly, he became deeply angry. "You inveterate doer of this kind of thing! I told you not to do anything foolish. You, Coyote, were about to establish the practice of returning from death. Only a short time from now the human race will arrive, but you have spoiled everything and established for them death as it is."

Coyote wept and wept. He decided, "Tomorrow I shall return to see them again." He started back the following morning and as he went along he began to recognize the places where his spirit friend and he had passed before. He found the place where the ghost had seen the herd of horses, and now he began to do the same things they had done on their way to the shadowland. "Oh, look at the horses; it looks like a roundup." He went on until he came to the place where the ghost had found the serviceberries. "Oh, such choice service berries! Let us pick and eat some." He went through the motions of picking and eating berries.

He went on and finally came to the place where the long lodge had stood. He said to himself, "Now, when I take hold of the door flap and raise it up, you must do the same." Coyote remembered all the little things his friend had done. He saw the spot where he had sat before. He went there, sat down, and said, "Now your wife has brought us food. Let us eat." He went through the motions of eating again. Darkness fell, and Coyote listened for the voices and he looked all around. He looked here and there, but nothing appeared. Coyote sat there in the middle of the prairie. He sat there all night but the lodge didn't appear again and the ghost never returned to him.

"See Bat's eyes!"

▼▼▼▼▼

39

BAT AND COYOTE

MANY PEOPLE dwelt near a river, including an old woman who had a daughter—a beautiful maiden. Across this river, on the other shore, Bat lived alone. He was young and he was known as Bat Youth. He owned all kinds of good things such as soft, furry robes and skins. He had all kinds of things.

Coyote thought up a scheme in connection with Bat. He, Coyote, built a canoe and paddled across the river to Bat's lodge. He arrived there and addressed Bat with these words, "I came across only to see you. How is it, Bat Youth, that this state of affairs exists? Across the river there is a maiden who lives with her mother. A long time ago you had an older brother, and his wife was the eldest daughter of this maiden's mother. And now, this maiden, the youngest daughter, and you are rightfully mates according to marriage custom." "Yes," Bat replied, "it is only that I did not know these things about myself." Coyote continued, "Here you live in a good lodge, you have all kinds of valuable possessions, and why should you not bring this maiden here?"

As a matter of fact, Bat was a very homely youth and that is why Coyote lied to him and convinced him of these matters. Bat said, "Yes, that is what I will do. It has only been that I did not know about myself before. It is good that you have told me. I will go across the river to this maiden." "Yes," Coyote replied. "But exactly when will you come? I will speak to the maiden and have her meet you." Then Bat told Coyote when he would go across the river.

Foolish Bat began to prepare for his departure. He packed up cushions, skins, and many other things. "Now I am going," he finally pronounced. He went down to the shore and began to shout in his own peculiar words to summon someone across the river to come after him.

"There is somebody over on the other shore shouting to be ferried across. I wonder who he is?" the people commented to one another. But Coyote knew.

(Recited by *Wàyi'làtpu*; originally published in Phinney, 1934.)

"That is he coming," he thought, and he went over to the maiden and said to her, "You should paddle across. I am very busy myself. It is Bat, and you can ferry him across." So the maiden went down to the shore and put out in a canoe. In a little while she landed on the shore and put the canoe in position for her passenger to step aboard easily.

There stood Bat, but he made no move to get into the canoe. Then he began to waggle his head as if to tell the maiden, "Point the bow of the canoe upstream." She did what he seemed to want. Then Bat waggled his head by way of saying, "Pull forward a little." The maiden did this, and now the canoe rested flush against the ground along its whole length. Bat was most elaborately dressed. Suddenly he ran over to the maiden where she sat in the stern of the canoe, jumped on her knee, and sat there. There he was—perched on her knee. "What is he doing?" the maiden thought. She tried to paddle the canoe but she was so encumbered by Bat's presence on her knee that she could scarcely make headway. She managed at last to paddle across.

The canoe had no more than touched shore when Bat jumped ashore ahead of her. There was a sudden jangle of his adornments as he alighted on the ground. The maiden got out of the canoe and tied it up. Then she started home, but Bat followed her—followed her right home.

The maiden entered her lodge and sat down. Bat followed her inside and again he hopped on her knee and sat there. There sat Bat when Coyote arrived. Coyote began to whittle shavings from a piece of cedar wood. He said to Bat, "So this is what you have decided to do, Bat? It is good that you have come. You must have thought, 'Because they were thus once,' and that, of course, is what is always done." There sat Coyote busily cutting cedar shavings.

But now the old woman, the maiden's mother, wondered, "What is he talking about? There were never any such relations. I never had a daughter like that." At this point, the maiden began to weep. "So this is what they are doing," she realized. Bat leaned over to her and said, "Do not weep. I still have many other skins there across the river. Let them take these." Bat thought she was weeping because they were taking things that he had brought. So Bat talked to the maiden and tried to soothe her feelings. Coyote talked incessantly while he whittled cedar shavings. He kept lying as he talked. The woman wondered, "Whatever is he talking about?" Bat sat there, his eyes indiscernible. Then, Coyote took his cedar shavings and thrust them into the fire. There was a sudden *crackle, crackle, crackle* of burning cedar. "The place is on fire!" shouted Coyote. The flames leaped high. "The place is afire!" shouted Coyote again. Bat, alarmed, suddenly lifted his head and looked up. Oh, his tiny beadlike eyes came into view. "See Bat's eyes! See Bat's eyes! See Bat's eyes!" Coyote howled in glee. "Ha ha ha! ha ha ha!" He laughed uproariously. Bat rushed out of the door and ran pell-mell down toward the shore, his adornments jingling at every step. He ran right up to a canoe, jumped aboard, and pulled for the opposite shore. There he landed, and with a push of the foot he sent the canoe back across. Then he went home—nor was anyone likely to see him again. He still lives there.

At the maiden's lodge, Coyote continued to laugh and laugh. "That he should think, 'Let me marry by prerogative!' " he declared. Thus Coyote played a practical joke on Bat. But when did Coyote ever show respect for anyone!

▼▼▼▼▼

40

CUT-OUT-OF-BELLY BOY

THE LAND PEOPLE and the denizens of the air engaged in war. One old woman's daughter was on the side of the land people and she was killed. The old woman knew that her daughter was with child. She cut open her daughter's belly and brought forth a boy, Cut-Out-of-Belly Boy. The boy grew, and grew, and grew.

One day Cut-Out-of-Belly Boy said to his grandmother, "Where did I come from? Where are my mother and father?" His grandmother wept and said to him, "Long ago there were many people and they engaged in war. They killed your father and mother, and I cut open your mother, took you out, and raised you. That is how you came to be, Grandson." "Yes," Cut-Out-of-Belly Boy replied, "it is good that you have told me." Then he purified himself. He bathed every day, every day, every day. "Now I seek vengeance. Now I prepare to go. I will go forth to attack them."

One morning he said to his grandmother, "I am leaving you now." His grandmother wept and said to him, "You are doing a foolish thing; you defy dangerous ones. Your wish to avenge yourself all alone is hopeless. They are many and they vanquished all the people." The old woman continued to weep. He said to her, "I am leaving you now." He began his journey.

The denizens of the air were holding many land people in slavery (among them Coyote). All those who had been conquered were being held in pitiful subjection. Cut-Out-of-Belly Boy knew where many people of the air were living. As he went along, he heard the drumming and words of a black brush pheasant. "Why do they say Cut-Out-of-Belly Boy is greatly to be feared? Thus I am going to do to him." And he drummed viciously. Cut-Out-of-Belly Boy went in that direction and he suddenly he seized the pheasant. "This one made

---

(Recited by *Wáyi'látpu*; originally published in Phinney, 1934. See also Watters's "Cut-Out-of-Belly Boy" in Aoki and Walker, 1989.)

a waif of me!" He plucked out all the wing feathers and threw them all into the bush. "This pompous one tries to make himself fearsome."

He went on from there. He heard shouting as he went along; he heard boys saying, "Get him from the other side for the terrible one! Get him from the other side for the terrible one!" He thought, "For what terrible one are they doing this?" He came upon them suddenly and said to them, "What are you doing, boys?" "It is for Owl, the terrible one. He is holding us and he makes us hunt for rabbits. Even if we bring in some rabbits, he alone eats and tells us, 'If you ever take any, I will kill you.'" They had sores all over their bodies; they were burnt and beaten, very pitifully so. Coyote was among them.

Cut-Out-of-Belly Boy said to them, "Pick up wood!" Then he built a fire. "Now give me rabbits!" Then he prepared food for them and anointed their chapped skin. They were frightened. "Owl will kill us; he is very terrible." "I will follow you later. Hurry, eat!" he assured them. He made them eat heartily all they had caught. "Now go home empty-handed." He followed them. "Now go inside." He waited outside and listened.

Owl had a conical lodge. He sat there and with large eyes glared at them. "So you ate your own kill! So you ate your own kill! Ate your own kill! Then eat your own kill! Then eat your own kill!" he chanted to them. They stood agape with fright. Owl had a dried mouse filled with pebbles. Its mouth was pried open. He rattled and rattled it to frighten them. Cut-Out-of-Belly Boy, outside, thought that they had been frightened enough. He entered gently; he went inside. There Owl glared. "Oh, so it was you then who caused them to eat! Caused them to eat! Then cause them to eat! Then cause them to eat!" He held his dried mouse up to Cut-Out-of-Belly Boy's face and rattled it and rattled it. Cut-Out-of-Belly Boy moved his face from one side to the other. "Aside with it! You might strike my eyes. Aside with it, Owl!"

Now Cut-Out-of-Belly Boy seized him. Then in the same manner as he had done to the pheasant, he plucked the feathers from Owl's wings. "This one talks himself into fearsomeness! This one made a waif of me!" He threw Owl out through the smoke hole and caused Owl to fall into the brush, to hang there, and to moan. "In only a short time the human race will come. People will say, 'Already it is this time of the year for the moaner is moaning.'" Cut-Out-of-Belly Boy addressed him and turning to the boys he said to them, "Tell me what you know!" "There are many people of the air living over there in that direction."

Then they all went from there and followed Cut-Out-of-Belly Boy. Coyote placed himself in front to inform him of the situation. They arrived. Oh, so many lodges there were laid out in a great circle. They arrived, but the people already knew that Cut-Out-of-Belly Boy was greatly to be feared. He had two arrows. He shot one arrow in one direction and demolished all; he shot the other arrow in the other direction and demolished all—exterminated them all.

When denizens of the air had learned that Cut-Out-of-Belly Boy was coming, they had lined up in a two-deep formation, thinking that from such a position they could charge best. But, instead, he shot all the men because they were in exactly the right array for him. Now all those who had been conquered before rushed out to the scene of action and went into the lodges to capture the women who were left unprotected. Coyote charmed himself: "Become a man handsome and big." And a great many of the Air People women became his wives. Thus it was that Cut-Out-of-Belly Boy avenged himself.

41

WEASEL WRESTLES

FOR A WIFE

THERE ONCE LIVED Weasel with his older brother. And he used to make sun-flower cake. He used to pound it and mix it with grease, and that was their food. His brother warned him, "Don't ever go over the hill from here." He gathered up everything that was there, and he asked himself, "For what reason did he forbid me to do that?" So he went over the hill from his place, and he saw many happy people shouting. And he went toward them and watched them.

There a girl was wrestling with them, and she said, "Whoever throws me down will be my husband." Even though Coyote tried to throw her, she grabbed him by the back of his head and threw him over instead. It looked like no one could beat her. Then they said to her, "Oh! Here is Weasel Boy. Let him try!" Weasel Boy said, "Oh no, not I!" But they insisted, so Weasel Boy said, "All right." Then Weasel Boy wrestled her, and lo! he threw her down. When he started to go home, the girl got ready to leave and caught up with him.

The elder brother of Weasel had a wife. The four of them spent their days there for some time. At long last, Weasel's elder brother and his wife had a boy. Weasel Boy thought a lot of the baby, and he rocked it and entertained it often. His sister-in-law would go out to dig roots, and the young man would take care of his nephew. One time his sister-in-law told him, "Go down and throw your nephew into the river." So he brought the baby down. He loved it so much, but his sister-in-law had said to throw it in because it was dirty with excrement. He stood a long time by the river. But his sister-in-law had told him what to do, so for the last time he petted him and rocked him to his heart's content, and then he closed his eyes and threw him in.

Then Weasel Boy became scared that the woman should have had his

(Recited by Watters; originally published in Aoki and Walker, 1989. See also "Weasel" in Phinney, 1934.)

nephew thrown into the river. Her husband came by just then. Weasel Boy told her husband that he had thrown his nephew in, and the older brother whipped the boy. He whipped him so hard that the end of his tail came off. Then Weasel Boy was sad. Older brother and his wife went looking for the baby, and they found it. It drifted ashore, and they took it out of the water. They worked on it, and somehow it was revived.

Meanwhile, Weasel Boy was sad. He would play, but when he missed the tip of his tail, he would become sad again. "Now I am going to kill myself," he thought, and he stuck his arrow into the ground and threw himself on top of it. But it fell apart and he could not kill himself by any method. Then he came upon a group of ants. He took a feather, which was on his arrow, and he lay down on it. But the ants took it and ate it up (and he could not kill himself). "Ah! Now I've got it," he thought. "These ants will certainly eat me up." Then he threw himself down, and the ants devoured him.

When he did not come home, his brother worried, "I wonder where he went." He looked for him, and finally he found him. Only his bones were left. Then he took up the remains and carried them back, thinking, "This is what happened." Older brother's wife said to him, "Yes, he had been very sad since you whipped him and knocked his tail off."

Then they wrapped his bones up in white buckskin, and Weasel Boy came back to life. When he was alive again, he told his brother, "Why did you do this to me?" And Weasel Boy's sister-in-law told him, "Don't say that! Your nephew has been very lonesome for you." Then the boy answered, "I have no way of entertaining him." And his sister-in-law said, "You lie still there," and she took the end of a deer's tail and attached it to his tail. Since then that has been the way Weasel's tail looks. From then on, Weasel Boy was happy.

▼▼▼▼▼

42

COYOTE MARRIES

HIS DAUGHTER

ONCE THERE LIVED Coyote and his friend Fox. Coyote had five daughters. His wife had died sometime before, and he became a widower. Then he started to desire his daughters, most of all the eldest. He thought, "I wish she were my wife," but she was his daughter. That's the way he spent his days.

One day he went over to the Flathead country, and he wandered around there. When he came back, he told his daughters this news, "I made a friend in the Flathead country." Whether or not this was true, Coyote went there every summer. He told his children, "I am going over to see my friend." This went on for two or three years.

One day toward spring he pretended to be sick, and he was sick in bed for a long time. He was pretty sick, and his daughters cared for him. Then he told them, "Yes, daughters, now I am going to die from this long illness. If ever my *yelépt* comes [*yelépt* means friend], you, my eldest daughter, will marry him. He will be your husband." And finally he died. But before he died, he told Fox, "My friend, go and bury me, but don't bury me too deep—just near the surface of the earth."

And that's exactly what Fox did. When Coyote died, Fox carried him away and buried him, just at the top of the ground. When Fox was out of sight, Coyote dug himself out. Then he wandered away from there. He traveled for a long time to a far away place. It was now a little past midsummer. Sometime toward the fall, Coyote came back, getting closer to his home, where his daughters were still living. Then he transformed himself, saying, "Let me seem just like the Flatheads, the same clothing and everything, including the way they speak." The Flatheads had blankets and buffalo robes, and that's how Coyote came to his daughters.

(Recited by Watters; originally published as "Coyote Marries His Daughter-in-Law" in Aoki and Walker, 1989.)

Coyote thought, "I wish she were my wife," but she was his daughter.

The daughters were surprised as they saw him approach. Then he asked them, "Where is my friend?" The eldest one told him, "Sometime ago he started to get sick. He was sick in bed for a long time, and finally he died. Then his friend buried him. He has been gone for some years." Then Coyote started to cry, and oh! he cried on and on. He would go outside and go around crying, and then he would come back. And the daughter said to him, "This is what my father told me, his eldest daughter; 'Whenever my friend comes, you will marry him. He will be your husband.'" Coyote kept on crying, and he said, "Yes, if that is the wish of my friend, I could not turn away from his wish for anything. Now we are together."

From that day she, his daughter, became his wife. And in this way they spent their days, but immediately the youngest daughter suspected him. She thought to herself, "He looks just like my father, not like a Flathead." Right next door there lived lots of different people. Somewhere close by lived Duck Man, and he recognized Coyote. He saw Coyote when he was hunting, and he thought, "That is Coyote there, hunting mice and picking berries. That is surely Coyote." When Coyote came back near to his house, he transformed himself, turning himself back into a Flathead by magic. That's how he returned to his daughter to become her husband.

Once again Duck Man thought to himself, "Surely that is Coyote." And one morning Duck Man started to sing, saying, "Coyote has slept with his daughter" several times. And all the birds that were flying around answered, "Coyote is so thoughtless." Duck Man sang for a while, and Coyote, when he heard it, became worried. So he went and gathered up his aunts, the mice. He told them, "I am going to sing to you, and you answer me." Now Duck Man was singing his tune, but he stopped. Then Coyote started singing, "Duck Man is sleeping with his daughter," and the mice yelled back in answer, "Yes, because he doesn't have any sense." This went on for several days, and the daughter started thinking, "It does sound like it's true. It might be so. My father is, or was, a thoughtless one."

When Coyote would leave, she observed him unnoticed from the distance, until quite a distance from there, sure enough, he turned into Coyote, catching mice and eating roseberries. "I thought so!" she said, "He is indeed Coyote. My younger sister saw through it. She said that he looked like our very own father." Then she came back from there, and she got ready. She told them, "I am going to leave, since I am ashamed. My father did a shameful thing to me." (I forgot what she turned into.) When Coyote came home, she wasn't there. The daughters told him, "Our sister left because of the shame of what you've done to her. All the people know the shame. She felt ashamed and left, and she'll never come back again." Then all of his daughters left him too.

So Coyote and his friend Fox were living together once again. Fox asked, "Why did you do these saddening and shameful things? All the people know about you, for you have acted shamefully. I shall go away also. What should I stay for?" Then Fox left for the Buffalo Country. Coyote left for the Buffalo Country, too, to forget his shameful acts. He never did return. He went there to the east, and finally he disappeared. That's all.

$$\blacktriangledown\blacktriangledown\blacktriangledown\blacktriangledown\blacktriangledown$$

43

COYOTE AND

HIS DAUGHTER

Now I am going to tell a story.

Coyote was living with his daughter. A river flowed nearby, and on its bank the poor ones had their tepee. Coyote was sickly; he wasn't strong, and his daughter took care of him. He had a good daughter, a nice girl, and she took good care of her father.

Coyote was always hungry for something, saying, "Go look for wolf leavings or meat upriver. Go and get some of that, and then make broth with it." Then his daughter would go and gather all of the wolf leavings, such as bones with some meat on them, that were scattered here and there. And she would bring them home and make broth for Coyote. He would say, "Thank you, my child, I ate well, and I feel good." He was ailing and weak. Every day she would go upriver and bring home meat leavings for her father.

One day Coyote's daughter went down to the river. She saw five big steelhead salmon lying in a pile by the hole in the ice where she usually got water. A young man appeared, and he told her, "These are yours. Take the steelheads. We want to take you for a wife. What do you think? We'll take you to our good home under this river. There you'll live peacefully." The maiden told him, "First, I'll ask my father for his views. For that reason I cannot say yes right now. We'll see what my father says, and then in a few days I'll let you know." The young man answered, "Yes, you shall come and answer us." Their proposal was to take her and marry her.

She had decided to take one steelhead to her father, but he said to her, "That's bad. No, I don't want any steelhead. No, no. I want only good deer

---

(Recited by Wilson; originally published in Aoki and Walker, 1989. See also "Coyote the Interloper" in Phinney, 1934.)

He cried out loud, "My daughter, my daughter, my child, my child!"

meat." She took the steelhead away and kept it for herself. In a few days the girl went down again to get water. There was Otter, that handsome-looking youth. "How did it turn out?" he said. (But earlier she had told her father that they had proposed to her, and he had said, "No, you aren't going to marry them, no!") So she said to him, "My father said I couldn't marry you." Then Otter gave up and went back under the ice.

The girl went home. Later she went upstream and she looked for meat. She found some bones with a little meat on them that the wolves had left after eating, and she took them home. "Oh! This is good," Coyote said. "This makes me feel good and strong." One day she went out again, and she found a whole deer on the ground. Five wolf brothers came upon her. They proposed marriage, and she told them, "I'll tell my father. There is no way I can answer you now. It is up to him to answer, and he'll decide." They took the whole deer home for her. She dried it, and she cooked the deer meat for her father. She said, "Father, the wolf brothers proposed to me. They want to take me." He said, "Yes, that's good. You can marry them because, even though you go, you can still take care of me. They always have plenty of good meat. I like that kind. Being Coyote I want meat, not fish."

A few days later, she went looking for meat, and she went upriver to meet the wolf brothers. When she came upon them, they asked, "What's the answer?" She said to them, "My father says it's all right for me to marry you." They said, "Tomorrow, we will come to get you." Then she went home and got ready, and she told her father, "Tomorrow they will come for me," and Coyote answered, "All right. You can still come and see me now and then." So the next day the wolves came, and they took her far away into the mountains. They went up and on; then they went one more day. Oh, what a good tepee was standing there. There was a big, pretty tepee, lots of dried meat, and plenty of food. After she had arrived, she and the five brothers set up house there.

And now the otters were angry. They missed the girl because she didn't come for water any more. They thought, "That settles it." They suspected the wolves. They plotted: "We'll go one morning and make trouble." Then all five of them went up and saw the trail and followed the tracks. And there from a distance they saw the tepee. They stopped, thinking, "We'll stay here. We won't go any closer, for they'll see us. We'll hide." There they stayed until it was quite dark. They heard the wolves laughing and telling stories inside the tepee, and the girl was also laughing.

Finally it was quiet. And then they heard snoring. All inside were asleep. The otter brothers advanced. They had small sticks and pitch and dry pieces of wood. And they put lots of logs close along the edge of the tepee. Inside the wolves and the girl were sleeping, just snoring away. Then the otters put dry wood near the tepee and set fire to it. They had sticks ready, and when the wolves and the girl tried to get out, the otters pushed them back in. And all of them burned there: the five brothers and the wife. Then the otters went back quite satisfied, recalling, "We had the good fortune to destroy all of them."

Several days passed, but Coyote still had lots of meat so he didn't know what had happened. Then one day he heard up high, "Father! Now we are on a journey." "What?" Coyote said, looking up. Then again he heard, "Now we are going. We are going to live no more on this earth. Now we are spirits." Coyote answered, "No! What can I do here in this world, my girl?" And his daughter said, "Build a big fire and jump in. Eventually you, too, will be just like us, and you will be able to travel with us. If your body is just like it is, it will be impossible to come with us where we are going." So Coyote made a fire, and he jumped into it. Ouch! And he jumped right out again. Then he tried it again and again.

Finally he gave up, and his daughter said, "You can go the way you are. You can sense us traveling along. You will hear us high up." For several days they traveled, and they went over five mountains. Over that way they went. "This must be the place," Coyote thought. "It is the spirits' land." That is the way poor Coyote went. He went over five mountains. When they arrived, it was twilight. There was not a soul around. It became dark, and a multitude of people arrived. All kinds of men, all dressed up, were gambling in one place. And in another they were dancing, and in yet another they were racing. Everyone was doing something. Coyote was fascinated, and his eyes were rolling. "Oh, this is so wonderful," he said. He stood watching. Then he saw his daughter [and the spirits]. They looked just like humans in the dark. Soon it became lighter, and the sun rose. Gone! They were suddenly gone. Coyote was alone there all day long.

This went on for a month and more. He became restless and lonesome. In the daytime he was all alone, and at night he wasn't interested in the activities. One night he said to his daughter, "Now, my child, I am lonesome. I don't want to be here anymore. I wish I could go home!" She said, "Get some buckskin somewhere, or make something, and wrap us and carry us on your back. Go back up the same way you came, but don't look back this way. Don't look back."

Coyote agreed, and he got some buckskin ready. He bundled them up and packed on his back. He went up the hill. "Oh, this is nothing," he thought. "They are light, not heavy." He walked fast, and now and then he rested. He ate whatever he had. When it got dark, he slept. On he went, but the load began to get heavy. Now he barely could get over the top, and he rested often. Then it rained, and the trail became slippery. Poor Coyote was barely making any headway. There was just one more hill to go over. As he was going, he slipped, and he looked behind him. The pack disappeared, and he heard them, "Now we are leaving you forever." His daughter laughed as she went. They were gone forever. He never saw them again.

The poor thing finished his climb, and there he sat. Then he cried out loud, "My daughter, my daughter, my child, my child!" His tears ran down. Then he became quiet and said, "All right. I am not the only one that will overcome sorrow. In a short time human beings will come. These days will be no more. Through the generations they will be sorrowful, just as I am sorrowful. They will lose their last child and feel the pain of sorrow. I am not alone in having this sorrow. Through the generations this sorrow will come to them." Then he wiped his tears and went home, looking for his friend Fox, and he came to him. There the two friends lived forever. That's all.

The fire landed and scooped up Coyote with a sizzling sound.

▼▼▼▼▼

44

ELBOW BABY

COYOTE WAS LIVING on the north side of the stream. He had five daughters, and Fox had five daughters, too. They all lived in one place, and they spent the winter there in their winter quarters.

One day Coyote developed a boil on his elbow, and he thought, "What is this?" It grew enormous. "Maybe it's a boil." It pained him all the time, and then one day it burst open. He had been touching it, and then, poof! it opened and a boy fell out. "My!" said Coyote. "It's a baby boy. Thanks!" He made a baby board for him and took care of him. He gave him food—soup made of all sorts of things.

The boy kept growing, and then one day, Coyote went to his daughters and said to them, "Come take care of your brother while I'm busy cutting wood and such." They took care of him. Many times he told them to care for the baby. Then one day Coyote was again busy doing something by himself; he was catching mice. Perhaps the daughters were tickling the baby or doing something—he had gotten very big; he hadn't yet started to walk but he wasn't small. They tickled him, and he laughed. His half-sisters laughed, "Oh, how sweetly he laughs." They tickled him again and again. They kept on tickling him. Finally he became limp, and he dropped dead. He had become exhausted from laughing. They were scared. They wrapped him up and left him there, and they went home.

Coyote arrived home saying, "My child, my sonny boy, where is he?" And he came in and saw him motionless. He went to him and felt him. "Oh, he's cold. Oh, is he dead?" He picked up his baby and held it in his arms. "Oh, son, what happened?" Then he lamented, "Oh! My child, my child, my son. He was going to be a rich man! My child was going to be a young chief. My child, my child, my child. He was going to be a rich man! He was going to be a young chief."

(Recited by Wilson; originally published in Aoki and Walker, 1989. See also "Coyote and Elbow-Child" in Phinney, 1934; and "Katstainomiots, or Elbow Baby" in Spinden, 1908.)

He cried. He wore himself out crying. Finally he dried his tears, and he took the child. "I will lay him to rest in some good place." He took him up on the hill where a bridge comes ashore across the river. From there he carried the child a little ways up the hill and buried him.

When Coyote came down from there, he planned. "I wonder how I can avenge his death?" He was angry. "How shall I get even with and punish my daughters?" Fox's daughters were there also. He planned, and one day he said, "I'm ready now. I'll go when they are sleeping at night, when they are dead to the world. Then I'll destroy them. I will get rid of them." He waited until midnight, and he got close to them as they were sleeping. There was an opening—in the winter quarters they climbed up to the opening on top to get out. He blocked the opening with logs that were firm and strong, and there he stood. Then he urinated on them, drip, drip. Finally the level of the liquid inside rose. Then he sensed them, running around scared below him. The water was getting deeper, and then they started to quiet down. The youngest one dashed up the ladder made of a little pine log with twigs. "Oh, I'm blocked in," she thought. "Coyote is standing on the other side." The girl was strong, and she pushed the logs. Coyote was knocked over backward. She told him, "I will come back. Now I'm going where the sun sets. One day in the fall I shall come. I will come back and see you people." That's what Coyote heard as she went away.

Coyote went home, and he told Fox what he had done to his daughters. Fox became sad for his daughters were also in the crowd. Then they moved from that camp in order to weather the winter. They made their winter lodging, and they cut wood for winter use. They got ready. They got lots of wood, for it was late in the fall. They were content, for luckily they had food and whatever they had gathered. They said, "We will comfortably spend the winter here."

One day they heard the noise of wind coming. "What could that be?" said Coyote. "It's loud, just like thunder." The wind was blowing, and it made a loud noise. Then they saw a fire. The wind was coming with fire. They heard it coming, and a young girl was singing, "I'm going to scoop up the hateful old man in fire. I'm going to jump over the cute old man. I'm going to scoop up the hateful old man in fire. I'm going to jump over the cute old man." "Listen," Coyote said, "do you hear that? She says she'll jump over the good old man with fire. That's me, the good old man. You, Fox, are the bad old man. She is going to take you." Fox thought to himself, "Nothing doing. But let him think that." The fire landed and scooped up Coyote with a sizzling sound. It took him a little way. He was completely burned up. It jumped over Fox. Coyote's daughter was traveling on it. And Fox was left alone now that Coyote had burned up. Then Fox bunched his things together, thinking, "This is where I'm going to winter alone."

The winter came and Fox lived there. It became spring, and the grass grew this high. Now it was late spring, and Fox was lonesome. He walked out to where poor Coyote had burned. He went around chanting, "I wonder if my friend's jawbone was left by the fire. I wonder if my friend's jawbone was left by the fire." All at once Fox heard a fast chattering, mocking him. It mocked him again and again. He went in the direction of the sound, and there was a gaping mouth, yawning at him, just bones. He went over to it, and he stepped over it. That was the custom of the people of the legend days. Then Coyote got up. Oh, the poor thing was so weak. Poor Coyote was so weak that his friend could hardly brace him up. He put his friend to bed, and he cared for him and gave him food. Finally Coyote got strong, and they started to live with the same people. "Oh, thank you!" Coyote said. His strength came back to him, and he went looking for mice. Again they lived together for a long time. That's all.

▼▼▼▼▼

45

CIXCIXÍCIM BOY

TWO BROTHERS were living together, and the elder had a wife. One day when she was working outside, the younger brother, who had used up his arrows, told his older brother, "You go hunting alone. I'll go and get some serviceberry twigs to make more arrows." (They [serviceberry twigs for arrows] are called *kayá·kaya.*) And that's what he did. The elder went hunting, while the younger got serviceberry twigs, and when he brought them home, he peeled their bark and put them around the fire to dry. When he went to get some more twigs to finish his arrow-making, he called his pet to come along. But it didn't move; it just lay there, so he left him by himself.

Meanwhile the elder brother returned from his hunting trip. But while he was away, his wife had told the younger brother, "There is a cute bird. Kill it for me." And he shot it for her, "Here it is. I killed it for you. Whatever did you want it for?" Then he left her, and right afterward she went into the house and scratched herself all over her face with the bird's claws. When her husband came home, she told him, "Your brother insulted me like this." Then her husband got mad, and he gathered all the serviceberry twigs and threw them into the fire. When he was through, he lay down.

When the younger brother came back, he couldn't find the twigs; finally, he found one charred piece. "What happened?" he thought, and he went outside and left. His pet dog followed him and told him, "You killed a bird for your sister-in-law and gave it to her. When you left her, she went into the house, and she scratched herself with it. When your brother came back, she told him, 'See how your younger brother scratched my face and thus insulted me.' Your brother became angry and burned everything all up, and then lay down on his back. That's how you saw him when you came in."

(Recited by Watters; originally published in Aoki and Walker, 1989. See also Wilson's "Cixcixícim Boy" in the same volume and "Elder Brother and Younger Brother" in Phinney, 1934.)

Because of this, the youth thought, "It is not right for me to live here. I disturb my elder brother." So he said, "I'm leaving. We are parting now, my dog, You stay here." His dog answered. "No, I'm going with you. There is no reason for me to stay here either." So the younger brother's dog went with him. They traveled on and went over five mountains.

Then the youth felt sorry for his dog, and when a grouse flew up the boy killed it for him. But the grouse got caught in the branches of a tree. So the boy took off his clothes, put them down, and told his dog, "I'm going up to get that grouse for you. Don't look up." So the dog hung his head down, and the boy climbed up. But the dog was hungry, and he wanted to know whether the boy had reached the grouse yet. He glanced upward, and just then the grouse moved farther up the branches. Then the boy said, "You looked up. Don't do that!" And thus he continued up the tree. Finally when he was farther up, the dog looked up and howled, *woo, woo,* and a tear rolled down his face. Thus the boy kept going farther and farther up, and the dog sat down and cried for several days.

At home his elder brother finally got lonesome. He said, "Now I am lonesome for my brother. I wonder where he went." He went looking for him, and he found tracks going off in one direction. He thought, "Oh, they went that way." He tracked his younger brother. He went over the first, second, and third mountains, and from there he heard what seemed to be the dog's howling from somewhere. He went in that direction over the fourth and fifth mountains, and he finally reached the dog. The dog was at the foot of a tree. He was sitting and looking up, howling, and his tears were rolling down. The elder brother asked the dog where his master had gone, but the dog wouldn't answer for a long time. Finally the dog said, "You're a nuisance speaking to me, asking about that. Your wife's lying caused sadness for you two. Your younger brother didn't do anything to her. She told him, 'Oh! How cute that bird is! Come and kill it for me.' That's what he did for her. He got her the bird and went to finish his supply of arrows. She went in and scratched her face with the bird and told you that your brother insulted her. She lied to you. He never touched her. It is a pity that she made you lonesome like that."

Then the elder brother said, "Yes, now I understand." He took the clothes of his younger brother and swallowed them all. Then he told the dog, "Now let's go home." But the dog answered, "Not me. I'm not going back. I'll stay right here. I shall never go with you again." The brother tried to persuade the dog for a long time, but he wouldn't follow. So the older brother said, "Now we are parting." Then he took out a pure white feather and tied it on the dog's crown, saying, "Now we are separating, my companion. This will be your home here in the mountains. Here you will roam and find different kinds of food, and from this time on you will be known as Grizzly Bear." Thus the grizzly bears are found throughout the mountains even to this day. There the man and the dog parted, and the man went home.

When he got back home, he found his wife scraping dry hide outside, and she was making a scraping noise—"*teep, teep, teep.*" Then he tipped his quiver and took out his bow and arrow, walking toward the woman as he aimed. She laughed suddenly, "He, he, he! You must be kidding. You might accidentally shoot me like that." Her husband answered, "Who's joking?" and he shot his wife and killed her. Then he took off her dress and swallowed it. From that time on, the bird she used to scratch her face is called *Teepteepnoo.* He went to his house, a buffalo-hide tepee, and tore it down, rolled it up, and swallowed it. And he swallowed all his other possessions as well. His belly was swollen now, and he shrank and became a little boy whose name was Cixcixícim.

Then he left, saying, "Now I'm going to my grandmother's, where the people are camping." He went in that direction for several days, and finally he arrived at his grandmother's. In some way she already knew what had happened. When he came, his grandmother was happy. Her tepee was just a small one. His grandmother made a bed right across from his. He stayed there, I don't know how long. Then he did a somersault, and *blam!* ha ha ha! that boy defecated.

A chief heard about the boy's arrival and that he was staying with his grandmother. The chief wondered, "Where does he come from? I think he must come from where there were two young men known as good hunters." He arranged the feathers of many birds in front of him and picked out two. From there, puff, he blew them to the top of a tepee, and high up there they turned into two eagles. The chief called Coyote and told him, "There, you see that there are two eagles. I shall give my two daughters to the one who shoots them down." Coyote went out and announced, "This is what my chief says. Whoever kills both those eagles sitting up there will be given both of his daughters. Now get ready."

The men came and each in turn aimed at the eagles. Grandmother made a bow out of rib for Cixcixícim, and he practiced outside, just playing around. Coyote spit on his hand and pointed two fingers at the boy, saying, "You can't shoot anything. Nephew, there are the eagles. Shoot them. Can you kill them? Go on, shoot!" He went on like that. And from that spot—pock!—the boy shot the eagle, and it came tumbling down. The old man picked it up. Then another one, and the boy killed them both. Then Coyote said, "My nephew just told me, 'If I kill the eagles, I won't have any use for the girls. Let them become your wives.'" But the chief said, "No, I have decided that they shall have this boy for their husband." The boy went home to his grandmother's. Then he somersaulted and, *poof,* he defecated.

The chief got his daughters ready. He told them, "You are going to him. Just walk in without peeking first. He lives there." And so they went, the elder leading. When they were almost there, she said, "Let's peek in, younger sister." And the younger said, "But our father said that we should not peek in." But in spite of her father's warning, the elder peeked in at them. Then she said, "I'm going to that handsome Raven instead. You go on in there alone." So the younger one went in. The old woman said, "You sitting over there, what are you up to?" "This is what our father told us to do," said the younger one, "but my sister went that way, so I came here alone."

The old woman said, "All right," but the boy was sitting hiding behind his grandmother, and he told her, "Give her some food, so that she can go home." His grandmother answered, "No, Grandson, she has come here to you." The boy thought that over and said, "Grandma!" after the girl went outside again to walk around or whatever she was doing. "Build a strong tepee. Then tie a strong piece of wood across the top, and tie me right up there by the foot. I will hang down there. Then give her buckskin for moccasins and send her back to her father and mother's. Then she can make moccasins for me there. She can use her father's foot for the pattern."

When the girl came back, the old woman said, "Here is our buckskin for moccasins. He says for you to make him moccasins; you can use your father's foot for the measurements. Now take this and go home, and make the moccasins there. Take your time, though. Don't be in a hurry. You can come back later." And that's what she did.

After the girl had gone, the boy told the old lady, "Now tie me up and hang me head-down. Then close the door tight and don't look in, even though you may hear something unusual. Close the door tight and don't look in, and then sit down outside and don't let anyone come in." When she was through closing the door, she sat down in front of it, blocking the way. In a little while she heard something landing—*thump!* And then another, different sound—*thud!* He was vomiting everything he had swallowed. Then he told her, "Now I feel numb. Come and untie me." The old woman went in, and there were lots of things in a pile, all his personal belongings and the buffalo-hide tepee. She untied him and he stood up. He was no longer a big-bellied boy but a slender, well-dressed young man. And he told her, "Now make a good tepee with this one here!" She took her old tepee down, all of it, and a huge new tepee was set up. After it was completed, all their belongings were put in the proper places, and good flooring was put in.

And so the youth was lying on his back when his wife returned. "But there was a tepee here and it isn't here anymore." She just stood around outside. The young man told his grandmother, "The woman is puzzled about coming in.

Tell her to enter." So the old lady came out and told her, "Come in, my grand-daughter-in-law. Come in, this is it. This is our home now. Come in." The girl went in, thinking, "Someone must have moved in with us." She looked for her husband, but couldn't see the somersaulting boy anywhere. The old lady told her, "This is your bed. That is the way he turned out to be, a handsome- look-ing young man." So the girl settled down there to make a home with her hus-band's folks.

At this time the chief called Coyote again. Coyote came, and the chief told him, "Tomorrow morning they are going to start on an early hunt after buf-falo, and they are going to kill them." Then Coyote, acting as camp crier, told the people, "This is what our chief says: 'Tomorrow morning those men living with their in-laws are going hunting, and will bring the buffalo in. We will kill them. Thus say I, the chief.'" Coyote was making fun.

In the morning the young man went on the hunt. He told his wife, "When we arrive with the buffalo, you will meet me with water mixed with white clay." Raven told his wife the same thing, except, "Mix charcoal in the water that you bring to meet me with." The boy went hunting, I don't know how far, and then he found some buffalo dung. He piled it up and ran around it many times. The dung patties all stood up and became buffalo. And then the people brought the buffalo in. They encircled them, and all the men brought them in.

The people in the village saw that the men were coming, and the women brought water to them, thinking that they must be thirsty. All of a sudden, the two sisters met. The older sister told her younger sister, "I wonder who you are taking the water to. Your husband is way back there somersaulting." The younger sister didn't pay any attention, and she didn't answer her. The return-ing hunting party was in plain sight, and the older sister was holding the char-coal solution for her husband, Raven. Then she saw someone coming and she thought, "It seems she is going directly to meet him." And she said to her younger sister, "It looks like you're taking your water to him." The younger one said, "Yes, certainly, that is my husband. That's how he turned out to be. He's no longer a boy; he has turned out like that."

At that moment Raven was still walking toward them, so the older one beat her sister to the young man and offered him some water. But he knocked the water over, saying, "I am the soiled boy whom you rejected." And the younger sister received him, while the older one cried. Then the older met her husband, Raven, with just a little water, even though he was dying of thirst. "*Caw caw,*" he was saying as she arrived.

Near the house the youth killed two fat buffaloes, and he butchered them and took them home. He told his wife, "Now take this meat to your father." Just before this the older sister had gone home. Raven had picked up the leavings, the head of the buffalo somewhere, and the other sister brought this to her father. And the old man was trying to cut this meat. Then the younger sister came in, bringing instead the choicest meat. She told her father, "You might hit your hands and bruise them on this," and she picked up the buffalo head and threw it up the smoke hole. It fell where Raven and his wife were, thump! in the fireplace. Because of that, Raven was infuriated. He told his wife, "We are leaving," and they left the camp. He took all of the deer and birds that could be hunted away with him. Then the people began to get hungry. There were no deer anywhere, even though the young man and other good hunters looked.

Then, just when they were about to starve, the people decided to have a council. At that time Raven was pure white. When the Raven family lived there, they had a child, a girl. Raven used to go around the people's campsite and snoop on them, and the people would say, "There's Raven. Look after him to see which way he's heading." But because Raven was pure white, when he flew high enough, he was invisible. So they considered the problem. Beaver told them, "Split me in half, and put me like that by the shore of the river where it's easy to spot me. Then I'll catch him. Then we'll make a really strong house, and we'll blacken him with smoke. After that we'll see him for sure wherever he goes."

And that's what they did. When Raven came circling around again, he thought, "My! It's so quiet. All of them must have starved to death." All of a sudden there was Beaver near the water, split in half. "I wonder how he starved," thought Raven, "for he never lived on meat. He eats things like willows. He must be fat." He dove down and landed right near Beaver, thinking, "The inside of his house is full of fat; so he can lie on his back." He went up to Beaver, thinking that he would eat him first. Just then Beaver grabbed him and hollered, "Now I've caught him! Rush over!" Then they grabbed Raven and tied him up, and they took him into the house. They built a fire there and directed the pitch toward him for some time, and finally Raven turned black. And thus the black color that he has today was caused by firing pitch.

The people asked him where he lived, but he did not answer. "*Caw,*" was all he said. Then the rope broke from the heat, and through the smoke hole Raven quickly escaped. He flew around and the people saw him going. And Coyote said, "There he goes like that!" He made the two-finger gesture at Night Owl, who was sitting there, and Coyote said to him, "You don't see anything. You're just a round ball." But Night Owl alone followed him with his eyes and saw where he landed. He told them, "I saw where Raven landed." Then the men gathered and selected the ablest among them. "Who can go?" "Let me go," said Racer Snake. And so said Little Fox, and I forget who the third one was. The three of them went.

Raven told his child, "When we leave the camp, don't go back to it. Don't go picking any leftovers." Their daughter was old enough to understand. Then they moved on. But the girl was playing, and she wandered back toward the old camp, to the place they had moved from. Suddenly she saw something: "Oh, what a cute dog!" She caught it, and then she saw something else. She said, "Oh, my mother left my digger behind," and she picked it up, and she picked up a pounding basket too. She took them home and hid them under her pillow. When they were eating, she would bend over toward her pillow and feed them. And they would all eat the food.

Somewhere toward morning those under the pillow got ready, and then Basket said, "I, the Basket, am going straight from here." On the other hand, Racer Snake who had turned into the digger, went to the south. The dog, who was Little Fox, chose the north. That's what they settled on. Toward morning Little Fox started sniffing something: Sniff! Sniff! Sniff! The smell became clearer and clearer and right away they found the deer. Then all the deer were taken away from there. They took back the deer and bird-game from Raven, all that he had been keeping out of sight. Then Raven told his daughter, "I forbade you to pick up anything anywhere and bring it back. But you brought them here, and now they have taken our game away from us."

From then on Raven was black from the smoke. Originally he was white. And that's the way they took back from him everything that he had been keeping out of sight. That's all.

▼▼▼▼▼

46

WARMWEATHER
AND COLDWEATHER

COYOTE WAS WANDERING around, and on his way down he thought something like a butterfly was flying around. He caught it and ate it. Then he became thirsty. Just then he realized that the thing that was flying around was poisonous. He went and drank water from the spring, but all of his teeth fell out. He became toothless. He continued on foot, and then he saw, "Oh! A wonderful tepee is standing there." He went up to it and peeked in. A beautiful girl was sitting there, sewing. He came back and transformed himself, "Let me be a handsome man with good long hair, painted handsomely with clay, a tall man. Let me become dressed up in good buckskin. Let me be a handsome person." And that's what he became.

Then he went and knocked on the door. "Come in." Coyote entered. The girl saw him, "Oh! What a handsome man." She said, "Sit down across from me. Sit down there, and I will prepare some food." She prepared food—dried meat—and she served it. Coyote was hungry. He started to eat, but then he realized, "I have no teeth." He ate a little, but he couldn't really eat. Then he became sleepy and went to sleep. The meat was left there. She saw it, wondering, "Why didn't he eat very much?" He was sleeping and his mouth was open, and the girl saw that he had no teeth. "That's why he didn't eat the meat." Then she took out all of a deer's teeth and brought them in and fitted them into Coyote's mouth. When Coyote woke up, the meat was still there, so he picked one piece up. "Oh, what sharp teeth!" Then he said, "I am Coyote, good at everything. These teeth grew in as I slept. Surely my teeth have grown in." And he sat there.

(Recited by Wilson; originally published in Aoki and Walker, 1989. See also Watters's "Warmweather and Coldweater" in the same volume, "Gusty Wind and Zephyr" in Phinney, 1934; and "Yayakye, the Girl Who Killed Her Own Brother" in Spinden, 1908.)

The Warmweather People went and met the freezing cold with sunshine.

It was dark now, and he heard five brothers coming. The ground was cold, and there wasn't much snow. They made sounds with their feet as they came. Then they put their meat pack down. The oldest one came in, "Move over a bit, guest." So Coyote moved over a little and sat down. Then the second came in, "Move over a little, my guest." Coyote moved closer to the place where the girl was sitting. Then he moved a little bit. Then the third came in, "Move over a little, my guest." It went on like this. The youngest came in and said, "Move over a little that way, guest Coyote." "Don't say that," the older brother said. Then Coyote was right next to the girl. Then she became Coyote's wife forever.

The next morning the oldest brother said, "Now we are going hunting again." Then Coyote said, "I am going too." They said, "It is very difficult. Maybe you shouldn't go." "I am going anyway." Then they gave him things for lunch, such as biscuitroot. They went out and came to a lake, and they said, "It is hard to cross. You sit here on top of us. Don't say a thing, no matter what. It's dangerous and we might get drowned." They went, and the geese were honking, "*hu' hu*." When they were crossing, Coyote said, "*hu' hu*." "No," they said. "No!" Then they lost altitude, and they told Coyote, "Don't say that," and they went up again and flew across.

They went hunting, and they shot many fine deer with antlers. Coyote was hunting by himself, and he went after a fawn, a small deer. The brothers came by on the way home, and they saw the fawn lying there. "Oh, Coyote must have shot this small one." They took the dead fawn and threw it into the bushes. Then they took the many big deer and Coyote on top of them—the load was very heavy. They said, "*hu' hu*," as they went, and Coyote said it also. Then they went down and went splash! over the water. "Don't say that," they said. They barely got ashore, and then they went home. They came home and told their sister, "Coyote is not going again tomorrow. He is acting very dangerously. Talk him out of going. We won't take him."

Next morning they went again. Coyote's wife said, "You stay right here." "No, I'm going. I'm going hunting too." Again he went with them. In the same way, they crossed the lake again. The geese cried, "*hu' hu*," and Coyote was happy, and he also called, "*hu' hu*." Then they flew lower and barely made it to the shore. Again they went hunting and shot big deer. Coyote shot a small one again, and they threw it into the bushes when they came back. Then they told him, "Coyote, you keep quiet. You are acting recklessly. We will drown and lose all the game. Now be quiet." They started again, heavily loaded. They made the geese's cry, and Coyote honked, "*Hu' hu*," and they started to lose altitude. "Don't say that. Keep quiet." They rose up, but Coyote again honked, "*Hu' hu*." They spread out, and Coyote dropped and splashed into the water. He called out, "Let me be a feather!" Saying, "Let me be a feather," he rose up high and did not fall into the water. But then he said the wrong words, "Let me be heavier," and the poor thing drowned. He did not come up out of the water again. They went home without Coyote.

The girl knew something was wrong because her needle broke when she was sewing. Then again it broke. She said, "There is something strange. I wish I knew what it was." When the five brothers came home, she saw that Coyote was not with them. They said, "He drowned. He went into the water. He was acting too recklessly." The girl got angry. She had a huge knife. She took out her heart and put it there [moved it to another part of her body]. She killed her brothers with the knife; she stabbed them. One, two, they lay on the ground. Only two were bright. They said to each other, "Somewhere she has her heart. Shoot her heart." One brother shot, and she dropped dead. There were now two brothers left. "Now surely we must leave. Let's leave everything here."

They left, and eventually they came to a house. Lots of smoke was coming out. There was a fire, but it was not burning well. "I wonder who lives here," and they looked in. There was an old man and a girl maybe fifteen years old. "Come in," they said; so the brothers went in. It was cold—a fire was going, but it was only smoking. Then the father told the girl, "Daughter, make soup for the guests. Make soup quickly." Then she took a big kettle. "Oh, we will eat well," for the two were hungry. They were very hungry indeed. "Thank you. We will eat well." When she finished making the soup, the father said, "Bring it over here. Let us taste it." Then the father and the daughter ate, and the boys sat and watched them eat it up. The soup was all gone. Then the father told the daughter, "This time make some for the guests." The brothers said to each other, "Let's go." They left. All the people there were *xálpxalp*—Coldweather People. They were winter coldness—this father and daughter.

The two brothers went on, and they traveled over many ridges. They saw a good tepee standing, "Oh! What a good tepee." Clear smoke was coming out. "I wonder who they are." Let's go over." They looked in. "Come on in." A good old man and his daughter were sitting across from each other. "Just sit down, guests, whoever you are. Daughter, make soup for them." She took a small kettle and made soup for them. They thought, "That's too small. We won't eat very much. It's not enough." The girl served them, and they ate. The kettle did not become empty. There was just as much as before. They ate enough, and then they sat there. The old man told them, "We know who you are. You are the brothers who killed your sister. You are Geese." "Yes." Then he told them, "Stay right here. You can hunt lots of deer here." That's what they did. Then the old man said, "I am going to give this girl to you." There they spent their days and hunted.

Meat was drying all over outside. Coldweather girl went snooping around there, saw the meat, and told the others that there was lots of meat there. Old man Coldweather got angry. The daughter said, "Now we are going to fight them, and we will kill all the Warmweather People." Then they took ice and snow. They let the wind blow and the snow fall, and they froze things.

The Warmweather People saw them coming. "Now let's do something." These people are known as *takakacya*—Summerweather. The father and daughter are Warmweather. Now they were fighting with the Cold. The Warmweather People went and met the freezing cold with sunshine. They met and fought—the heat and the cold. Ice would come, but the sunshine and heat would melt it. Snow would come, but the sunshine would melt it too. The warmth defeated the cold. Coldweather gave up and begged for food. The Warmweather People gave them liver, meat, and other things, and the Coldweather went home. Thus these two spent their days, and they lived there from then on. That's all.

Coyote insulted Bobcat by making a two-fingers sign at him, saying, "You're sitting bunched up like a ball."

▼▼▼▼▼

47

BOBCAT AND PINE
SQUIRREL'S DAUGHTER

THERE ONCE LIVED lots of people under Chief Pine Squirrel. He had an un-married daughter, and all the men wanted her, but they could not get close to her. Bobcat also lived in the same place. One day he saw the girl going to uri-nate. He followed her and saw her urinate. Then he urinated exactly at the same place. The girl became pregnant, and after some time she had a baby; but she didn't know who the father was. Even though her father, mother, and rela-tions asked her, she just answered them, "I just don't know who it is. I don't know how I became pregnant."

From the moment the baby was born, it cried; it never stopped crying. It cried and cried all the time. This worried the chief. He called Coyote and said, "This crying baby worries me. Whoever quiets the baby by picking it up will be known from that time on as the true father." Coyote went out and an-nounced in a loud voice, "Listen, people. The chief says that all the men who are here shall come forth and sit in a circle. The baby will be carried around. Whoever stops this baby's crying by picking him up will be known as the true father."

And that's what the people did. All the men who were there sat in a circle. The baby was still crying, and they passed the baby around. While they were sitting there, Coyote broke some bones and took the marrow out. When they gave the baby to Coyote, he let the baby chew on the marrow, which quieted it. When the baby had eaten it up, it started to cry again. His friend Fox said to him, "You'll make the baby choke. What are you trying to do?" Then Coyote said, "You'll never quiet this baby as I did," and they kept passing the baby around.

(Recited by Watters; originally published in Aoki and Walker, 1989. See also Wilson's "How Bob-cat Found a Wife" in the same volume, and "Bears and Coyote" in Phinney, 1934.)

At that point Coyote insulted Bobcat by making a two-fingers sign at him, saying, "You're sitting bunched up like a ball. You'll never quiet him by picking him up." They brought the baby to Bobcat, and when he received it in his arms, it stopped crying and went to sleep. "Yes, this is my decision," said the chief. "Bobcat is the father of the baby." This decision dissatisfied Coyote. He kept coming to the chief, saying, "It's not right for my niece to have such a husband. I'm thinking this: In the morning whoever brings meat earliest to this baby— when it is morning, the very first to bring meat—he will have her as wife. That truly is its father." And he announced, "This is what chief says. 'Tomorrow morning all the men will go hunting. Whoever brings in the meat first to the chief will give it to his daughter, and this will be the true father of the child.'"

When he was through with his announcement, Coyote went hunting all day and somewhere he shot a yearling deer and he hid it. "I will carry it from here early in the morning to a short distance from the village." Bobcat saw what Coyote was doing the next morning, and he pulled out a whisker and shot it up into the air. It became dark with fog, and nothing was visible. When all the hunters went out, Coyote looked for his kill, but he couldn't find it. "I put it here," he would say, going from place to place. He looked all over.

Meanwhile Bobcat went out and killed a deer. Nobody else had returned yet, but Bobcat had already brought in his meat. Now Coyote found his, and he carried it in. His children ran to him. "Daddy, you are taking it to the wrong place. You are passing our place. This is where we are." Coyote said, "You are not the children I am getting this for. I am taking it to still another child of mine." Then they told him, "Bobcat brought his in long ago. Where are you going? You are acting pitifully." He carried it back from there and scolded his children, "Why didn't you tell me I was going in the wrong direction? No, it is too ridiculous, my niece could not have such a man."

Then Coyote came to the chief and said, "This won't do. Lastly, whoever brings in an animal with the whitest fur will be the husband. We will make *qícex* [white fur]. Now all men will make it. Whoever brings in the whitest wolf of all will have her as wife." The chief said, "All right," and Coyote made the announcement. Then men went out to make white fur.

In the morning he found *céxle* [a kind of wolf?], and it was one that was dull-colored, almost black. He went to look over the ones of the others, and he found the one owned by the cougars and others, which was almost white. So Coyote exchanged his with Cougar's, and he left his and took Cougar's away.

Now the others were bringing their kills in. They were all dull in color. Then Coyote brought his in, saying, "Oh! Mine is white. Take it now, chief. Don't waste time." The chief said, "No, one is still not here." After a while Bobcat brought his in. It was the whitest of them all; there were no dirt spots. Bobcat's surpassed Coyote's, who stole and exchanged. The chief said, "All right, this is the third time now. This is truly the father of the baby. I cannot say anything more."

Coyote incited those who had feelings for the woman like this: "This simply cannot be. Let's kill him." They agreed, and they took Bobcat and killed him. "Let's do a thorough job on him," said Coyote, "and then we will move our camp away from here." But Coyote went too far. His actions were too violent. He pounded Bobcat to pieces, and he mixed them with dirt. Not even the bones were visible. He broke up all the bones in his pounding. Then he said, "We're going to move," and the people left.

The young woman told her father, "I caused all this misery to that man. Therefore I shall not move. I'll stay right here. I'll spend my days here with my child." Even though the people tried to persuade her to leave, she refused; so they left her. She made a tepee to live in. Then she went to where Bobcat was killed, and she gathered up all his flesh, hair, and bones, thinking, "I wonder if I got every bit of it." She picked it all up and wrapped it up and put it under her pillow.

The bundle remained there for two, three, four, five days. The fifth and sixth nights, she heard the first groaning. On the seventh day she felt his movement. He was now moaning without stopping. The ninth and tenth day dawned. Then he sat up, revived, and came back to life. "Well," Bobcat said, "what did you do, for they have left you." She said, "I am the one who caused you this misery, and this is what I decided—I will not go any place, and I shall not leave him to go anywhere. I picked up your body and everything. Then I wrapped it with tanned buckskin. I hoped and believed that someday you would come back to life. And that happened to you." There they spent their days, and finally he got completely well. He went hunting. He shot game and lived in abundance. The son grew to be a big boy.

Some time later, the people got hungry. Magpie would leave from time to time and go looking for the girl they had left. "Yes, they are still there, they live there," said Magpie. He was the grandfather of the Pine Squirrel Woman. Then one day, when the boy was playing outside near the garbage and leftovers, which had been thrown out. Magpie was eating the leavings, and the boy said, "There is someone here, so come and see, Mother." Then she looked out and said, "Oh, that is my grandfather! Grandfather, you have come. Come on in! Why are you eating those leftovers? Come in, you can eat here." Then he came in, and he made a pack. She told him, "You must come back here. You are having a hard time."

And that's what he did. Magpie took the pack, and he arrived with it, and the magpie children ate noisily while they enjoyed their meal, saying, "Large intestines are easy to break, large intestines split easily." They ate noisily. The others said, "My! Why are they making so much noise eating?" They would go and see the magpies, but the magpies would pretend they were eating pine moss. And they would say, "Pine moss is easy to break, pine moss is easy to break." This went on.

Then Mosquito told the others, "I, Mosquito, am going to see what those magpies are doing." He simply flew up in the air and he looked inside; there he saw the magpies eating big intestines, good side fat, and many other things. He thought, "That's what was causing them to eat noisily." They heard his rustling and quickly picked up the moss. But Mosquito had seen it. "They are eating meat. I wonder where they got it."

Then the people came and asked them, "Where did you get it?" Finally Magpie told them, "Right at that place where you killed Bobcat. He has completely recovered. They live at the same place, and they are well off. Now we're getting ready and gathering our things, so that we can move in the morning." Coyote announced, "She is inviting us back over; she is inviting all of us. We will move back over to her place. They live in plenty over there." That's what they did, but she only wanted her grandfather to come. But she said, "You can come over and stay." That's all.

▼▼▼▼▼

48

THE DISOBEDIENT BOY

AMONG A LARGE GROUP of people, there was a very mean and unruly boy. He would always make the children scream and cry by hitting them. Every so often he would pick on Coyote's son, Cicéqi, hitting him and making him scream.

Coyote was very upset about this behavior, and one day he called some boys together. He said to them, "Take that boy along with you to make twigs in the forest. There you should spit on the twigs, and when you do, one of the twigs will speak in answer to him. While he's preoccupied with that, you can leave him there. Then all of us will leave and run away from him."

So the boys took the disobedient boy along to make the twig branches. While they were making them, the boy began acting mean again. He went into the thicket, and he said to the others, "All this is mine, and don't any of you fool with it!"

The boys spat on each of the twigs, and the boy scolded them as they worked cutting the twigs off. By and by the mean boy sensed that he was alone—everything was silent. He hollered at them, "Where are you?" The twigs called out, "Ho" from both sides of where the mean boy stood. This went on for quite some time and, finally, while muttering to himself, "They're answering me from somewhere!" he saw the twigs gaping at him with their mouths open. "Oh," he exclaimed, "is this what is answering me?" He tore the twigs off and broke them to pieces. "You'll never escape! I'll hurt you when I get you," he shouted.

Then he went home, and when he got there he found it completely empty with no one around. He went around to the houses, and there was nothing to be seen there either. Then he shouted, "I'll hurt you when I get you!"

He went around to his home again, but when he got there he found it still completely empty and there was still no one around. Once again, he went

(Recited by Watters; originally published in Aoki and Walker, 1989. See also Wilson's "Naughty Boy Becomes Good," and "The Disobedient Boy" in Phinney, 1934.)

One day when the boy was fishing again, the Water Woman grabbed the hook.

around to the houses, but still there was nothing to be seen there either. Then he thought, "I'll go to my maternal grandmother's house—she may have left something there."

When he got to his grandmother's place, he saw a pounding basket there. He opened it up and moved it this way and that. There, at the bottom, was a hole, from which he took out some sunflower seeds and other foods and things that she had left for him. He ate them, and then he found a fire way down inside the basket. Coyote had put out all the fires in the village, and no one had left a fire anywhere for the boy. But he did find the fire there in the basket. From that fire he built up a larger fire.

He spent his days at the mudbath. He had no food and soon began to get hungry. He found his grandfather's fishhook and went fishing with it. He caught a fish and cooked it, and in this way he spent his days.

Now the Water Woman enters our story. The poor boy was having quite a bit of trouble, and, seeing this, the Water Woman rowed ashore. She tied herself under the water, and one day when the boy was fishing again, the Water Woman grabbed the hook. The boy raised up the pole with too much force, and it broke. "I'm about to catch a big one!" he thought, and he made another line and fastened the hook to it. He began fishing again and then slowly pulled her out. He could hardly pull the line up, but finally a canoe appeared on the surface, in which a woman was sitting. At this he let the fishing rod and everything go and ran home. The woman rowed ashore and tied up her canoe. Then she went looking for him here and there, but he was nowhere to be found. Finally she came upon him by accident.

She said to him, "Boy! What are you running away for? I've come to stay with you because I feel sorry for you. Let's go and bring the things ashore from my canoe." And so they went and unloaded all the things, including different kinds of food that she had. They spent their days together in a good tepee, which they had made.

The people in the village who had left the boy were living somewhere together, but they were having a hard time because they had very little to eat. They were not able to kill or shoot anything, and they did not catch any fish.

One day, while he was working, Old Man Magpie saw something smoking over among the pine moss (where their old village had been). He said to his wife, "I'm going over there to see them—or him (or whoever is making that smoke). It looks like there is smoke coming from the place where we were." "Go!" she said to him.

So Old Man Magpie came to the place where the boy and his wife were living. They already had one child, a girl. The child was playing with something outside the tepee. Old Man Magpie took the girl's toy and bit it. She ran to her parents, crying, "Daddy! Somebody's out here and he looks hungry! He started to eat my toy!" So the young man got up and came out, whereupon he saw Old Man Magpie. "Oh!" the boy exclaimed, "There's my paternal grandfather! He's your great-grandfather, child. He's come to visit us. Come in!" So Old Man Magpie went in. He told his wife, "Prepare some food—this is my grandfather. The poor man, he's come to see us."

When he finished eating, the old man said to his grandson, "Grandson, we're really having a hard time over there. We're just living on pine moss." The boy replied to his grandfather, "When you get back there, move your things back here. There's a tepee here that you can move into. In the meantime, pack up as much as you want from here and take it back with you—as much as you can carry." So the old man packed up as much as he could carry and headed home.

The old man had quite a few children. These children were eating what their father had brought for them that evening. The children were making quite a lot of noise as they ate. Some of the other people, hearing this, wondered, "Why do those magpies make so much noise in their eating? Let's go and see."

The children, hearing the people come, hid their food and grabbed some pine moss in its place. They began chattering to each other, "Pine moss, loosen up! Pine moss, loosen up!" The people who had come to snoop around went back home, and they told the others, "They're just fussing over pine moss." But most of the people still said, "That's not likely!" So Blue Racer Snake decided to go and see for himself. When he got to where they were, he found them snatching sides of meat and lots of other food from each other. They screamed and yelled gleefully as they fussed over the food. To this day, whenever magpies eat, they still make a lot of noise.

Blue Racer hurried back to the people, and he told them. "They have lots of food that was brought back!" Upon hearing this report, Coyote proclaimed, "I'm going to go ask them myself." When he got to them, the magpies told Coyote, "We're just fussing over this pine moss. Where would we get any food anyway?" Finally Coyote told them, "He plainly saw you eating such-and-such. Where did you get it?" But the magpie children just answered, "Oh, over there," evasively.

Finally, after a long time Old Man Magpie told Coyote the truth: "Yes, we got it over there when I went to visit my grandson. He fished a woman out of the water and is living in grand style over there with her! He said, 'Move over here,' to me. So tomorrow at daybreak we are going to move over there."

Coyote went back and announced to the people, "My nephew, the disobedient boy, surely told me, 'Coyote, you will be the one to come over here and have this house full of food.' Tomorrow we'll go back to that place." So from there all the people traveled back to the old village. They came to it some time before Magpie did.

Coyote was about to move into the tepee when the boy said to him, "That's my grandfather's tepee—you'll have nothing to do with it!" But Coyote answered him, "Why, I was doing this for your benefit!" And the boy said again, "No, never! My grandfather left me a fishhook, and my grandmother left me some food and a fire, but you went around putting out all the fires. The woman was watching you do all this, and for that reason she took pity on me, and she came here to me."

And so the people came back to camp to live there, back to the boy who was disobedient and who caught a Water Woman for his wife.

Just then her pinching made Cicéqi cry out, and she scratched him.

▼▼▼▼▼

49

FROG AND
CRAWFISH DANCE

THERE LIVED SOME PEOPLE, and they made a long house. Coyote made an announcement, saying, "Now get ready; we are going to dance." Then he said, "Where is my Aunt Frog? Let her dance and sing." His aunt sang, "Nephews, ʔi'ya'qoqo, nephews, ʔi'yá'qoqo." Her singing caused the fire to die down. "What kind of dance are you doing? Take her away!" said Coyote. Where is my Aunt Crawfish?" Then she, too sang, "Oh! nodding, nodding being." In her movement she pinched them. Just then her pinching made Cicéqi cry out, and she scratched him. Coyote said, "What kind of person are you putting on to dance? Throw her out!!" That's all.

(Recited by Watters; originally published in Aoki and Walker, 1989.)

With these shoes he went up the bluff without any difficulty.

▼▼▼▼▼

50

COYOTE VISITS

WHITE MOUNTAIN

ONCE THERE WAS Coyote, and he had a daughter. She married someone downriver at Mt. Adams, and he took the daughter as a wife over there. She spent the winter there, but in the springtime she returned to her father. She had a boy when she came back to see Coyote, who was still living here. And they stayed for a while.

Then the daughter and her son said, "Now we are going back home to White Mountain." Coyote hated to be left behind, and he said, "Daughter! I am lonesome being left alone here. I'm going with you." She answered, "It's difficult. It won't be easy for you to get over there. The trails go over the bluffs; their home is there. They live in bluffs and caves. There is no way to make it easy for you to get there.But maybe there is some way you can." Coyote insisted, "I will come with you anyway, and I will stay somewhere near you." They told him, "All right." So they started from there. When they were close to White Mountain, the daughter said, "This is pitiful; it's impossible for you to get up there. Your son-in-law will make shoes for you." Son-in-law finished the shoes and put them on Coyote. With these shoes he went up the bluff without any difficulty. He told himself, "Oh, this is wonderful. They'll see me at qú'lpeqele'sp [Fish Dam]. How easily I climb up the bluffs. I have good shoes." Then they traveled on.

They traveled on and came to a cave, and they went in. When they were inside, it was completely dark, and Coyote couldn't see anything. His daughter kept telling him, "Come this way," and he stumbled over them, even though he opened his eyes wide. When they stopped she told him, "Sit here." There he sat, and across from him was an old woman, some sort of in-law. That old woman could not resist laughing when she saw Coyote. He was looking down the aisle,

(Recited by Watters; originally published as "Coyote and His Daughter" in Aoki and Walker, 1989.)

opening his eyes wide. The old woman laughed, "My! How funny you are, opening your eyes wide like that!" And Coyote thought to himself, "Your saying such a thing, woman, makes me want to make you my wife and get even with you. I will sleep with you." The old woman laughed, "Ha ha, that's what he's thinking!" She had read his thoughts. Meanwhile it had become evening. "My, he's so pitiful," his son-in-law thought and smeared Coyote's eyes with salve. Coyote's eyesight cleared right up, and he looked down the aisle and saw lots of people. "So this is the kind of place I came to," he thought.

Coyote had no place to go. He would go out and come right back in. He became restless, for he had never stayed at one place this long. Now, sometime after he had become restless, he said, "Daughter, I am restless. This place is too boring." She told him, "Yes, anytime you want to, you can leave, if you want to go back." Coyote said, "I'm lonely for my friend Fox. He must be over there somewhere. All right, now I'm leaving." Then he left, and as he did, his daughter gave him something, saying, "Take this with you." He brought that thing (it was a goat) with him from there, and he came right down to the bottom of the bluff. He brought them when he came back here. From that time the goats have been found throughout the mountains, for what Coyote brought was his grandchildren, although he didn't realize what he was bringing over. That was what his daughter gave him to bring. Those shoes that he had intended to show off at *qú'lpleqele'sp* disappeared when he came down the mountain. Since that time, we can find goats throughout our mountains.

▼▼▼▼▼

51

SEA MONSTER

Sᴇᴀ Mᴏɴsᴛᴇʀ Bᴏʏ from the downriver people heard that Young Coyote was to be feared at hoop-spearing. Sea Monster Boy then plotted against Young Coyote, and he came from down the river. They had a spear-throwing contest against each other, and Young Coyote defeated the boy. It so happened that Sea Monster Boy had a sister who was the very hoop target which they were spearing. Sea Monster Boy said, "Young Coyote, you have defeated me and now I am giving you my sister." Sea Monster Boy then went home, while Young Coyote came into possession of a wife. Then they (Young Coyote, his wife, Old Coyote, and Fox) moved to the mountains. There they shot much game, which they prepared by drying. In the meantime a baby was born to Young Coyote and his wife.

Old Coyote was making a spoon. "With this I will sup huckleberries and bitterroots at the Wedding Journey feast." Fox was making pure pitch, a pipe, and a spearhead. Old Coyote was thinking only of eating and therefore was making only a spoon. They came down from the mountains, and they said to one another, "We are going on the Wedding Journey." They brought all the meat and all other kinds of things [for gifts]; they packed and placed them all in a canoe. Their canoe was made of a pine tree trunk. And they embarked downstream.

Sea Monster Woman sat in the bow and Fox, Old Coyote, Young Coyote, and his son, sat in the bottom. Thus they proceeded to the lower reaches of the river. They were going along when they saw the woman in the bow start making the boat dive. Just before they submerged, Fox said to them, "Hurry, let us get into the pipe," and all four of them got in and shut the door. The canoe and all in it traveled along under the water. Sea Monster Woman thought, "They will be drowned." They were underwater a long time and the woman thought, "They must be drowned by now." They rose to the surface again and behold!

(Recited by Wàyi'làtpu; originally published in Phinney, 1934.)

At very close range Young Coyote speared the monster under the armpit.

she saw them dancing their grandson about. "What have they done? I thought they would be suffocated by now," she said to herself. She did the same thing again farther downstream, but she could not drown them.

At last she took them to their destination far down the river and there she said to them, "We have arrived now." They drifted ashore. The woman was the first to disembark, and immediately she left them and went home. They unloaded their goods, built a fire on the lowlands by the riverside, and there all alone by the water's edge they made for themselves whatever in the way of food they found. In the evening the woman came to them and said, "Here you are. Here is a spear, for every evening something swims here. I don't know just what it is, a person, yet not a person, and you will spear it with this. That is what my people said." But she was lying to them. She wanted only to kill them, and when she had gone home earlier, she had said to her people, "They are powerful; from the first I wanted to destroy them, and in no possible way could I do it." And then they had told her, "Take this spearhead to them [it was small and worn] and father will kill all of them when he swims."

The woman now gave them the spearhead saying, "He comes in the evening and be sure you do him in." Before leaving she gave them what appeared to be pure pitch but it was really false pitch, which is worthless for burning. Then the woman left them. And evening came. Presently they heard him coming and they lit their torches to watch his coming. Just like a huge person he came along in the water, crawling and grabbling about aimlessly. To all appearances he was a person, yet gruesome, and they knew he was Sea Monster. Close by he came and Young Coyote took up their good, large, sharp spearhead of Fox's making, and at very close range speared the monster under the armpit. The monster struggled and writhed in death agony. Young Coyote struggled with him for a long time and finally managed to kill him.

In the morning the woman came to them again and said, "Well, how? Did he swim?" "Yes, we killed him," they replied. They had hidden their own spearhead and now they showed her the one she had given them, which they had smeared with blood for the occasion. The woman then took the dead one and, departing, said to them, "This evening again you will do this; another monster will come to you." [They had already killed her father and now she was referring to her father's sister's husband.]

But there sat Coyote disconsolately holding his spoon, not having supped at all. Again in the evening in the same way the dangerous one came to them, and Young Coyote killed him, too. In the morning the woman came to them again and said, "Again, a monster will come to you."

Now Fox said to his friends, "We have already killed two of them, and soon she herself will come. She will come upon us in vengeance; she is very ferocious.

She will very likely kill us." Soon it was evening, and now she, herself, Young Coyote's wife, became a great gruesome thing. They saw her coming, and now they lit their torches because this light stood for their strength, and should their light go out, at that moment the sea monster would take them all under water. For that reason they were holding their torches high and singing increasingly louder, "It is glowing, it is glowing, it is glowing, it is glowing." The boy, too, Young Coyote's son, was singing increasingly louder. Now they saw her coming, and at once Young Coyote recognized her, "It is my wife, all right." She was crawling along, hair straggling this way and that. Young Coyote speared her, hitting her perfectly true. She struggled very fiercely, and then she turned on them. The boy was still loudly singing, "It is glowing, it is glowing." Then in the midst of the struggle Young Coyote said to them, "Now, hurry, go ashore, flee, for she will kill us." Even though he had speared her well, she attacked them ferociously. As they fled at Young Coyote's word, the water rose and pursued them in torrents. They ran on as the water surged to their knees. Then Young Coyote shouted to them, "Now she is killing us! She is carrying us under! Release the boy, for on his account she is doing this to us." In their flight Coyote and Fox were holding him by his hands—one on each side—and they were running. The water now came to their armpits, just barely allowing them to step. Young Coyote again shouted to them, "Now she is taking us under! Release the boy quickly!" They let go of the boy, and immediately the water receded and the flood that had pursued them ran off dry. Thus Sea Monster Woman took the child away from them and never again ever did they see her.

▼▼▼▼▼

52

HOW COYOTE'S PENIS
BECAME A DAM

ONCE UPON A TIME Coyote was wandering about, and all at once he saw some girls swimming on the other side of the river. He thought to himself, "I wish I could have those girls somehow!" He began pounding his penis, and he tried to see if it would reach to the other side of the river. It wasn't quite long enough, so he pounded some more. Finally it almost reached the other side. The girls were swimming around unconcernedly. Coyote entered the oldest girl. She felt something, and she screamed, "He's done something to me!"

The girls tried to get Coyote's penis out of her, and finally the girl became so uncomfortable that one of them suggested, "Cut it off!" So they tried to cut it off, but they had little success. They worked on it for a long time, and after a little while Coyote hollered over to them, "Use the split [meaning obscure] that's already there." The girls found the split, and with it they cut his penis.

And to this day, there is a waterfall at Lewiston where this incident occurred. The name of the place is *Tukeyú'tpe.*

FOR THE EXPENSE OF THE material

(Recited by Watters; originally published in Aoki and Walker, 1989. See also "Coyote and the Mallard Ducks" in Spinden, 1917.)

PART TWO

A DESCRIPTIVE INTERPRETATION OF COYOTE'S CHARACTER

Introduction

IN THIS SECTION, we construct a portrait of Coyote's character. Because his appearances are scattered throughout the narratives and range from that of central actor to merely a peripheral cameo player, consistency and continuity may
not be immediately apparent. Nevertheless, certain actions and situations are
important, because they are repeated throughout the narratives. A consistent
pattern of actions and motivations becomes apparent in particular interac-
tional contexts, and these are the basis for describing Coyote's character. Our
analysis considers Coyote's relationships with virtually every other mythic
character, including interactions that may seem minor and atypical.

The myths that have been referenced or reprinted in this volume come from
several sources. The most recent collection is Aoki and Walker's *Nez Perce Oral
Narratives* (1989), which Deward Walker began collecting in 1962. It includes the
narratives told by Samuel Watters and Elizabeth Wilson. Watters's repertoire is
more extensive and less sanitized than Wilson's. Phinney's *Nez Perce Texts* (1934)
were collected from his mother, *Wayi'latpu*. The original publications of both
collections include an interlinear translation plus an English-only version ad-
justed for syntax. Earlier collections are Spinden's "Myths of the Nez Perce Indians" (1908) and "Nez Perce Tales" (1917), which were originally published as
English-only translations. Spinden's narratives are generally more abbreviated
than those in the other collections, but several unique myths are included. Raconteurs freely abbreviate or expand portions of the myths from one recital to the
next, so one version may differ from another version that is vague or abbreviated.
Our more comprehensive treatment also helps ensure that our conclusions have
not ignored potentially contradictory evidence. We do not presume to represent
what he specifically means to the contemporary Nez Perce people.

Our analysis of Nez Perce Coyote reveals a degree of similarity with the
Coyote who appears in other Native American cultures. William Bright's *A*

Coyote Reader presents a collection of Coyote myths arbitrarily drawn from various Native American cultures, and arranges them into categories according to specific character traits. Because Bright's work draws from many different cultures, the resulting image of the Coyote character in Native North America is at best a generalized hybrid and not entirely accurate for any particular culture. Although the image of Coyote drawn by Bright is reminiscent of Nez Perce Coyote, it omits various distinctive features, especially the complex interactions and contradictions among the many aspects of his character. For example, the primary factors motivating Nez Perce Coyote are his lust for food, power, and sexual gratification. Nevertheless, his abilities are generally inadequate to fulfill these desires. His attempts to bridge the gap between his inadequate abilities and his lustful desires by use of deception, evasion, trickery, and disguise are frequently humorous; these actions transform the world, but these transformations are almost an afterthought of his often unsuccessful efforts to satisfy his appetites.

We believe that interpretation or explanation of Native American myths must begin within the context of the other narratives forming the myth corpus. Some books, such as *Voices of the Winds* by Margot Edmonds and Ella Clark and *American Indian Myths and Legends* by Richard Erdoes and Alfonzo Ortiz, are also anthologies of myths from many different Native American cultures. Although these anthologies provide a sampling of a wide range of themes and characters, they do not explain or interpret the myths in relation to either the culture from which they came, or more importantly to other myths from the same culture. Other works, such as David Rockwell's *Giving Voice to Bear*, focus on a particular character as it appears in the myths, rituals, and other areas of several cultures, but again its broad scope precludes a detailed treatment of the character of Bear within any particular culture. Donald Hines's *Tales of the Nez Perce* includes some of the tales included in our present work; it consists of a standard classification of various motifs for the purpose of folkloristic comparison and does not examine characters or other aspects of the myths in any depth. Dell Skeels's "Style in the Unwritten Literature of the Nez Perce" attempts to explain the myths using psychoanalytic schemes which we reject. Mythical characters are not human beings, so it is problematic to assume that they exhibit human psychological traits.

We have drawn much inspiration from Melville Jacobs's *The Content and Style of an Oral Literature*, which examines Clackamas myths in the context of Clackamas culture. Jacobs stressed the importance of examining social relationships among Clackamas mythic characters as a means of understanding Clackamas personality structure. He realized that such studies must remain within the context of myths from the same culture. Theodore Stern has employed similar methods in "Ideal and Expected Behavior as Seen in Klamath

Mythology." Stern argues that exceptional as well as everyday events occur in myths and that mythic variants in the cultural norm are also important in pointing the moral. He suggests that the consequences of the actions of mythic characters reveal the values a society places on such actions, that happy outcomes follow sanctioned actions, and that misfortune follows socially disapproved actions. We employ Jacobs's and Stern's general principles but our specific goals and methods differ from theirs. Our goal is to describe Coyote's character in terms of the consistent behavior and motivations demonstrated in his relationships with other mythic characters. The myths operate according to their own rules. We suggest that the descriptive methods employed below are also applicable to other mythic characters, and that a thorough descriptive analysis must precede any attempt to explain the deeper meanings of the myths by reference to psychoanalytic or other theoretical schemes.

Coyote and Monsters

Many of the characters Coyote encounters in the myths are monsters. Some of the interactions constitute discrete narratives; some are incorporated into other stories. Many of Coyote's encounters with monsters are highly formulaic in terms of the sequence of events, the type of incidents, and the actors in the episode. Other incidents with monsters are not formulaic, but the monsters share a personality common to all Nez Perce monsters. Most monsters (especially those in the formulaic encounters) do not know Coyote's identity until after they have killed him, which makes them all the more terrifying, because they are clearly indiscriminate killers.

Another typical feature of most monster myths is that the monster is rendered harmless to the future human beings. When Coyote kills them, he often tells them that they will no longer be killers and transforms them from their former dangerous nature to their harmless form in the present world. This motivation does not seem to be Coyote's initial one; instead it seems to be an afterthought.

The formulaic episodes typically share the following structure: Coyote encounters the monster; he is killed and thrown into the river; he is revived by Magpie; he is advised how to defeat the monster by the excrement children; he returns and kills the monster. (This sequence also occurs in stories that involve female monsters and the killer baby.) In general, the monsters have very limited roles and do not appear in any other myths (with the minor exception of White-tailed Buck). Variation occurs mainly in the motivations of Coyote and the particular monster, but the consequences of the interactions remain determined by the formula.

The formulaic monsters are all killers but may be divided into the categories of "provoked" and "unprovoked" killers. The unprovoked killers kill Coyote simply because he wanders into their presence. Butterfly (see "Killer Butterfly") and Mussel-Shell Women (see "Mussel-Shell Killers") lure Coyote by appealing to his sexual impulsiveness. They apparently do not recognize him until he is dead, because they say, "Oh, it's just Coyote" before dumping him into the river. He does not recognize them either but learns their identity from third-party informants (Magpie and the excrement children). It is not indicated whether he has previously transformed himself before meeting them, as he does in other encounters with sexually desirable females, or, if they simply do not recognize him, but his appearance seems irrelevant to these women. Their sexual behavior is not intended to create a relationship at all but instead is used as a tool to lure victims to their death.

Mountain-Sheep Girl (in Spinden's "Coyote's Wars") also lures Coyote to his death. She requests Coyote's assistance from afar, so she does not know who he is. She pretends to need help in killing her game, and when Coyote comes she pushes him over the cliff with a forked stick. Coyote's motivation is that he sees an opportunity to obtain food. The Killer Baby (in "Killer Baby") is a formulaic monster who sucks Coyote to death when Coyote attempts to nurse him with his finger. Coyote kills him by shoving a bone down his throat.

Male monsters may kill Coyote simply because he encroaches on their territory. The hummingbirds ("Coyote and the Hummingbird") challenge Coyote to battle well before they know who he is, and it seems indicated in both versions (Wilson, and Phinney, 1934) that they do this to anyone who comes near. The excrement children tell Coyote that White-tailed Buck ("Coyote Breaks the Fish Dam at Celilo") killed him as he jumped across the river simply because "that is what he does to people."

The other formulaic monsters are also killers, but Coyote provokes their hostility through his actions. Rock ("Coyote Breaks the Fish Dam at Celilo") kills Coyote, for example, for inadvertently urinating on him. Often the monster has some power that arouses Coyote's envy. Grasshopper (in "How Coyote Lost His Eyes") fascinates Coyote, because he has the ability to detach his leg. Phinney's version indicates that Coyote attempts to imitate him and gain this power in order to impress the shamans. However, the imitation apparently steals the power from Grasshopper, who realizes what is happening and kills Coyote. In the same narrative, the eye-juggling man (Bobcat in Wilson's version) also inspires Coyote's imitation for identical reasons; but instead of killing Coyote, Bobcat simply causes Coyote's eyes to become lost. Thus, the monster formula is not applicable in this case (see our discussion below on relationships emphasizing body parts). Imitation is a threat to these actors' special powers, and it provokes their protective reaction. Coyote's motivation for meddling with the Blindworm ("Blindworm Killer") is less clear; he marvels at Blindworm's counting game and steals the counting sticks. In Spinden's version he simply thinks it would be fun to hide the sticks. It seems possible that he intends to learn Blindworm's power (which is unspecified, yet seems present because Coyote marvels at it) and to steal this power by stealing the sticks. Coyote's disruption provokes Blindworm to kill him. Coyote's attempts to acquire powers possessed by others is not limited to monster narratives, but these episodes illustrate the hazards of his meddling with powers that he does not understand.

A main difference between the formulaic and nonformulaic monster myths lies in Coyote's awareness of the nature of the monsters. When he is unaware of the danger, he is killed—and the formula (being revived and advised before returning to confront his adversary) must be invoked. This lack of forewarning also allows his personal motivations to lure him to the encounter. Once he is advised and prepared to react, his actions explicitly make the world safer; yet the motivation for personal revenge cannot be ruled out. By contrast, his encounters with the nonformulaic monsters seem more heroic, because he is not killed. Hence, personal revenge seems an unlikely motive for his actions.

The monsters in the nonformulaic myths share many features with the others, including their nature as killers and their ultimate transformation into harmless forms (with the exception of Grizzly Bear, who remains dangerous). Mosquito Boy ("Killer Mosquito") kills his grandmother which seems to be reason enough for Coyote and others to plot his death. Coyote lures Mosquito to his death by offering him blood, the one thing that Mosquito cannot resist. Frog ("Frog and Coyote") is a threat to the river, because she blocks its source, and Coyote decides to fix the problem. Frog seems more similar to Grizzly Bear than to other female monsters (except she is not a killer) which seems appropriate, because she is portrayed as being particularly unattractive and thus would not interest Coyote sexually. Frog appears again in "Frog and Bluejay," where she is killing the birds in a rigged contest. Coyote does not directly confront her in this narrative; rather he persuades the people to come up with a plan and carry it out. When Coyote encounters Sun and Sun's father ("Coyote Defeats the Sun"), he knows exactly what to expect and makes elaborate plans in order to defeat the monsters. No specific motivation is given for his desire to battle them except that he knew that Sun was a killer. In the end, he announces that he has made the world safer for the coming human beings.

The Monster ("Coyote and Monster") is defeated when Coyote has foreknowledge of the Monster's danger to the people. (Spinden's version is consistent but vastly abbreviated and leaves out the creation of the various peoples. Coyote only rescues the myth people.) The anonymous informant is probably Meadowlark, who advises him on how to proceed, although the details are not explicit. Coyote deliberately loses the inhaling contest as a ploy in order to gain access to the Monster's heart and kill him. In Phinney's version, Coyote's motivations explicitly help the people and/or the coming humans; he is interrupted from building the fish ladder which he was doing for the people who were swallowed by the Monster. (These seem to be the myth people, because when he learns of their absence, he says, "Then I'll stop doing this, because I was doing it for the people.") During the inhaling contest, Coyote creates camas roots and serviceberries, saying, "Here the people will find them and will be glad, for only a short time away is the coming of the human race." After defeating the Monster and rescuing the myth people, Coyote creates the various tribes from the Monster's body, almost forgetting to create the Nez Perce who are made from the remaining blood. Coyote is purely heroic in this myth. He engages a formidable enemy, acts solely in the interest of others (except perhaps to prevent his own loneliness), and he acts in a chiefly manner in directing the assistance of his fellows which seems appropriate because he alone has the plan to defeat the enemy. This episode contrasts with other instances in which he inappropriately attempts to act as leader.

Coyote fights Winter (Yaunyaiye) in "Coyote and Winter Have a War" when winter inexplicably challenges him. The narrative is so abbreviated that it is difficult to determine whether Winter is really a monster. He is similar to Hummingbird when he issues the unprovoked challenge, but there are no formulaic elements. The particular consequences of the battle are not given.

The most important feature of the monster episodes is that Coyote changes the world to make it safer for the coming human beings. This motivation seems accidentally heroic in the formulaic examples, because he is lured by inappropriate impulses (unrestrained sexuality, attempting to imitate another's special powers, and so on). Making the world safer for everyone seems to be merely an extension of making it safer for himself. In the nonformulaic myths, the monsters are threatening the people in general, either as killers or as threats to their resources. In these examples, Coyote explicitly acts in order to benefit everyone, and he only incidentally benefits himself.

Coyote and Grizzly Bears

Grizzly bears are monstrous in several respects, but they differ from all of the other monsters. They are Coyote's enemies in an ongoing conflict, whereas other monsters typically appear only once. The motivation behind a particular conflict episode is not always made explicit, perhaps because the raconteur assumes that the audience is aware of the relationship between Coyote and the grizzlies. Grizzly Bear's killer personality exists under a thin veneer of sociability and surfaces at the slightest provocation. Grizzlies are a threat to many other members of the myth community besides Coyote, which makes them seem especially dangerous. The male grizzly seems less threatening to Coyote than the female, who actually kills him. The male grizzly threatens but never manages to defeat Coyote. Grizzly bear children often suffer in the conflict as well (see the discussion of Coyote and children).

Male Grizzly Bears In the ongoing feud between Coyote and male grizzlies, both parties seem motivated to intimidate the other without provocation. Bear rushes furiously at Coyote when they are inside the Monster ("Coyote and Monster"), and Coyote kicks him on the nose, saying, "So! You make yourself ferocious only to me?" (This episode takes an unusual turn, because Coyote appears to physically overpower Bear; it is more typical for him to deceive and outwit Bear, sometimes with the assistance of a third party.) Grizzly Bear also initiates hostilities in "Coyote Kills Grizzly Bear's Sons," when the five grizzly bear brothers cause the death of Coyote's five sons. Coyote arranges a phony hunt and distracts father Grizzly, while Bobcat kills the grizzly bear brothers. Father Grizzly wounds and nearly kills Coyote who transforms his appearance to dupe Bear. Ultimately, Coyote shoots Bear as he flounders in the river. In Phinney's version this episode is linked to the one in which Coyote incites the murder of Lynx. Here Coyote plays his two enemies off against one another by lying, telling the revived Lynx that it was Bear's idea, not his own, in order to have Lynx killed. Thus, Lynx kills Bear's sons in the phony hunt which proceeds almost identically to Phinney's version with a similar conclusion.

In Phinney's "Coyote Bears He Killed" (not included in this volume), Coyote kills Grizzly Bear's son for stealing the people's meat, knowing that father Grizzly will attempt revenge. Coyote tells the people that he too is fearsome. He kills Bear by tricking him into swallowing hot stones, and he mocks him as he dies. Coyote then moves into Bear's lodge and takes it for his own. This method of killing, as well as the assumption of the victim's property, is similar to the conclusion of Wilson's "How Coyote Killed the Grizzly Bears." The beginning of Wilson's version is different, however. In it, Coyote is rather impressed with himself and shows off his new female acquaintance to the village. He sends for Chief Grizzly Bear's "prized" deer-hoof bell and is insistent when Bear declines to provide it. He knows that Bear will appear stingy if he refuses, so asking for it will infuriate Bear. Once Bear is enraged, Coyote entraps him into participating in a phony contest, which ends with Coyote tricking Bear into swallowing hot rocks. Coyote then declares himself chief and takes Bear's houses. Phinney's "Coyote and the Expeditioner" is comparable to the first part of "How Coyote Killed the Grizzly Bears," with Coyote insistently asking for Grizzly Bear's hand-drum in order to infuriate him. This episode, however, ends with Grizzly Bear calming down, apparently satisfied that the people are playing a trick on Coyote (switching Frog with Coyote's new girl).

It appears that the various raconteurs may freely associate the motivation for conflict between Coyote and Grizzly Bear to either party. The various outcomes of the conflict also seem to be interchangeable. Thus, particular provocations do not seem to imply particular consequences.

Female Grizzly Bears   Female grizzly bears do not appeal to Coyote. They are not sexually attractive, nor do they provide food, services, or information. In every instance, Coyote and female grizzlies are mortal enemies. Their animosity exists largely because all grizzly bears, especially females, tend to become ruthless murderers when their anger or jealousy is aroused.

Grizzly bear women, like Coyote, are repulsive to the opposite sex. We know Coyote is aware of this repulsion, because he lures the five Grizzly Bear sisters to their doom by telling them that a desirable young man is interested in them ("How the Grizzly Bear Sisters Were Fooled"). Their subsequent enthusiasm to participate in the dance indicates that the interest of a man is rare good fortune to be taken advantage of before the opportunity disappears.

In Phinney's "Bear Led Astray a Boy" (not included in this volume), Grizzly Bear becomes jealous of her husband when she realizes that he has been paying attention to other young women. Because he had been captured as a young boy and raised by Grizzly Bear in seclusion, he had no other women with whom to compare her. But at his first opportunity (a visit to his village of origin) he becomes interested in other women. Grizzly Bear responds by killing the five women who have become her sexual rivals, and this act, in turn, inspires Coyote to help the people plan for her death.

In "Don't Crack the Bones," Grizzly Bear woman moves in with Black Bear and Coyote's son as the consquence of Black Bear's failure to obey a specific command from her husband ("Don't crack the bones"). Grizzly Bear, however unwelcome, seems intent upon performing the duties of a co-wife, and both she and Black Bear take turns cooking breakfast. Her magical transformation of her excrement into the morning meal reveals her inability to cook normally. Her anger at having her technique discovered is extreme, because cooking is integral to the role of a wife and failure as a cook is equivalent to failure as a wife. It is Old Coyote who exposes her secret, which seems appropriate because of his fondness for good food and his general animosity toward grizzly bears. She is so angered at being discovered that she kills everyone present except Fox.

Coyote's motivation for causing the death of the Grizzly Bear sisters is un-specified, but it is linked to the demise of the Woodpecker brothers ("The Five Grizzly Bear Sisters and the Five Woodpecker Brothers"). It seems that Coyote is inclined to destroy the Woodpecker brothers and simply finds it convenient to have the grizzly bears killed at the same time, even though they have not specifically provoked him. He expects to be rewarded for his actions, but it is not clear what the reward will be or if it would be granted for acting against either or both of his adversaries. This example demonstrates the ongoing feud between Coyote and all grizzly bears, because Coyote does not kill (or cause to be killed) other actors without specific reason. Therefore, his animosity seems based on some previous unspecified incident or incidents, which in turn im-plies a consistency in their relationship throughout the corpus of myths. Coy-ote's animosity goes so deep that after fooling the sisters into thinking the hunters' weapons are harmless, he not only cooks the first dead grizzly bear but also serves her meat to her unwitting sisters.

In Phinney's "Coyote Bears He Killed," Coyote kills Grizzly Bear's wife, who attempts to kill Coyote because he killed her husband and son. Her demise oc-curs in identical fashion to that of her husband, whom Coyote duped into swallowing hot stones. In Phinney's "Bears and Coyote," Grizzly Bear woman runs away in fear after Coyote kills her husband. In Spinden's "Grizzly Bear and Coyote" (a brief version of Wilson's "How Coyote Killed the Grizzly Bears"), Grizzly Bear woman attempts to avenge her husband after Coyote kills him, but Coyote discovers her plan and sends out the hunters in groups in-stead of singly, and she is killed. Her sister and a brother are spared to perpet-uate the species.

In Spinden's "Coyote and the Grizzly Bear" (not included in this volume), Coyote reluctantly cures Grizzly Bear after she is sick from eating so many peo-ple. When she realizes that he knows the cause of her illness, she chases him. He eludes her by transforming himself, first into a buffalo, then into an old man with smallpox. (See "Coyote Kills Grizzly Bear's Sons" for a similar ending.)

Coyote defeats the grizzly bears in every instance except in "Dont' Crack the Bones." He relies on trickery and deception rather than physical prowess or fighting skill to achieve victory. This technique is consistent with Coyote's mode of action with other actors as well and is especially effective, because the grizzly bears seem to be particularly slow-witted. Other actors fear the grizzlies and avoid confrontations with them, but Coyote takes pride in his bravery against them. He may wisely run from the bears, but this merely allows him to create the opportunity to trick them. Grizzly bears are not transformed like other monsters, because grizzlies retain their dangerous nature in today's world. Instead, their numbers are reduced and they are confined to the mountains.

Coyote and Advisers

Some actors provide Coyote or other actors with information, either in support of or against Coyote's purposes. Advisers usually appear only briefly in the myths; their action is usually limited to providing information. Occasionally advisers also appear in other roles, but in this section we will discuss only their appearances as advisers.

The most frequently appearing male adviser is Magpie. This frequency is largely due to his appearance as part of the formula of several monster narratives. In this formula, the dead Coyote is revived by Magpie pecking for eyebrow-fat. Magpie then dispels Coyote's delusion of having been occupied with women upriver and rudely informs him of the truth of what actually happened to him. Coyote often scolds Magpie for disturbing his dreams of women, perhaps as an effort to save face. This formula is seen in Watters's narratives "Coyote Breaks the Fish-Dam at Celilo" (twice), "Warmweather and Coldweather" (twice), and "How Coyote Lost His Eyes"; in Wilson's narratives "Coyote and Hummingbird," "Blind Worm Killer," "Mussel-Shell Killers," "Killer Baby," and "Killer Butterfly"; in Phinney's narratives "Coyote and Butterfly," "Coyote and Humming Bird," and "Coyote and Curlew"; and in Spinden's narratives "Coyote's Wars" (twice) and "The Log Worm." Similar circumstances occur in Wilson's "Coyote, Fox, and the Wild Carrots" except that Coyote has been killed by accident instead of by a monster. Magpie also acts as adviser (against his intentions in this case) when he discovers the whereabouts of Disobedient Boy (see "The Disobedient Boy," all versions) and of Bobcat in "Bobcat and Pine Squirrel's Daughter" (Wildcat in Spinden's version), both of whom survived or revived to become successful again after being abandoned or killed. In these myths, Coyote learns that the magpies are eating well while the other people are starving, and he seeks an explanation. The magpies (the old man and his children) pretend to be eating pine moss, but Coyote is persistent, and eventually old man Magpie reveals the source of his food. Magpie is reluctant to divulge his secret food source which would benefit the others, including Coyote, and he succeeds in deceiving all but Coyote. Coyote's success in discovering Magpie's secret where others fail reflects his extensive experience with matters involving deception and hunger.

Mosquito acts as an adviser whose information serves either for or against Coyote's purposes. In "Coyote Breaks the Fish Dam at Celilo," Mosquito spies on Cricket to discover that Coyote's son had returned and informs the group (in Phinney's version Blue Racer Snake performs this function). Thus Coyote's deception is foiled, and he suffers the consequences of his incest. In "Bobcat and Pine Squirrel's Daughter," Mosquito provides the information that the magpies are eating well, which leads Coyote to find out why. In Watters's and Phinney's versions of "The Disobedient Boy," Blue Racer Snake performs the same function. In Watters's "Furred and Feathered Animals Have a Council" (not included in this volume), Mosquito informs the people that Wolf (previously thought to be dead) had recovered from his illness and was threatening nearby. Coyote acts on the information, advising the people in turn to secure their dwellings and remain inside, but they fail to listen and are killed.

Duck Man's sole appearance involves exposing another instance of Coyote's incest through deception ("Coyote Marries His Daughter"). He sees Coyote hunting and recognizes him (he had disguised himself in order to sleep with his daughter). Duck Man sings, "Coyote has slept with his daughter" and the birds add, "Coyote is so thoughtless." Coyote tries to evade the issue by saying the same about Duck Man. He sings, "Duck Man is sleeping with his daughter," and he gets the mice to add, "Yes, because he doesn't have any sense." Coyote's humorous attempt to cloud the issue fails, and his daughter becomes suspicious, eventually discovering the truth.

When Coyote's plan to kill Grizzly Bear's sons unfolds, ("Coyote Kills Grizzly Bear's Sons"), Pinion Bird (or Marten in Phinney's version) witnesses the death of the young grizzlies and announces the fact loudly enough for Father Grizzly to hear. This interference complicates Coyote's scheme, and he narrowly escapes Bear's anger.

Women also serve Coyote as a source of information. He asks Aunt Mouse where Grizzly Bear is living, and she tells him without incident in Phinney's "Coyote the Expeditioner" (not included in this volume). Meadowlark is often a source of information for other actors, and Coyote uses her services twice. Meadowlark's appearances are usually formulaic, with the actor accidentally breaking her leg, then offering to repair it on the condition that she give specific information. She is also addressed as "aunt," an example of a kinship term being applied to strangers to indicate the type of relationship expected from them. Within the framework of this formula, Meadowlark ("Coyote and Monster") gives Coyote information about where the people have gone (they were swallowed by the monster). He arrogantly replies that he knew this already and leaves her. In the second instance, again following the formula, Meadowlark tells Coyote how to succeed at keeping the salmon he has acquired for dinner ("Coyote Breaks the Fish Dam at Celilo").

Children may also serve as advisers, as demonstrated by Coyote's "excrement children" (sometimes called simply "children" or in Spinden, "little creatures"). They appear as advisers in Watters's narratives "Coyote Breaks the Fish-Dam at Celilo" (twice), "Warmweather and Coldweather" (twice), and "How Coyote Lost His Eyes"; in Wilson's narratives "Blind-Worm Killer," "Mussel-Shell Killers," "Killer Baby," and "Killer Butterfly"; in Phinney's narratives "Coyote and Butterfly," "Coyote and Humming Bird," and "Coyote and Curlew"; and in Spinden's "Coyote and Salmon." The excrement children occasionally appear in other capacities, (see our discussion of Coyote and children). As advisers, the excrement children form part of the formula associated with Coyote's interactions with most monsters. He is first killed by the monster, then awakened, and advised as to what happened by Magpie; then he consults the excrement children about how to defeat the monster. The consultation proceeds by Coyote hitting his hip so the excrement children tumble out fighting and/or poking at each other's eyes. Coyote sends them back inside himself, but blocks out the youngest who usually scolds him for making them chilly and then tells him the course of action he is to take to defeat the monster.

Some of Coyote's minor interactions with children also center around his need or desire for information. Inside the monster ("Coyote and Monster"), Coyote asks the boys where the monster's heart is, and they tell him without incident. Coyote asks the magpie children ("The Disobedient Boy") to tell him where the good food they are eating came from. Their answer is evasive, and Coyote eventually learns the answer from their father. These two scenes show that children realize that it may or may not be in their interest to divulge certain information. The boys in the monster have nothing to lose by telling Coyote what he wishes to know, and in fact their information contributes to their rescue. The magpies know that they may lose their secret source of food if they tell Coyote where it came from, especially since they are familiar with Coyote and his greed for food. Coyote seems to hope that the magpie children will be naive and divulge their secret to him, but they hold out until their father can handle the issue. Conversely, children may provide unsought or unwelcome information. His own boys indicate that he is slighting them when he bypasses them to deliver his kill to a prospective wife ("Bobcat and Pine Squirrel's Daughter"). Coyote seems unconcerned until they add that Coyote's rival has already won the contest; then he realizes that his clever plan has backfired.

Advisers seem limited to telling the truth, which may work for or against Coyote's purposes. When Coyote simply needs to know something, the truth of a situation is beneficial to him. When Coyote relies on deception or disguise to accomplish his goals, the exposed truth usually works against him. The role of advisers is so limited that very little is revealed about their character, although they tend to rebuke Coyote if he deludes himself or others.

Coyote's Interactions with Groups

There are many instances in the myths in which Coyote interacts with groups of actors who are generically referred to as the people. This term usually indicates the mythic people, which this section addresses, but sometimes indicates the coming human beings (occasionally, the two are indistinguishable). The interaction between Coyote and the people may take different forms. Coyote often employs the people's assistance in his schemes. Sometimes he joins them in a mutual endeavor. Other times he acts as their benefactor. The people may act as his conscience, and we see situations in which they collectively ostracize him.

On the many occasions when the people assist Coyote in his schemes, he and the people may have a common interest in the proposed action. In these cases, the people simply comply with Coyote's instructions. In "Mosquito and Coyote" (Phinney's version of "Killer Mosquito"), the people fill five pails of blood to help Coyote destroy Mosquito, a youth who has killed his own grandmother. In Phinney's "Bear Led Astray a Boy," Coyote decides that Grizzly Bear must be killed because she killed the maidens who made her jealous; the people carry out the plan to kill her. In Phinney's "Wild Goat a Woman Carried Away" (not included here), Coyote assembles the people in his lodge and tells them of his plan to kill the skulls who have been tormenting everyone. The people carry out the plan. In Watters's narratives "Coyote Kills Grizzly Bear's Sons," "The Five Grizzly Bear Sisters and the Five Woodpecker Brothers," and in Spinden's "Grizzly Bear and Coyote," the people agree to kill the grizzly bears as part of Coyote's plan. Coyote announces that the people will go east to avoid being killed by the cannibal in "Cannibal." In Spinden's "The Diving Beaver" (not included here), Coyote assembles the people and requests that they make a plan to kill Beaver, who has been killing the diving people.

These examples illustrate Coyote's success at leading the people to act against monsters. Even when the people do not assist him against some monsters, they benefit from his actions. It is appropriate for Coyote to expect their assistance and cooperation when he fights common enemies. The people risk negative consequences if they do not cooperate in such situations. In Watters's "Furred and Feathered Animals Have a Council" (not included here), the scared people fail to obey Coyote's instructions to bolster their dwellings and stay inside, and all of them are killed by the dangerous wolf. In another myth, the people are skeptical that Coyote can kill the grizzly bears (Phinney's "Coyote Bears He Killed"). They inform Father Bear that Coyote has killed his son, presumably fearing that Bear will win and take revenge if they ally themselves with Coyote. After he defeats Bear, Coyote refuses to share the spoils of his victory with them.

Following Coyote's instructions does not always have desirable results. In the narratives about the Disobedient Boy (see "The Disobedient Boy," all versions), Coyote encourages the people to abandon the boy. After the people endure a long period of hunger, the grown boy is discovered with his stores of food, and Coyote leads the people to live with the now-grown boy again. Coyote tries to put the blame on the people for the decision to abandon the boy when it was actually he who conceived the plan. Similarly, in "Bobcat and Pine Squirrel's Daughter," Coyote tells the people to move away after Bobcat (Wildcat in Spinden's Version) is killed, and he leads them back after Bobcat is rediscovered with plentiful food. In Wilson's version, the people leave, but decide to return on their own.

Coyote occasionally cooperates with the people even when the plan is not his. In Phinney's "Elder Brother and Younger Brother," a version of "Cixcixícim Boy," Coyote is briefly seen participating in the communal effort to capture Raven. In "How the Grizzly Bear Sisters Were Fooled," it is the people's plan to kill the Grizzly Bear sisters, and Coyote assists by luring the sisters to the camp and distracting them with his incessant jabbering. In Watters's "Turtle and Squawfish" (not included here), Coyote is a peripheral actor who participates in the search for the chief's killer and spots him.

There are several groups of people who tend to be either friendly or antagonistic to Coyote. Those who might be considered Coyote's enemies include (1) the downriver people ("Sea Monster"), who give Sea Monster Woman advice on how to kill Coyote's family; (2) the Air People ("Cut-Out-of-Belly Boy"), who Coyote helps to defeat, taking some of their women as spoils; and (3) Mistoyno's people ("How Coyote Lost His Eyes"), who play with Coyote's eyes. Those who are friendly to Coyote are (1) the Shadow (or Spirit) People, who act as host to Coyote in "Coyote and the Shadow People" and "Coyote and His Daughter"; and (2) the People at White Mountain ("Coyote Visits White Mountain"), who also act as host to Coyote. Somewhere in between friends and antagonists lie the Warmweather People and the Coldweather People ("Cold and Warm Brothers Wrestle"). At first Coyote sides with the Coldweathers in a scheme to acquire food; then he switches allegiance to the Warmweathers when a worthy adversary appears against the Coldweathers.

Coyote frequently acts as benefactor to the people. When he destroys monsters (including Grizzly Bear), it is explicitly or implicitly because they are killers (see our discussion on Coyote and monsters). Sometimes he tears down dams or fish traps ("Coyote and Monster," "Coyote Breaks the Fish Dam at Celilo," Phinney's "Coyote His Son He Caused to be Lost," and Wilson's "The Five Swallows and Coyote"). Coyote does this to facilitate the freedom of the salmon, which he recognizes as a valuable resource for the people.

The people may pass judgment on Coyote, as determined from their reactions to his deeds in various situations. When Coyote gloats over his newly acquired female companion, the people signal their disapproval by switching the girl with Frog as Coyote reclines on her lap (Phinney's "Coyote the Expedi-tioner"; in a similar situation, the men also switch Frog for the girl in "How Coyote Killed the Grizzly Bears"). In "Coyote Marries His Daughter," the peo-ple discover Coyote's shameful incest with his daughter and abandon him.

Coyote and Children

Coyote has a negative effect on children who are often caught up in his inter-actions with adult actors and are frequently abused, neglected, or killed in those situations. Some children have skills or powers superior to Coyote's or possess knowledge that he desires. Children are often exploited for Coyote's schemes, and if they annoy him, he can be a merciless disciplinarian.

In several instances children are killed as the result of Coyote's interactions with other actors. As a part of Coyote's plan, Grizzly Bear's sons are killed by Bobcat in "Coyote Kills Grizzly Bear's Sons" (by Lynx in Phinney's version). In Watters' version, the death of Coyote's sons provokes his vengeance, which leads to the death of Grizzly Bear and his sons. In Phinney's version, Coyote makes Grizzly Bear the scapegoat for his deeds against Lynx, again leading to the death of Grizzly Bear and his sons. In "How the Grizzly Bear Sisters Were Fooled," the eldest Grizzly Bear sister's son burns to death with his mother and aunts when the people carry out Coyote's plot against the sisters. Flint Man kills Coyote's sons in "Coyote and Flint," and Coyote kills him in return. Por-cupine kills Coyote's son Cicéqi as partial revenge for Coyote's attempted theft of the buffalo carcass in "How Porcupine Went to the Plains." In Watters's ver-sion, Cicéqi is abused by being force-fed by Porcupine before falling from the tree, perhaps as an indirect retribution for Coyote's unwillingness to share the carcass. In "Coyote Bears He Killed" (Phinney's variant of Wilson's "How Coy-ote Killed the Grizzly Bears"), Coyote is angered by the grizzly bears' theft of the people's choicest kills, and he kills one of the young bears, causing the fa-ther to seek revenge; the father, in turn, is killed. These examples demonstrate that when adults are enemies of Coyote, their children may also suffer unfor-tunate consequences. They may be killed as an indirect insult or injury to an adversary or to provoke an adversarial relationship; or they may be killed (in-tentionally or not) as a result of such a conflict.

Even Coyote's family members may become enemies as the result of the death of children. Coyote's daughters inadvertently cause Elbow Baby's death in "Elbow Baby," and Coyote exacts a cruel revenge by urinating on them and trapping them in their lodge to starve. The severity of his vengeance reflects the severity of the injury he feels they have caused. They betrayed his trust in kinswomen to take care of his special child. Elbow Baby's death, however, did not really result from the daughters' neglect. In fact, the opposite was true; the girls played too exuberantly with Elbow Baby and he laughed himself to death. Coyote's failure to draw this distinction leads to his own death, because the daughter who kills him is rightfully indignant for being unjustly punished. In Spinden's version ("Katstainomiots, or Elbow Baby"), after Elbow Baby helps Coyote get new eyes, Coyote simply kills him and throws him away, because he does not "want to be bothered with him."

Some children suffer negative consequences that are not fatal as the result of Coyote's interactions with other actors. Coyote nearly chokes Pine Squirrel's baby to death in "Bobcat and Pine Squirrel's Daughter" by stuffing marrow in its mouth in order to quiet it and be wrongly recognized as its father (and thereby become Pine Squirrel's husband). In Watters's version, Coyote also neglects his own children by attempting to use his kill to win a hunting contest (again to win Pine Squirrel as his wife) instead of sharing it with them, and they express their objections accordingly. In "How Coyote Killed the Grizzly Bears," Cicéqi is sent to fetch Grizzly Bear's prized deer-hoof bell for Coyote, an action designed to infuriate Bear, presumably at considerable risk to Cicéqi. The excrement children are instructed to pose as decoy "victims" in Coyote's plot against Sun, and they would certainly be killed if Coyote's plan were to fail in "Coyote Defeats the Sun." Cicéqi serves as a "guinea pig," in effect testing magical food prepared by Elk and Fish Hawk that Coyote is hesitant to try in "Coyote and His Guests" (Phinney's version of "Coyote Visits Elk and Fish-hawk"). Although Coyote does not force Cicéqi to do this, he does not prevent Cicéqi from doing something which he is afraid to do himself.

Occasionally Coyote encounters children who have special abilities or powers. Cixcixícim Boy, also called Elder Brother in Phinney, outshoots Coyote and other adult males in a contest for the chief's (or old man's) daughters in "Cixcixícim Boy." Cixcixícim is actually an adult who has transformed into an ugly boy but retained his adult hunting skills. This scene, which demonstrates Coyote's inferior hunting skills, is humorous, because he is fooled and defeated by a child in an adult contest. Coyote is unable to admit his defeat and tries to lie or cheat in order to win the wife. Just as Coyote transforms his appearance to dupe others, he is also vulnerable to being duped by characters who disguise their appearance.

A similar situation occurs in "Weasel Wrestles for a Wife," where Coyote competes with Weasel Boy in order to win the maiden (Sunflower) for a wife. Coyote is humorously unable to throw down the maiden, and to have a boy succeed where he has failed further emphasizes his inferiority at this skill. However, Weasel Boy has a hidden advantage over the other contestants in Phinney's version, where Weasel had gnawed Sunflower's roots before the contest, thus weakening her. The contests with Cixcixícim and Weasel are both tests of adult male skills (shooting and wrestling), with a wife as the prize. These skills are the main criteria for deciding the appropriate husband for the young women. Coyote's inferiority is humorous when contrasted with his high opinion of himself; elsewhere, (for example, in "Warmweather and Coldweather"), he says, "I am Coyote, good at everything," taking credit for the Goose Maiden's magic when he discovers his new teeth. His vanity makes it difficult for him to admit defeat.

Cut-Out-of-Belly Boy (Phinney's version) saves Coyote and some other boys from Owl's enslavement in "Cut-Out-of-Belly Boy." Because the boy is able to defeat Owl when Coyote and the other boys are unable to do so, his powers are clearly superior to theirs. Coyote recognizes this superiority and gets out in front of the others to act as adviser to Cut-Out-of-Belly Boy, an action that demonstrates Coyote's tendency to associate himself with actors of superior status (see our discussion of his relationships with chiefs). Cut-Out-of-Belly Boy acts in Coyote's favor, but his rescue of Owl's slaves seems incidental to his plan to defeat Owl and the Air People. Coyote's attempt to associate with him amounts to merely "tagging along," but he eventually benefits from this association by sharing in the spoils of the defeat of the Air People.

All of these children with special powers and abilities are the central actors in the myths in which they appear. Coyote's roles in these stories constitute brief or cameo appearances, which seems to reduce his importance or stature in relation to the child actor and at the same time increase the importance or stature of the child. Coyote appears to be a pest who is easily swept aside by these children, which is exactly the opposite of his expectations.

The youngest sibling often has unusual perceptive clarity in Nez Perce myths. The youngest Goose brother (in "Warmweather and Coldweather"), Mistoyno's youngest granddaughter (in "How Coyote Lost His Eyes") and the youngest Swallow sister (in "Coyote Breaks the Fish Dam at Celilo") all recognize Coyote when others are fooled by his disguise. The special knowledge of these children does little harm to Coyote, because the others remain duped by his disguise and seem unwilling to listen to the children's advice.

Coyote has little tolerance for children who misbehave or make nuisances of themselves. In the case of the Disobedient Boy, also called Naughty Boy in Wilson's version ("Naughty Boy Becomes Good"), Coyote becomes upset when the boy physically abuses other children (especially when his son Cicéqi is abused). In Phinney's and Watters's versions (both titled "The Disobedient Boy"), Coyote decides on his own to abandon the nuisance boy with the aid of some other boys. In Wilson's version, the boy abuses children who are not Coyote's; yet Coyote decides on and carries out the plot to abandon the boy in a similar manner with the approval of the offended children's parents. In all three versions, the boy's abandonment is facilitated by Coyote's deception, in which objects (reeds, twigs, or trees) are magically enabled to speak by being spat on, thus helping to conceal the withdrawal of Coyote and his accomplices.

After abandoning the boy, Coyote and the other people enter a difficult, hungry time in contrast to the boy, who becomes a wealthy, successful hunter with the assistance of the Water Woman. The punishment of the boy seems to precipitate the ill fortune of those who participate in it, and the boy receives assistance from a mysterious benefactor (the Water Woman) who reverses both his fortune and character. This combination of events suggests that the punishment, or at least its severity, was inappropriate.

Upon the rediscovery of the now successful young man, Coyote lies about his role in the abandonment in order to move back in. There is no remorse on Coyote's part, however, because his motive for reuniting with the former boy is primarily to obtain food, as demonstrated by his persistence in locating the source of the magpies' meat. Coyote tries to be perceived as being on good terms with the young man, because after stealing supplies from him, Coyote tells the others, "My nephew . . . surely told me, 'Coyote, you will be the one to come over here and have this house full of food.' Tomorrow we'll go back to that place." This is an example of Coyote's desire to associate with those of higher status or ability in complete opposition to his original relationship with the boy.

The former disobedient boy allows Coyote and the others to move back in with him in spite of Coyote's lies and thievery, although in Watters's version he rebukes Coyote's lies (because the Water Woman told him of Coyote's actions). Coyote is forbidden to occupy the boy's grandfather's tepee, but it is unclear whether Coyote is allowed to remain in a different tepee. By reprimanding Coyote, the boy indicates that Coyote's actions were improper. In the versions in which Coyote is unconditionally allowed to return with the others, Coyote lied about his role in the abandonment; either the boy believes him or he knows Coyote is lying and decides not to make it an issue of contention. Either way, Coyote appears to be shamed, because he has no rightful claim to associate with the boy again. The boy is certainly well off without the company of Coyote and the others. Either the boy forgives Coyote and/or the others or he merely tolerates their return, but his response also seems to acknowledge his disobedient behavior as inappropriate. The reconciliation also serves to end the hunger "punishment" of Coyote and the others, as though the boy decides that the situation is even once again.

In "The Disobedient Boy," Coyote employed the services of some boys in the abandonment of Disobedient Boy. In a reversed situation, some boys are instructed by Coyote's son to help abandon Coyote in retribution for his improper sexual relationship with his daughter-in-law ("Coyote Breaks the Fish Dam at Celilo"). Boys may act as accomplices both for and against Coyote's interests. Whether acting for or against Coyote's interests, the boys assist in deceiving the victim by concealing the plot from him. Because of their age, as well as the casual, everyday activity in which the plot is couched, the boys do not arouse the suspicion of the victim.

In Phinney's "Wild Goat a Woman Carried Away," Coyote's relationship with the skull brothers is in part similar to his relationship with Disobedient Boy and in part similar to his relationship with monsters. The youngest skull brother arouses Coyote's ire by tormenting the other children. The older brothers become nuisances by eating all of the food. Coyote plots the destruction of all of the brothers by appealing to their vanity and duping them into attempting to smash the cliffs. This is similar to narratives in which Coyote appeals to the grizzly bears' vanity in order to dupe them and cause their demise. The offense of the young skull is similar to that of Disobedient Boy, as is the punishment, if abandonment of a child is presumed to lead to its death. One difference is that the skulls are foreigners whose behavior is entirely inappropriate to their role as in-laws or guests. The punishment is seen as appropriate by the other characters who agree with Coyote's judgment. Even the skulls' wife agrees to the plot. Since Disobedient Boy's punishment appeared to be too severe and his offense was no different from that of the skulls, it would seem that misbehavior is to be far less tolerated from foreign children (or adults).

The egg-hunter boys in "Coyote Breaks the Fish Dam at Celilo" play a trick on Coyote as he sleeps (cutting out his anus and eating his salmon). Coyote's revenge does not seem extreme; indeed it is almost exactly reciprocal. He eats the boys' food (eggs) while they sleep, and he physically alters them. In Phinney and Watters's versions, the wolf boys instigate the anus-cutting, and it is they who incur the least desirable reaction from Coyote. Their appearance is negatively changed (painted and smeared to give them the ugliest possible appearance in Phinney; wrinkled noses and mouths in Watters). The other boys who participate are also altered physically but not in a negative fashion. Raccoon and Fox's faces are painted handsomely. When the boys discover Coyote's deeds, they chase him in vain, but he allows Fox to catch up, the two continuing as friends. In other narratives, Fox is always very close to Coyote (usually referred to as "friend" or "brother"). This tale is an example of a joking relationship in which insults are minor and result in "tit-for-tat," (that is, the punishments seem carefully chosen to avoid escalation of the situation). Once the series of events has concluded, the characters are even. Certainly in Fox and Raccoon's case, Coyote's actions are restrained and seem to reflect the prior affection between them.

The predominantly negative relations between Coyote and children reflect their value to him. Other actors attract Coyote, because they have abilities or things that satisfy his desires (above all, for sex and food); children typically offer neither. In these terms they are of neutral value to him, but if their own actions or motivations negatively affect Coyote they are treated as pests or enemies. This is true even with his own children, which illustrates the weakness of his paternal bond. Coyote's many sexual encounters, thus, do not reflect a desire to become a father.

Coyote's Relationships with Adult Female Characters

The factors that seem most prevalent in Coyote's relationships with female characters are sexual relations, the maternal role, food, and the provision of specific services. Coyote's motives in these relationships are often unidimensional in that usually only one of the above factors constitutes the foundation of the relationship.

Sexual Relations

Coyote's sexual successes and failures follow several patterns. When he is successful, he has usually transformed himself into a handsome young man. Transformation seems necessary for Coyote's sexual success, because he is undesirable to females who recognize him. Mistoyno's youngest granddaughter recognizes him and says, "This is Coyote! I wouldn't carry him for anything!" In this example (in "How Coyote Lost His Eyes") Coyote copulates with the girl's unsuspecting older sisters as they take turns carrying him, but the youngest girl has a special knowledge (also in Spinden's version) of what is occurring. (The special knowledge or wisdom of the youngest sibling is a common motif in Nez Perce mythology.) Therefore, her refusal to carry him is also a refusal to copulate with him. Similarly, the youngest Swallow sister recognized Coyote and avoided copulation with him ("Coyote Breaks the Fish Dam at Celilo) in contrast with her older sisters. In the same narrative (and the corresponding versions by Wilson and in Phinney), Cricket realizes that the disguised Coyote is not her real husband and avoids him until her husband returns. In contrast, Cricket's co-wife fails to recognize him and suffers disastrous consequences. In another instance (Phinney's "Coyote and Butterfly," not included here), Magpie rebuffs Coyote's complaint about having his dream about women interrupted, saying, "Then, too, why should you think that any woman would desire you?"

When Coyote's sexual encounters are within a marriage relationship, they are typically short-lived. These include his marriages to his daughter-in-law, Duck (in "Coyote Breaks the Fish Dam at Celilo" and in Wilson's version, Swan in Phinney's version), to his own daughter ("Coyote Marries His Daughter"), to the injured maiden ("How Coyote Killed the Grizzly Bears" and in Phinney's version), Goose ("Warmweather and Coldweather," all versions), and to the unnamed wife ("Coyote and the Shadow People"). The other wives are Mouse (in "Coyote Visits Elk and Fish Hawk" and in Phinney's version, and in "Porcupine and Buffalo" which is Wilson's version of "How Porcupine Went to the Plains"), the unnamed wife ("Coyote and Flint"), the Gopher sisters ("Coyote Defeats the Sun"), and the Air People women ("Cut-Out-of-Belly Boy"). Coyote's episodes with these wives are not specifically sexual and will be discussed below.

In all of the versions involving Duck (Swan), Coyote gets rid of his son, transforms to take his identity, and takes up marriage relations with his daughter-in-law. Duck (Swan) is duped into becoming Coyote's wife, because she fails to recognize that he is not her true husband. Upon the return of Coyote's son (the true husband), the woman transforms into a male duck (in Watters's and Wilson's versions) and leaves in shame (all three versions). Coyote is clearly an inappropriate husband for his daughter-in-law, which is emphasized by her reaction upon discovering his identity. This inappropriateness is reinforced by Cricket (the other daughter-in-law coveted by Coyote) who knows his identity all along and steadfastly avoids him. Coyote instinctively knows that the marriage is inappropriate, because he does not attempt to keep his wife upon the return of her true husband.

In "Coyote Marries His Daughter," Coyote's wife dies and Coyote begins to desire his eldest daughter. He spends years setting up an elaborate plot to marry her and fakes his own death. He transforms into the handsome Flathead man whom Coyote commanded her to marry upon his death and proceeds to marry her. Duck Man recognizes Coyote and sings, "Coyote has slept with his daughter," and the birds reply, "Coyote is so thoughtless." When she discovers his identity, the daughter leaves in disgrace. Coyote's other daughters and his usually faithful friend Fox also leave him in disgust. This instance affirms that Coyote's sexual success continues only as long as his identity remains concealed, and that it must be concealed because the relationship is incestuous and morally inappropriate. His ostracism reflects the severity of his offense.

An inappropriate marriage relationship seems implied in the story of Coyote and the injured maiden. In Phinney's version, Coyote transforms into a handsome man before he meets the maiden; in Wilson's and Spinden's versions, he does not (these versions are significantly more abbreviated than Phinney's). Phinney's version states that she will become his wife as a condition for his assistance. In all versions, Coyote heals the girl and helps her rejoin the people. In Phinney and Wilson, he shows her off by singing while leaning against her and resting his head in her lap (this act seems to imply bodily, i.e., sexual, familiarity). The maiden is switched with Frog (Wilson's version) or lady Bullfrog (Phinney's version) as Coyote reclines, by the young men who dislike Coyote or by the people, respectively. The switching seems to be an unspoken expression that Coyote does not deserve to be with an attractive maiden, but should instead be with Frog who is described as a rather unsavory female in other narratives.

When Coyote is transformed, he is recognized not by the maiden but rather by the people who remove her from Coyote. Once he is recognized for who he is, the relationship is terminated. When he is not transformed, the maiden does not seem to realize Coyote's intentions (she makes no promises of marriage or sex to secure his assistance), but then he reclines on her and she takes the first opportunity to escape. No protest is indicated from her when she is switched with Frog by the young men. In Spinden's version, she simply elopes with another mate. This comparison indicates that the untransformed Coyote is tolerated by females until his sexual intentions become evident and, conversely, that the transformed Coyote's sexual intentions are tolerated until his identity becomes evident.

Coyote transforms into a well-to-do, handsome man when he discovers Goose alone in her house. She treats him well by feeding him, providing him with new teeth and allowing him to stay and rest. Upon the return of her brothers, she and Coyote become husband and wife. Goose never discovers Coyote's identity and remains faithful to him to the extent that she kills some of her brothers after they kill him. Coyote's interactions with his brothers-in-law doom his marriage. Coyote proves to be an inferior hunter who bags only small prey which causes the goose brothers to scoff at him; his inadequate hunting skill would be a detrimental quality in a husband. He also fails in the cooperative etiquette necessary for group hunting, for he disobeys instructions to keep quiet while riding on the backs of his brothers-in-law. This disobedience demonstrates a lack of respect for the wishes of his newly-acquired kinsmen and puts the entire group in danger of drowning as well. Thus, Coyote is an inappropriate husband for Goose, because he lacks husbandly skills, the ability to hunt and to behave appropriately in the company of his wife's relatives. The youngest brother-in-law recognizes Coyote from the beginning, and after Coyote's disrespectful behavior, the other brothers also come to realize that he is indeed Coyote. Once his true identity is revealed through his actions, the relationship with the female is terminated, even if she was not the one to end it.

Coyote's sexual appetite prevents him from reuniting with his dead wife, again ending the relationship. The Death Spirit offers to allow Coyote to take his dead wife back to the world of the living on the condition that Coyote follow certain instructions exactly. He has been deeply pining for her, so he agrees. He obeys all of these instructions until he is on the verge of success, but then violates the last instruction of not touching her until the journey has been completed—"But suddenly a joyous impulse seized him; the joy of having his wife again overwhelmed him. He jumped to his feet and rushed over to embrace her. His wife cried out, 'Stop! Stop! Coyote! Do not touch me. Stop!' Her warning had no effect. Coyote rushed over to his wife and just as he touched her body she vanished." In this case, the relationship itself is not necessarily inappropriate; indeed, of all the instances where he has a wife, this one seems most appropriate. He longs for her in her absence, goes to extraordinary lengths to secure her return, and so on. Yet he knowingly risks a permanent reunion by failing to restrain his impulse toward physical contact, which was the only condition placed upon his relationship with his wife. It seems appropriate to assume that his longing was for renewed sexual relations. Under the conditions of the prohibitions, this type of relationship with her was inappropriate and is terminated by the Death Spirit.

In a similar situation, Coyote is prohibited from having tactile contact with the buffalo he acquires by aiding the defeated buffalo bull ("Coyote's Trip to the East"). As a reward for his aid, Bull gives Coyote a buffalo cow (Spinden's version) or thirty cows (Wilson's version) to take with him when he leaves the Buffalo Country. In Spinden's version, the cow is explicitly intended to become Coyote's wife; in Wilson's version, the buffaloes' future relationship with Coyote is not explained. Both versions include a prohibition against touching the buffalo for a certain length of time which Coyote obeys until he has almost succeeded; but he gives in to his impulsiveness just before the time is complete. In Wilson's version, he cannot resist "touching" the buffalo as they are sleeping, and they become scared and run away back to the Buffalo Country. In Spinden's version, the buffalo cow gradually turns into a Coyote female, making it impossible for Coyote to refrain from "touching" her while she sleeps, which causes her to change back into a buffalo and return to the Buffalo Country. In both versions, Coyote's impulse to "touch" these females while they sleep seems to be a metaphor for sexual relations, as it also seemed to be with the spirit wife. The prohibition against "touching" (sexual relations) involving the buffalo and the spirit wife are tests of Coyote's worthiness to remain with these female characters; his failure causes them to run away. Self restraint is a desirable quality in long-term relationships between males and females. A general inference can be made that sexual relationships are appropriate at certain times and not at others and that Coyote is incapable of refraining at inappropriate times.

In the stories in which Coyote is not transformed or disguised and attempts to acquire a wife, he takes advantage of situations in which the female has little choice about the outcome (or so he believes). Pine Squirrel's daughter (in "Bobcat and Pine Squirrel's Daughter"), also called the Well-Behaved Maiden in Phinney's version, is made the prize of various contests (quieting the baby, bringing in first kill from the hunt, capturing the animal with the whitest fur) to see who is the most suited to be the father of her son (the actual father needs to be discovered). Coyote cheats quite cleverly but fails. The chief's daughter is similarly offered as wife to whoever can shoot the eagle. The unnamed wrestling girl (Sunflower in Phinney's version) will be wife to whoever can throw her down, but Coyote fails in "Weasel Wrestles for a Wife." These examples show that Coyote is not adept at skills a woman finds attractive in a potential mate such as fathering, hunting, or fighting. Thus Coyote seems to have few if any qualities that might be considered attractive to women.

When Coyote accompanies his daughter to the cave in "Coyote Visits White Mountain," he encounters an old woman in his everyday form. She makes fun of his wide-open eyes as he tries to see in the dark. Coyote then thinks to himself, "Your saying such a thing, woman, makes me want to make you my wife and get even with you. I will sleep with you." The old woman reads his thoughts and laughs, "Ha ha, that's what he's thinking!" This episode is unusual in that Coyote's motivation for sex is to punish or assert control rather than to satisfy his impulsive arousal as is usually the case. It is possible that such a motivation underlies his sexual relationships with other females (such as Mistoyno's granddaughters and the swallow sisters) when affectionate relations seem inappropriate in the context of the rest of the story and Coyote's motivation is not explicit. The old woman is unusual because she seems to welcome Coyote's sexual attention in spite of its negative tone. She seems to be flattered that someone would think of her sexually. She is presumably unattractive because of her age, so if she desires sex she would not be in a position to be particular concerning her sexual partner. Thus Coyote would serve her desires regardless of his attractiveness (or lack of it) and regardless of his motivation. In the sense that the old woman is unattractive, she is similar to Frog. Both females accept Coyote in his undisguised form, presumably because no other males are interested in them. Coyote rejects Frog and throws her out, and it is unclear whether he carries out his intention with the old woman. The myths imply that both women are appropriate mates for Coyote, because they accept him in his untransformed state.

Coyote remains untransformed in the episode with the unnamed girls in "How Coyote's Penis Became a Dam" (mallard ducks in Spinden's version). In this myth, the girls on one side of the river remain unconcerned, even though they see Coyote on the other bank. The eldest sister does not suspect Coyote's intentions until his penis actually enters her from across the river, so being able to recognize and possibly refuse him (or his intention) is not an option.

The unnamed women in Coyote's dreams occur as part of a larger formulaic pattern, in which Coyote has been killed, is thrown into the river, and is revived by Magpie (see discussion of Coyote and Monsters, Coyote and Advisers). When Magpie wakes Coyote by pecking at his brows or eyes, Coyote scolds Magpie for interrupting him when he was helping some girls or women across the river, typically upstream. In Wilson's versions they are girls (six instances) or the chief's daughter (one instance); in Phinney's versions they are the head of the valley's daughter (three instances); and in Watters's versions they are generic women (five instances). Magpie usually exposes Coyote's lie, saying, "You were doing no such thing" or a similar statement and tells Coyote what really happened to him. Clearly, Coyote tries to "save face," deluding himself, attempting to delude Magpie, or both. This lie is an attempt to substitute a worthy fictitious activity in place of what actually occurred. He chooses to imagine himself as a ladies man, even assisting important women in some cases. Given the other instances of Coyote's relationships with women, he is obviously projecting his wishes rather than actual possibilities.

Some of Coyote's marriages do not seem to be based upon a sexual relationship. This may in part be a result of the economy of mythology in which unnecessary information tends to be excluded from the narrative (that is, the sexual component of these relationships may be irrelevant to the story at hand). In the previous examples, however, Coyote's identity must be disguised or remain unknown in order for him to establish a successful sexual relationship. Correspondingly, in the examples to follow, if sexuality is not mentioned as part of the relationship between Coyote and a female, he does not need to transform or disguise himself.

The Maternal Role

Coyote's relationship with women rarely includes raising children and forming a family unit. Coyote appears with both a wife and a child in only a few instances: when he brings Mouse and Cicéqi to the buffalo carcass he has stolen from Porcupine ("How Porcupine Went to the Plains"); a brief mention that he is living with Mouse and their son when he visits Elk and Fish Hawk ("Coyote Visits Elk and Fish Hawk"); and a reference to Coyote preparing for a child when he is married to Goose, because he mentions that his kill will partly go toward making leather diapers ("Warmweather and Coldweather"). A common theme in these three myths is Coyote's failure as food-provider.

On several occasions Coyote impregnates young women who are enemies (for example, the swallows and Mistoyno's granddaughters). This desire to leave his enemies with children may reflect Coyote's general propensity to procreate, and impregnating enemies may be especially satisfying to him, because being pregnant with and giving birth to his children would constitute an insult or degradation for the duration of the ordeal. Whether these children are aborted, killed after birth, or are allowed to survive is not indicated. But since Coyote does not seem concerned about the welfare of his progeny, it seems more likely that the insult to the woman is at least as important as procreation or sexual satisfaction.

Coyote's appearance as an orphan baby, which is part of his scheme to destroy the fish dam at Celilo ("Coyote Breaks the Fish Dam at Celilo"), further illustrates his view of females. He seems to know the swallow sisters will adopt a helpless baby, and the sisters compete to determine which one will gain possession of the baby. Wilson's version indicates that the girls are relative strangers to Coyote, because part of the reason he takes the form of a baby is to learn about them. Thus it may be inferred that he counts on a maternal response, which is not specific to the sisters but rather to women in general—even with children that are not their own biological progeny. This may explain why he throws Crawfish out of the dance ("Frog and Crawfish Dance"); she pinches and scratches Cicéqi—actions that would be inappropriate for a woman with maternal impulses. Coyote's extreme response to his own daughters' part in the accidental death of Elbow Baby ("Elbow Baby") may also reflect Coyote's failure as a parental figure.

Food

Another frequent theme concerning Coyote's relationships with females centers around food. Coyote is constantly hungry, and his quest to obtain food underlies his motivations with many characters, both male and female. This section will examine how elements of food acquisition, preparation, and exchange are involved in Coyote's relationships with females.

We have already seen that Coyote is poorly skilled as a hunter in relation to the geese and that he fails at every contest involving tests of hunting skills. When he does kill game, it is small or inferior. In several myths, he hunts mice or goes hungry. He is attracted to females who offer food, because he is a relatively poor provider of food, both for himself and for others.

Gift-giving between strangers is a common motif in Nez Perce myths, and food is often given as gifts. In "Gusty Wind and Zephyr" (Phinney's version of "Warmweather and Coldweather"), Coyote meets three old women in succession, and each gives him a gift. The first two give him fleas and dung, which he finds repulsive. The third gives him venison, fat, and grease which he eats. He schemes to take advantage of her by disguising himself and "meeting" her over and over in order to obtain more meat, even though she has told him she is poor and has little. After making several caches of meat, he decides to kill her in order to obtain all of her meat. Upon her death, the old woman, her meat, and Coyote's caches of meat all disappear.

The first two old women are treated properly. Although they offer unwanted gifts, the turned back of the receiver precludes him from the possibility of embarrassing the gift-giver by declining to accept the gift. By contrast, it would have been proper for Coyote simply to be grateful and go on his way after meeting the third old woman, but Coyote's greed increases by degrees until he defeats his own purpose. His repeated, disguised encounters with the third old woman violate the ritual of gift-giving between strangers, because he is no longer a stranger.

The goose maiden's relationship with Coyote ("Warmweather and Coldweather") involves food in several ways. In all three versions, Coyote (disguised as a handsome young man) visits Goose as a stranger, and she offers him food. He had previously lost all of his teeth, so he eats only the softest items offered. He eats very little dried meat (Wilson's version) when it is the only item offered. Goose notices his eating behavior and seems concerned, perhaps because she is worried about her abilities as a hostess. (Her skills would be especially important to her because the "handsome young man" is destined to become her husband according to the edict of her brothers.) A young woman attempting to impress a prospective husband would wish to show her ability to perform her future duties in the role of wife. Her strong interest in having her guest eat her food is evident, because after noticing his lack of teeth, she puts deer's teeth into his mouth as he naps. Evidently Coyote's disguise cannot hide his lack of teeth, which could threaten the success of his deception if Goose chooses to be suspicious of him. Yet, rather than become suspicious, Goose simply corrects his inconsistency. Perhaps the prediction that her next visitor (Coyote) would become her husband has overridden any tendency to scrutinize a stranger's motives. Goose remains deceived by Coyote until her death, which is indirectly caused by his behavior being inconsistent with his appearance (this is the direct cause of his own death).

The motif of the young woman attempting to impress a prospective husband is reinforced later in the narrative when the surviving goose brothers visit the Coldweather and Warmweather families. Their decision to remain and marry the Warmweather daughters is based upon the generosity of the hosts, who prepare and provide plentiful food. By contrast, the Coldweather daughters prepare food, but young Coldweather and her father eat it all before the guests have been served.

When Coyote visits the Shadow People ("Coyote and the Shadow People"), his dead wife sits beside him for a time, then prepares food for him and the Death Spirit. Although he cannot see the food, he imitates the motions of the Death Spirit, who seems to be eating. Here the wife appears to be demonstrating her willingness to resume her marriage relationship with Coyote by resuming her duties as a wife, namely by preparing and serving food. This seems similar to Goose's (Swan's) behavior, differing only in that the spirit wife seeks to reestablish an interrupted relationship and Goose (Swan) was interested in establishing an entirely new relationship.

Coyote's wife, Mouse, suffers the consequences when Coyote attempts to host Elk and Fish Hawk in order to return their hospitality ("Coyote Visits Elk and Fish Hawk"). Mouse knows that it is improper for Coyote to invite guests, for they have little to offer. She says to herself, "Why does Coyote have them come? He will, without fail, do something stupid again." Coyote intends to perform the same magical food preparation he had observed earlier as a guest. When he attempts these things (Phinney's version), Mouse calls him an "imitator" and thinks to herself that he is "the doer of all foolhardy things." She loses a strip of clothing, which fails to transform into meat as it had when Elk performed the same magic. Mouse is struck in the back by the cherrywood stick that Coyote was attempting to transform into cooked intestines as Fish Hawk had done. Both Mouse and Coyote end up confined to bed from their injuries by the end of this version. Coyote's mistakes were to invite guests when he was not assured of being able to provide for them and to assume arrogantly that he was capable of the same magic performed by others. Mouse's mistake could be that she allowed Coyote to usurp the food-preparing duties.

Coyote's daughter undertakes the duties of food preparation for her ailing father ("Coyote and His Daughter") when Coyote's wife is inexplicably absent. In both versions, the daughter scrounges bones to prepare broth for Coyote. Thus, food preparation seems to be a duty of any woman in the domestic setting. (Presumably Coyote's wife, if she were present, would be chiefly responsible for this duty.) Coyote still manages to behave greedily in spite of his dependent position. The daughter is obligated to seek Coyote's permission to marry the otters who give her salmon as a token of their proposal. Coyote rejects their offer, because he seems to know that the wolves will also propose to her and that they will offer venison, which he greatly prefers. Certainly the salmon would have been better than the bone broth on which he has been subsisting, but he holds out for even better fortune. His fatherly power to grant or deny permission to his daughter's suitors is exercised in his own best interest without any concern for her wishes. If his plan succeeded, he would have sons-in-law to procure his favorite food (the wolves are always excellent hunters in Nez Perce mythology), and presumably he would remain with them and his daughter, who would prepare and serve the food. Yet he fails to consider that the snubbed otters might foil his plans, which they do by killing the daughter (who dutifully abided by his decision) and the wolves. Coyote's greed is the catalyst for ruining an otherwise proper relationship between father and daughter.

Mistoyno also feeds Coyote ("How Coyote Lost His Eyes"), but she does not seem especially interested in impressing him. She is pounding roots for biscuits, which she says are for her granddaughters, and she gives some to Coyote in order not to appear rude. While eating, he decides to kill her and assume her identity as part of his plan to reclaim his eyes. By eating, he implicitly assumes the obligation to behave properly as a guest, but this is merely a deception used to put her at ease so he can murder her. Again his greed arises, because after he kills Mistoyno, he eats all of the biscuits she has made. This complicates his plan, for he has to make more biscuits so that Mistoyno's granddaughters will not become suspicious after he assumes her identity. In this situation, food seems integral to the woman's identity.

After Coyote dupes Porcupine in the contest for the buffalo carcass, he goes to fetch his wife, Mouse ("How Porcupine Went to the Plains"). On the surface this act appears to be simply that of a husband sharing with his wife and family, but the disastrous outcome suggests that something was not done correctly. In most other examples of hunting, the hunters transport the kill to their home, or if it is a gift, it is transported to the recipient's home. This incident is unusual, because Coyote takes his wife (and son) to the kill. The purpose of the action is unclear; either he intends for Mouse to prepare the kill for consumption on the spot, or he is enlisting his wife and family to assist in the transportation of the carcass. The latter seems more likely, because Coyote's greed is emphasized in his refusal to share the carcass with Porcupine. Had he packed home as much as he could carry, he would have succeeded in providing for his family, and the remainder could have been left with Porcupine, thus avoiding the disastrous conflict. However, his desire to have more than he needed causes the demise of his entire family. It was also clearly inappropriate for him to bring his family to a place where enemies are present, thus placing them in danger.

Provision of Services

The role of females as providers of services is also a factor in Coyote's relationships to them. Coyote retains his true identity when he marries the five gopher sisters ("Coyote Defeats the Sun"). The details of this marriage are not explicit, but a certain obligation seems implied, because Coyote has just enabled the gophers to see. Perhaps their new sense of sight is simply not yet trained to distinguish Coyote as being unattractive. Coyote has a specific task in mind for the gopher sisters—to dig a tunnel so he can get to the sun. It is possible that he is not interested in them sexually, but while this cannot be ruled out, the issue simply is not relevant to the structure of the narrative. The tunnel dug by the gophers is a necessary device for events that come later in the myth, and by marrying them he can exercise control over abilities which they have and he needs.

In "Coyote and Flint," when Coyote decides to go after Flint Man, he "quickly told his wife to make him some moccasins and get him ready." Apparently this command is carried out without incident, indicating that it was not unusual or inappropriate. This episode indicates that a husband can expect his wife to make clothing for him and to supply provisions for journeys.

Upon healing the injured maiden, Coyote takes her to his Aunt Mouse's home. In Wilson's version ("How Coyote Killed the Grizzly Bears"), Coyote shows off his new woman in Mouse's home (described as "that ugly tepee" by the other villagers). Coyote feels free to impose upon his aunt's hospitality, even if she might not be able to provide well for guests (as is suggested by the "ugly tepee" remarks). But he also seems to feel obligated to provide her with better housing when he is able to do so, because after killing the grizzly bears, he takes Aunt Mouse and Cicéqi to occupy the grizzly bears' tepees. No particular emphasis is given to these events, so they seem to represent normal kinship relations of reciprocity between aunt and nephew. Phinney's version indicates a much more one-sided relationship. Coyote imposes on Aunt Mouse by arriving to visit and immediately commanding her to fetch Grizzly Bear's personal hand drum. She grumbles to herself about what a nuisance Coyote is and tries to point out the danger she would encounter by imposing on Bear, yet she obeys him nonetheless. Her obedience is due to a feeling of obligation rather than to a fear of Coyote, because when she hesitates to carry out his command, Coyote says, "Why you are not even afraid of me! Why should you fear him? Hurry, get it for me!" In Wilson's version, Coyote sends his son Cicéqi on a similar errand, to fetch Bear's prized deer-hoof bell. It seems that Coyote can issue unusual commands to his aunt or son with equal authority. These relationships imply that a visiting adult male kinsmen has authority over the host kinswoman, perhaps even to the degree that a father has authority over his son.

Coyote's relationships with female characters reveal much about the impulses that underlie his character. His sexual urges appear to be entirely unrestrained by even the most basic social rules or traditions concerning choice of partner, appropriate times, places, and so forth. He is aware of these social rules, however, for he will exploit courtship traditions in order to obtain food. He is also aware of the strong desire of women to care for children, and he exploits this desire to his own advantage. Because he is largely uninterested in raising children (see the discussion on Coyote and children), his satisfaction in producing children may simply be evidence of his sexual success. This achievement would be important to him, because his undesirability as a mate makes sexual success challenging. In order to succeed sexually, he must use stealth or disguise, which often leads to humorous situations. By impregnating enemy females he in effect leaves them with a negative token of the encounter. Despite his many sexual encounters, Coyote is hardly interested in females as companions; and he is not interested in or capable of acting as a husband, except as a means of gaining the specific things that females may offer. Prominent among these things is food, because Coyote's constant hunger is an urge comparable in strength to his sexual urge. Both hunger and sex are elements of his strong life force, and females are a primary means of sustaining this drive.

Coyote's Relationships With Adult Male Characters

Fox

The relationship between Coyote and Fox is the most elaborate of all of Coyote's relationships with individual characters. Fox is consistently referred to as being Coyote's friend, and the two often live together. The two characters frequently engage in the same activities, which invites comparison of their relative successes. Fox seems to be endowed with wisdom and reason in contrast to Coyote's foolhardiness and capriciousness; this difference in their natures often causes discord between them. Yet the two generally remain tolerant of each other in spite of their differences.

Because Coyote and Fox sometimes live together, their adventures are usually predicated on seeking food. Fox often discovers food by accident, and when Coyote typically attempts to imitate Fox's successes, he spoils the good fortune. The best example of this situation is in "Coyote and Fox" (all versions). The fullest version (included here) consists of four episodes in which Fox discovers four different sources of food. The first is salmon, which appears in place of the pitch Fox is gathering. The three versions that include this episode show that Fox succeeds, because he is intent upon taking only what he needs. Coyote attempts to repeat Fox's success, but his intention to outproduce Fox ruins the unknown magic that produces the salmon. Fox takes the salmon home before eating any, but Coyote greedily eats his on the spot, which spoils his second attempt. Sharing food seems to be important for preserving the efficacy of the magic. Greedily eating before returning home precludes any sharing; therefore Coyote fails. But in Watters's version Fox hides his find in a cache cellar, not because he does not wish to share but because he knows Coyote will want to imitate him, which in turn will ruin the good fortune and neither will have food. Thus, the difference may lie in self-restraint. Fox is hungry but returns home with his food before eating. Coyote is hungry and immediately eats—only then does he consider taking some food home.

In the next episode, Fox (Watters's and Phinney's versions) or Coyote (Spinden's version) wish for five packs of food to appear, and they do. In Phinney's and Spinden's versions, Coyote takes what appear to be the best three packs, although they turn out to be inferior meat. In all of the versions, Coyote spoils the good fortune by insisting on seeing the identity of the benefactor (Deer Tick).

Another sequence (in the versions of Watters, Wilson, and Phinney) involves Fox meeting a man and a boy who offer him food when they see that he is hungry. He follows the man's instructions to help himself and returns home with all the meat he can carry. Again Coyote tries to duplicate Fox's methods and goes to visit the man and boy. He does not follow the man's instructions to help himself; instead, he kills the man in hopes of taking his vast stores of food all at once. This greedy act results in all of the stores disappearing, including the remnants of Fox's previous acquisition. Coyote's greed of the moment again spoils a potentially long-term beneficial situation.

In the last sequence in this narrative, Fox obtains wild carrots (according to Watters and Wilson) or turnips (according to Phinney) when he submerges his tail in the river; he takes them home before eating them. Coyote decides to try and eats his first batch on the spot. On his second attempt (to have a surplus to take home), his tail becomes too heavy, and he is pulled into the river and drowns. As in the episode involving the salmon, Coyote's desire to immediately satisfy his hunger has dire consequences.

This narrative reveals much about the relationship between Coyote and Fox. Fox implicitly behaves properly in these unusual situations. He knows that Coyote tends to behave improperly, for he often says, "You don't do things right" or something similar when Coyote desires to know where he obtained the food. Fox does not attempt to press the advantage of his good fortune; he simply accepts it as it comes. Coyote's greedy personality seems to offend the various benefactors and ruins the good fortune. The friends share food, but Coyote tries to gain more than his fair share.

Coyote also seems jealous of Fox's good fortune which may be a sign that he is unwilling to admit that Fox may have access to magical power that he lacks. Rivalry over magical power seems to be the center of Phinney's elaboration of the turnip episode in which Fox declares his intentions using ancient terms that Coyote does not understand. Coyote intends to imitate Fox but does not wait to see what the ancient terms mean—in his haste to be first, he ruins his own turnips before he discovers the simple meaning of Fox's statements. In the rivalry between Coyote and Fox, it is Fox who seems to have the superior abilities. In "Coyote and Fox as Shamans," Fox is summoned to cure people with body swellings. Coyote insists on trying to help, and when he does the patients grow worse. The patients demand that Coyote desist. Fox also has the power to revive the dead Coyote by straddling him (Wilson and Phinney's versions of "Elbow Baby," and in "Porcupine and Buffalo," Wilson's version of "How Porcupine Went to the Plains").

In another narrative, the search for food centers around Coyote's plan to dress himself and Fox as women in order to receive food from their potential husbands, the wolves ("Coyote and Fox Pretend to be Women"). Fox agrees, and the plan works for several days. They realize that they cannot keep up the deception any longer and prepare to flee, but the outcome of the episode is unspecified. At best it can be seen that Coyote and Fox can cooperate in order to obtain food.

Food is also at issue when Coyote and Fox encounter the Sea Monster Woman ("Sea Monster"). While preparing for the wedding of Coyote's son and the Sea Monster Girl, Fox quietly and inexplicably prepares pure pitch, a pipe, and a spearhead, while Coyote makes only a spoon in anticipation of the wedding feast. Fox's preparations turn out to save his party when the treacherous Sea Monster family tries to kill them. Fox's wisdom and foresight stand in contrast to Coyote's desire for food which seems so strong he neglects all caution in a situation in which caution would certainly be appropriate. Fox is so wise that he realizes that Coyote would not take precautions appropriate of a father in such a situation. Coyote's son combats the sea monsters, which usually is Coyote's specialty; perhaps Coyote has no role left to play, so he eats!

Coyote and Fox are racing partners in "Coyote and Fox Run Races." Food is again associated with their actions as a benefit of winning the races. The races are set up so that the losers will be beheaded (the opponents are all large game animals: mountain sheep, elk, black-tailed buck, white-tailed deer, and mountain goat). The first race is won by Fox; therefore it is he again who actually acquires the food and Coyote merely shares in his good fortune. Coyote and Fox become fat by eating the losers' bodies, but they then lose the subsequent race. Fox remains true to his word by waiting to be beheaded after losing the second race, whereas Coyote attempts to escape and hide. Fox outperforms Coyote in both races, demonstrating his superior speed and endurance.

Fox's superior speed and endurance are also seen in other narratives. In Spinden's version of "Elbow Baby," Fox overtakes Coyote when he escapes with his eyes from the people who possessed them. Coyote sends Fox back, saying, "Who else will you get a chance to live with?" In Wilson's version ("How Coyote Lost

HIs Eyes"), Coyote rescues his eyes by jumping through an opening high up: "Then Fox followed him. He said, "Oh, you go wherever I go because we are friends. You can come with me too.'" Here Fox is clearly able to follow Coyote where others cannot, but rather than admitting this, Coyote pretends that he is allowing Fox to follow. In Phinney's "Coyote and His Anus" (see "Coyote Breaks the Fish Dam at Celilo"), the young egg hunters are chasing Coyote, because he altered their appearances. Fox alone is determined to overtake him, implying his ability to do so. When Coyote sees that the remaining pursuer is his friend, he waits for him to catch up.

Fox recognizes Coyote's superior ability to defeat monsters, and Coyote shares his victories with his friend. When Coyote kills Sun, he boasts of his victory to Fox ("Coyote Defeats the Sun"). When Coyote kills Flint Man, he gives a victory cry ("Coyote and Flint"), which Fox and others hear. Fox is confident that Coyote has won, although the others are not convinced by the sound, which apparently could have been from either combatant. In Phinney's "Coyote Bears He Killed" and "Bears and Coyote," the people fear that Grizzly Bear will kill Coyote, but Fox has confidence in him, saying, "Coyote is powerful. He and I will soon be pit-cooking Bear." Indeed Coyote wins, and Coyote and Fox share the cooked bear.

Fox is consistently portrayed as a wise man. He frequently exposes Coyote's follies, presumably as a friend attempting to spare his comrade further embarassment. In "Elder Brother and Younger Brother" (Phinney's version of "Cixcixícim Boy"), Fox points out that the boy, not Coyote, had won the eagle-shooting contest. Fox lets Coyote know that he is acting foolishly when he attempts to quiet the baby with marrow in order to be declared the maiden's husband ("Bobcat and Pine Squirrel's Daughter"). Fox tells him, " 'You'll make the baby choke. What are you trying to do?' Then Coyote said, 'You'll never quiet this baby as I did.'" Phinney's version contains similar bickering. Fox rebukes Coyote for making fun of Weasel during the wrestling contest with Sunflower (in "Weasel," Phinney's version of "Weasel Wrestles for a Wife"): "How could anyone such as he, a boy, throw her! There Coyote is, always in front!" Fox told him. "Yes, I see you throwing her too! Coyote snapped in reply." These examples show that Fox thinks it is inappropriate for Coyote to attempt to cheat in order to win, whereas Coyote thinks it is improper for Fox not even to attempt to win at the various contests.

When Coyote is inside the monster ("Coyote and Monster"), Fox asks Coyote what he intends to do to such a dangerous adversary. Coyote seems to think that Fox doubts his ability and sends him looking for wood with the other skeptics. Because Coyote's plan succeeds, he seems rightfully scornful of Fox's doubts. Indeed, Fox should have felt his otherwise consistent confidence in Coyote's ability to defeat monsters, but perhaps his doubt in this situation emphasizes the exceptionally formidable nature of this monster. Later in the narrative, Fox reminds Coyote that he forgot to create the Nez Perce when he created the other peoples. Coyote tries to save face by blaming Fox for the oversight: "'Well,' snorted Coyote, 'and did you tell me that before? Why didn't you tell me that a while ago before it was too late? I was engrossed to the exclusion of thinking. You should have told me that in the first place.'" Coyote does not question Fox's wisdom but is annoyed at the timing of the information.

Fox generally seems to tolerate Coyote in spite of his foolishness, with one exception. When Coyote disguises himself and marries his daughter, Fox scolds him and abandons him ("Coyote Marries His Daughter"). Fox asks, "Why did you do these saddening and shameful things? All the people know about you, for you have acted shamefully. I shall go away also. What should I stay for?" Fox's abandonment of his friend Coyote underscores the magnitude of Coyote's offense. In contrast, Coyote would go to live with Fox out of lonliness ("Coyote Visits White Mountain") or for consolation ("Coyote and His Daughter").

The friendship between Fox and Coyote is so strong that Fox remains with him even when Coyote kills Fox's daughters along with his own ("Elbow Baby"). Fox feels sorry for them and frees the eldest before she can die like the others. Fox knows that the freed daughter will have revenge on Coyote; he is incapable of defeating Coyote in combat. His compassion for the maidens is proper (in contrast to Coyote's improper murder), and appropriately the avenging surviving daughter deliberately passes Fox by in her vengeful attack on Coyote. Perhaps Fox thinks Coyote has been sufficiently punished, for in both versions he gets lonely and revives the dead Coyote.

Other Friends

Coyote's other friends are Elk and Fish Hawk ("Coyote Visits Elk and Fish Hawk"). In this story, like the narratives involving Fox, Coyote refers to these friends as "brothers" (in Phinney), and the central interaction involves food. In all versions, Coyote visits Elk and Fish Hawk, who provide food using special or magical means. Elk cooks a strip of his wife's clothing, which turns into good meat to Coyote's surprise. In Wilson's version, Elk also conjures a delicious camas dessert by inserting a stick into his anus. Fish Hawk turns a ring of wild cherry wood into perfectly cooked intestines and obtains salmon by diving from a tree (Phinney). In Wilson's version, Fish Hawk obtains salmon from a tree using a forked stick. In Spinden's version, it is Elk who turns a bent stick into "marrow-gut" and gets camas from his anus, Mountain Sheep makes meat from a strip of clothing, and both Otter and Fish Hawk obtain salmon in similar fashion. In all versions, Coyote invites his guests to return the visit, and when they do he attempts and fails to imitate their methods of food production. His failure results in humiliation, injury, or death.

In Phinney's version, Coyote would surely be humiliated when his guests pity him and provide the food that he failed to provide. In Phinney, the ring of cherry wood springs from the fire, burning Coyote and his wife. In all versions, Coyote hits his head on the ice, which proves temporarily fatal in Phinney. In contrast to the Fox narratives, Coyote's imitation does not affect the powers of those he imitates; instead, the failure results in injury to himself and his wife.

Other Beneficial/Cooperative Relationships

Adult males other than Coyote's friends may engage in cooperative relationships with him. These relationships are intended to be beneficial to one or both parties. In some cases a character may assist Coyote in achieving something that cannot be achieved alone, usually with certain conditions being attached. Coyote may also act as benefactor to certain characters, with or without conditions being attached. Still others cooperate with Coyote without their motivation being made clear.

Buffalo ("Coyote and Bull") reluctantly agrees to transform Coyote into a buffalo so that he too may eat grass and not go hungry. Buffalo places a condition on Coyote; he must hold still while Buffalo charges him and tosses him in the air with his horns. Of course Coyote moves, and the attempt to transform him humorously fails. Buffalo makes a second attempt, but only after much begging and pestering from Coyote. This attempt is successful, because Coyote fulfills the condition of not moving during Buffalo's charge.

When a second coyote requests the same service from the now-transformed Coyote, the first Coyote transforms back again during the attempt. The reversal of the primary transformation may be because Coyote's stated reason for being transformed was to enable him to eat grass—a desire that was fulfilled. Buffalo never agreed to endow Coyote with his special transformative power; therefore, Coyote's attempt to use this power would constitute an unwelcome imitation of Buffalo. As in many other cases, Coyote's attempts to imitate the special powers of others reflect his inability to understand these powers, and invariably his attempt to use the power has disastrous consequences.

In another Buffalo narrative ("Coyote's Trip to the East"), Coyote agrees to assist a wounded bull in return for cow(s) to take home from the Buffalo country. The bull orders Coyote not to touch the cow(s) until his journey is complete. At the last moment he takes a fancy to the best one and touches her. In Spinden's version, the cow turns into a coyote woman, and Coyote cannot help himself. In both versions, the cow returns to the Buffalo country.

The Death Spirit ("Coyote and the Shadow People") agrees to help Coyote retrieve his wife from the spirit world. He tells Coyote, "I could take you to the place where your wife has gone but I tell you, you must do everything just exactly as I say; not once are you to disregard my commands and do something else"; Coyote agrees. He follows every instruction except for the last. He loses control of himself and touches his wife on the return journey, even though he was explicitly told not to do so. Not only does he permanently lose his wife, but death becomes a permanent feature in the world as a result. The Death Spirit's motivation for assisting Coyote is unclear. Possibly, he merely felt pity for Coyote who pined miserably for his wife; or perhaps he knew that death was to become a permanent aspect of the world, and he actually counted on Coyote's failure in order to accomplish this goal.

Deer-Tick ("Coyote and Fox") acts as an anonymous benefactor to Coyote and Fox by providing them with the packs of food they wish for. The condition for his assistance is the maintenance of his anonymity, although it is not directly stated. Instead, Coyote realizes the condition only after he has violated it. In the same narrative, the old man at the sweatbath also acts as benefactor to Coyote and Fox. The old man gives two instructions to his visitor: to help himself to a meal in the old man's dwelling and, later, to pack home as much food as he could carry. Coyote violates both instructions. He does not help himself to a meal, and he intends to take all of the old man's stores of food, not just a packload, and kills the old man. Thus he spoils the benefits of the relationship.

Coyote frequently acts as benefactor in his relationship with the salmon, which in turn results in a benefit to the people. In "Coyote Breaks the Fish Dam at Celilo," Coyote tears down the swallows' fish dam. This is done explicitly so that the people will have salmon to eat (except in Wilson, where the reason is not specified). Coyote also assists the salmons' spawning efforts by indicating where a suitable place could be found "How the Salmon Found Out That They Shouldn't Go Up Potlatch Creek"). Coyote often expects a return for his efforts: In Wilson's "The Five Swallows and Coyote" and Phinney's "Coyote and His Anus" (versions of "Coyote Breaks the Fish Dam at Celilo"), he requests that a salmon swim up to him so that he will be able to eat. The salmon comply, because Coyote reminds them that he either "made them" (Phinney) or gave them freedom (Wilson). His concern for them does not seem to arise from any emotional affinity or friendship; rather, Coyote treats the salmon as a valued resource for himself and the people.

Relationships Emphasizing Body Parts

As seen in our discussion of monsters, Coyote is awed by characters who can detach their own body parts. This fascination is based on the powers residing in these parts and the ability to transfer the power by transferring the parts that contain it. Because Coyote is always interested in gaining new powers, he eagerly exchanges or otherwise acquires foreign body parts if he feels he will be empowered by them. He may also bestow changes on other character's bodies to enable them to assist his purposes. Bodily alteration may also be a sort of punishment.

Bobcat's (Lynx) ability to juggle his eyes inspires Coyote's imitation ("How Coyote Lost His Eyes," all versions), but the imitation annoys Bobcat, who causes Coyote's eyes to become lost as he juggles them. Coyote's impulse to imitate the eye-juggling demonstrates his reluctance to admit that someone else may have superior abilities (this seems true of most occasions where he imitates another character). Bobcat's whiskers are particularly powerful—he uses one as an arrow to kill Grizzly Bear's sons ("Coyote Kills Grizzly Bear's Sons"). Coyote seems to be aware of this power, but in this case he does not attempt to imitate Bobcat, perhaps because he is preoccupied with distracting father Grizzly Bear. Bobcat's whisker is also used to create a fog that foils Coyote's plot to win the hunting contest ("Bobcat and Pine Squirrel's Daughter"). It is interesting that Bobcat also uses his "moustache" to knock away Coyote's eyes in Wilson's and Phinney's versions of "How Coyote Lost His Eyes." It seems likely that Bobcat's whiskers hold a power superior to anything Coyote possesses, making it impossible for Coyote to imitate these actions.

Particular body parts are not only the foci of special powers, but the powers of the body parts can be graded according to their relative strength. This characteristic is particularly evident concerning eyesight. When Coyote loses his eyes, he is completely sightless. Through trickery he lures the curlew bird close enough to be grabbed, and Coyote takes Curlew's eyes and puts them into his own empty sockets. The little eyes allow him to see dimly (better than not seeing at all). In Wilson's and Watters's versions, Coyote similarly tricks Owl, who has bigger eyes that give him even better vision. With these he can see well enough to eventually recover his own eyes.

Coyote seems keenly aware of the relative strength of various characters' eyesight. When the people try to see where Raven is going (because he has taken the game animals), it is Owl who has powerful enough eyes to follow his progress ("Cixcixícim Boy"). In Phinney's version, Bat loses sight almost immediately and Coyote shortly thereafter; yet both pretend that they can still see Raven, because they are unwilling to acknowledge Owl's superior abilities. Bat is absent in Watters's version, but Coyote again pretends to be able to follow Raven's path. Here he gives Night Owl the "two fingers gesture" (presumably derogatory) and tells him, "You don't see anything. You're just a round ball." Owl's success presumably forces Coyote to realize that his own visual powers are inferior to Owl's, whether he admits it or not.

If Owl's vision is superior to Coyote's, Bat's vision is certainly inferior. This is explicit in the narrative discussed above and also seems to be central in Coyote's elaborate joke on Bat in "Bat and Coyote." Coyote gets immense satisfaction in emphasizing Bat's inferior vision. As the culmination of his joke, Coyote throws cedar shavings into the fire and yells, "The place is on fire," which causes Bat to show his beadlike eyes in the bright light. Coyote howls and laughs while Bat retreats to his home in embarassment. Bat's eyes also seem to emphasize his homely appearance, which makes him very unattractive to females in spite of his material wealth and considerate character. Coyote undoubtably derives pleasure from Bat's inferior physical appearance as well, for Coyote is very unattractive himself (see discussion of Coyote and adult females). Visual ability and physical attractiveness are attributes that Coyote lacks, so his pleasure stems from establishing that others may be even less endowed in these qualities.

Another example of Coyote's willingness to exchange a body part for one that he thinks is superior occurs in "Worm Penis," in which he trades his penis for a magical worm. The worm's owner is most happy to part with it, for he considers it a nuisance. Coyote is so anxious to employ it for cutting timber for his fish trap that he suspects nothing. It works only too well for when the worm runs out of timber, it gnaws Coyote to death, perhaps because it retains the urgency of Coyote's sexuality. His greed for an unusual advantage blinds him to the potential danger, and the consequence is death.

Coyote occasionally alters body parts of other characters and he transforms them into their present form (see the egg-hunting boys in the discussion of Coyote and children). He cuts eye slits on the formerly blind gophers ("Coyote Defeats the Sun"), presumably so they can assist him in his plan against Sun and Moon. He kicks Rattlesnake on the head when it confronts him inside the monster, giving it the current flattened appearance ("Coyote and Monster"). In the same narrative, Muskrat loses the hair on his tail when he is tardy in escaping from the Monster's anus. Coyote's scolding seems to suggest that this fate is at least an indirect result of Muskrat's failure to promptly follow Coyote's instructions to escape from the dying monster.

A body part may even contain the power to reconstruct the whole body from which it came. When Coyote's daughter kills him in a firestorm, only his jawbone remains intact, humorously chattering away ("Elbow Baby"). Fox finds it and straddles it, an action that revives Coyote. This sort of reconstitution requires the assistance of another party.

Hunting Relationships

Many of Coyote's relationships with adult males center around hunting, an activity strongly associated with male identity. Hunting competitions are often used to determine a male's relative desirability as a husband. Coyote also manipulates hunts in order to defeat enemies and rivals, even though he is an inept hunter.

When Coyote marries Goose, he goes on hunts with her brothers ("Warmweather and Coldweather," all versions). The Goose brothers are superior in every aspect of hunting. They are able to travel to better hunting grounds, and they kill superior game. Clearly envious, Coyote sabotages their return trip by imitating their honking, which causes them to lose their ability to fly. Coyote's motive may be to sabotage the superior ability of the Geese. If they return without game (which is discarded to maintain their flight when he interferes), the result is as if they had never killed the game in the first place. This would put him in a superior standing with the Goose girl. Her brothers, who were previously her providers, could thus be supplanted from this position, and Coyote would become her sole provider. Presumably Coyote would prefer this situation, because he would otherwise be constantly reminded of his inferiority if the Goose brothers continued to serve as her providers.

A similar theme occurs in "Bobcat and Pine Squirrel's Daughter." The father of Pine Squirrel's child (and her future husband) needs to be determined. Pine Squirrel's father arranges hunting contests so he can decide who will marry his daughter. The true father is Bobcat, and he wins the contest(s) even though Coyote attempts to cheat by various means. Coyote also tries to cheat Cougar by stealing the game from Cougar's trap, but Bobcat's catch turns out to be superior in spite of Coyote's theft. Despite his trickery and deception, Coyote cannot overcome his inferiority in the company of accomplished hunters, and he does not win Pine Squirrel for a wife.

Coyote may also use the occasion of the hunt to further his own purposes, even when he does not hunt himself. In these instances he acts as the organizer of the hunt and declares the enemy Grizzly Bears as the game to be hunted. If possible, he places other rivals in such a position that if the grizzlies cause any problems, it will be Coyote's rivals who suffer the consequences. Coyote seems jealous of the Woodpecker brothers ("The Five Grizzly Bear Sisters and the Five Woodpecker Brothers"), who are highly respected by the other people. Coyote knows the dangerous power of the Grizzlies, and it is unclear why the Woodpeckers agree to this event; perhaps they would lose their respectability if they declined to do so. The result demonstrates the success of Coyote's scheme. Only one grizzly and one woodpecker survive.

A similar situation occurs when Coyote arranges a hunt in which Lynx is directed to shoot the Grizzly Bear brothers while they hunt ("Bears and Coyote," Phinney's version similar to "Coyote Kills Grizzly Bear's Sons"). In the prior scene, Lynx was Coyote's rival for Pine Squirrel, but Coyote lies about being the cause of Lynx's death, saying it was Grizzly Bear who caused it, in order to convice Lynx (who had revived) to cooperate. If any problems had occured in this part of Coyote's scheme, it would have been Lynx who suffered the consequences. Regardless of the outcome, Coyote would have disposed of either his enemies or his rival by pitting them against each other in this fashion. Because of the information provided by Marten, Father Grizzly learns that Coyote is ultimately responsible for the death of Bear's sons, and attempts revenge on him instead of Lynx.

Coyote's encounter with Porcupine also involves hunting; Porcupine has killed Buffalo but is unable to prepare the carcass ("How Porcupine Went to the Plains"). Coyote tricks Porcupine into giving him the carcass. In this story, both parties are inept hunters. Porcupine only manages to kill Buffalo through cleverness, not through any skill at hunting (he pierces her heart with a quill when she agrees to transport him across the water inside of her). His inability to prepare the carcass reflects his inferiority. Coyote is able to prepare the carcass, but leaves it relatively unprotected, resulting in its loss. Because transporting the game home is part of the hunt, he too is shown to be an inferior hunter, even though he did not kill the game.

Competition For Women

In our discussion of Coyote and adult females, we noted that Coyote is generally unsuccessful in acquiring mates because of his homely appearance and general lack of qualities desired by women. Thus, Coyote sometimes has to compete with other adult males for females as potential mates. He may also resort to deception, disguising his true identity in order to hide his undesirability.

Coyote competes with Bobcat and other unspecified males to be recognized as the father of Pine Squirrel's child, even though he is fully aware that he is not ("Bobcat and Pine Squirrel's Daughter"). The father would become Pine Squirrel's husband. Hunting contests are used to decide the competition, because Coyote is dissatisfied with the baby-quieting contest. Coyote is so enraged at his defeat that he plots to have his rival (Bobcat/Lynx) killed. Like the story in which he pits enemies and rivals against each other in the hunt, he incites Robin, Bobolink, Eagle, and the other flying people to kill Lynx. In other stories, the flying people are among Coyote's enemies (e.g., Phinney's version of "Cut-Out-of-Belly Boy"), even though he finds their women attractive. Therefore, Coyote benefits even if Lynx should overpower his assailants.

Coyote competes with his own son in an effort to steal his daughter-in-law as his own mate ("Coyote Breaks the Fish Dam at Celilo"). He proceeds by magically causing his son to become marooned in the clouds when he is tricked into climbing a tree. Coyote then transforms to appear as his son, but people begin to become suspicious when he fails at the duties of hunting leader at which his son excelled. The son receives assistance from his grandfathers, the Spiders, and is enabled to return to his wives. Coyote's deception is soon revealed, and the son appropriately maroons him by tricking him into attempting to carry game back to camp using sabotaged ropes. Coyote's desperation for a mate surpasses the father-son bond, both because he is generally unsuccessful with females and because he may be jealous of his son (who is admired as a skilled hunting chief).

Coyote's Relationships with Chiefs

There are several ways in which Coyote interacts with chiefs. In some cases, Coyote himself is a chief. Occasionally he behaves as the subordinate of a chief should behave. Conversely, he may depose an existing chief if the chief is somehow an inappropriate leader.

There are relatively few instances in which Coyote is specifically referred to as chief. In Spinden's "Creation Story" (not included), Chief Coyote foretells the coming of people (humans) from the ground. His only action is to name the various peoples; the title of chief seems mainly to sanction his right to do so. Coyote is hunting chief in Phinney's "Bears and Coyote" (a version of "Bobcat and Pine Squirrel's Daughter"). He officiates in the hunting contest to determine the husband of Pine Squirrel (and of course he plans it so that he will be able to cheat). Similarly, in the same narrative and in "Coyote Kills Grizzly Bear's Sons," he officiates in the hunt in which he arranges Grizzly Bear's death. It is unclear why he would ever be a hunting chief given the lack of hunting skills he demonstrates elsewhere. Predictably he uses his position to further his own personal agenda. In "Coyote and Fox," Coyote considers himself to be a chief (this is his opinion only in this myth), and hence refuses to serve himself as his host had directed. This haughty attitude proves to be inappropriate, for upon the host's return, he assumes that Coyote has followed his instructions and does not offer to serve him. It is likely that the host does not recognize Coyote as a chief. Whether he is really a chief may be irrelevant, for it seems that whatever his status, he is for the time being a guest and a guest is obligated to follow his host's instructions.

Coyote knows what behavior is appropriate for a chief. He tells Sun, "You are acting badly for a chief" and transforms him into the Moon ("The Sun and the Moon"). Sun had been so hot that he had nearly killed everyone, which prompted Coyote to assemble a council to discuss the problem. This demonstrates that the chief should act for the benefit of his people. Coyote exposes Chief Grizzly Bear's stinginess by demanding to borrow his prized deer-hoof bell, a ploy designed to infuriate Bear and set Coyote's plot to destroy him in action ("How Coyote Killed the Grizzly Bears"). Once he defeats the Bears, Coyote declares himself to be the chief and moves into the Bears' lodges. It would seem that his only subordinates are the Mice and Cicéqi. A chief seems entitled to certain special priveleges, a fact that Coyote exploits when he plots to destroy Chief Grizzly Bear, of whom he is jealous (Spinden's "Grizzly-Bear and Coyote," a version of "Coyote Kills Grizzly Bear's Sons"). Coyote lures Bear to the spot where his assassins wait because the chief is supposed to be where the hunting is best.

Coyote seems to have a special interest in the daughters of chiefs. In one of the instances in which Coyote dreams of women while he floats dead down the river ("Coyote and Hummingbird"), he says to Magpie, "Oh, you disturbed me. I was just helping some girls get across the headwaters. I was helping a chief's daughter get across in a canoe." He seems to be trying to impress Magpie with the status of the girl he claimed to be with. This impulse to be associated with those of higher status may lie behind the great lengths Coyote goes to in his attempts to win Chief Pine Squirrel's daughter for his wife ("Bobcat and Pine Squirrel's Daughter"). After losing one contest, Coyote begs the chief to hold additional contests to ensure that he indeed has identified the worthy man. Eventually the chief refuses to hold any more contests. Similarly, in "Cixcixícim Boy," the chief holds a marksmanship contest to determine a husband for his two daughters. When Coyote loses he tries to lie, saying that the winner has bequeathed the girls to him, but the chief stands firm on his decision. It appears that once a chief makes a firm decision, Coyote must abide by it like everyone else.

Sometimes Coyote acts as a chief's subordinate. Coyote acts as messenger for the chief, telling the grizzly bear sisters that the chief's son wants to look them over as potential wives ("How the Grizzly Bear Sisters Were Fooled") in order to lure them into the people's plot to kill them. Because Coyote is always interested in defeating the Grizzly Bears, his assistance may simply be offered to further his own purpose rather than to simply serve his superior. Coyote is a messenger in Wilson's "Naughty Boy Becomes Good" (a version of "The Disobedient Boy"); the Chief and Coyote tell the people to move back in with the now-grown boy they had abandoned. Once again, his assistance seems to reflect his own interest, which in this case coincides with the interest of the Chief and the people.

Coyote's relationships with males are largely based on competition and rivalry. He attempts to be superior to other males, regardless of his actual abilities. These attempts often result in humorous failures. He is also always interested in acquiring special powers or abilities from friends and rivals alike, although he does not understand how to use them. Usually his lack of understanding results in failures that further emphasize his inferiority. He fails to measure up in competitions that test specific male skills, such as hunting, shooting, and wrestling. Because Coyote is unable to compete successfully, he resorts to cheating or deception. These methods may work temporarily, but most such attempts usually fail. In noncompetetive relationships, Coyote fails to achieve the benefits offered by the other party, usually because he cannot refrain from a specifically forbidden action.

Conclusion

Although Nez Perce Coyote is selfish and foolhardy, his importance is paramount. Coyote is the creator of the Nez Perce and much of their environment, yet his personality is in no sense a role model. His actions are often humorous, but their consequences have serious effects concerning the transformation of the world into its present form.

Nez Perce Coyote possesses impressive magical powers, the most important being his ability to transform his physical appearance and that of others. His ability to disguise himself is often employed in his schemes to trick, deceive, or evade his opponents. He is always interested in obtaining new magical powers but fails to acquire or use them properly and is thus usually denied their benefits. Coyote's frequent resurrection from death is accomplished only through the assistance of other actors (Magpie and Fox), suggesting that he lacks the godlike immortality attributed to him by certain writers. Although his magical powers and physical abilities are not unlimited, his ultimate survival parallels the ultimate survival of the Nez Perce people.

Coyote prefers to eat the choicest portions of big game, but his hunting prowess is only suitable for capturing mice and fawns. Other mythic actors are able to procure food through magical means, but Coyote's greed confounds his own attempts to use the same magical methods. If he manages to acquire food by taking advantage of his fellow beings, his good fortune typically ends when he fails to uphold his social responsibilities. His powers of strength, speed, visual acuity, and his hunting and shooting skills are inferior to those of other mythic characters. Because he is not physically powerful or skilled, he resorts to trickery, evasion, deception, and disguise in order to compete with those who possess superior powers and skills.

A consistent feature of Coyote's character is his constant mobility. He is generally restless, wandering, or traveling about; these activities parallel his curiosity and his opportunistic tendencies. (In a few myths, for example, as he wanders he destroys monsters to protect the coming human beings from their ravages.) His mobility, however, prevents the formation of long–term social ties with most other characters as seen in his insistence on accompanying his daughter to her new home in order to avoid being lonely. Yet once there, he quickly becomes bored and decides to leave. He rarely stays in one place for long, even though he feels lonely and desires social contact and interaction. As soon as his loneliness abates, his need for mobility and change resurfaces. Likewise, once a need or desire is satisfied, another arises that requires his attention, action, and frequent movement or travel.

Coyote's movements upriver generally signal a coming adventure, whereas movement downriver symbolizes defeat. His movement along the river is consistent with both Nez Perce prehistory as well as traditional Nez Perce settlement patterns in which villages are usually situated in linear fashion along streams. The people and places Coyote encounters during his travels encompass most of the traditional Nez Perce homeland. Likewise, there are various expeditions eastward to the Buffalo country (the Plains of Montana), which correspond to known expeditions undertaken regularly by large parties of Nez Perce. His journey to his son's wedding on the Pacific coast suggests the western boundary of the traditional Nez Perce subsistence range of movement.

Coyote's compulsive mobility affects other aspects of his character. His transitory membership in various groups allows him to violate customary mores and etiquette without serious concern for consequences. He evades most social sanctions by not being a permanent part of any group. Despite efforts to impose sanctions against him, such as abandonment or death, he lacks any real fear of social sanctions and remains largely amoral throughout the myths. In fact, Coyote seems incapable of successfully fulfilling any social role. He is the father of many children but is unwilling or unable to provide for their welfare. He seems content to forget them entirely after the act of conception. For him, children are a burden and an annoyance, and he will even kill them for trivial reasons. Other children are tolerated as long as they are of some use to him, but if they annoy him they are abandoned or killed.

Coyote's relationships with females are similarly impulsive and usually involve sex or food. He has many sexual encounters, often takes wives, but seems disinterested in long–term relationships. From a female perspective, Coyote is physically unattractive (hence his need for disguise), and he is a failure at being either a father or husband. When he does appear with a wife (Mouse) in what could be a long–term relationship, she is either complaining about the relationship or suffering the negative consequences of Coyote's activities. His other wives come and go so quickly that relationships do not have a chance to develop. Coyote's nonsexual relationships with females seem entirely based upon their ability to satisfy his other needs of the moment—usually food, information, or shelter.

Coyote's relationships with males are also driven by his immediate needs. He often competes with other males in contests where either food or women are the prize. He seems disinterested in acquiring the respect or admiration of his male competitors, for his schemes and tactics involve cheating and deception. He wishes to win at any cost and usually fails. Other males are generally depicted as Coyote's competitors in physical appearance, physical abilities, hunting prowess, and magical powers. Likewise, Coyote's relationships with his friends are far from ideal. He is aware that his relationship with Fox should be based on sharing and cooperation and often reminds Fox of this ideal. He even tries to rival Fox's special magical abilities but ultimately fails because of his selfishness. Similarly, his other friends (like Elk and Fish Hawk) have special abilities that he mimics unsuccessfully. What at first appears to be reciprocity usually becomes rivalry, with Coyote wanting to show his friend, "If you can do it, I can do it better." In fact, Coyote's friends almost always become his rivals just as do strangers.

Coyote even violates the basic rules of family and kinship when he eliminates his son in order to have his daughter–in–law for himself. He exhibits no hesitation, and once his actions are discovered shows no guilt or remorse. His immediate desire for sexual relations overcomes any moral restraints of a father or father–in–law. His failure to maintain any social roles for an extended period of time allows him to avoid the moral responsibilities associated with them. As a result of severe breaches of morality, he is often abandoned by the group; but he actually loses very little because he moves on to the next adventure.

Coyote is at his best when he confronts the monsters of the mythical prehuman era. Although his reliance on deception, disguise, evasion, and trickery reflects his shortcomings, these skills also make him ideally suited for confronting monsters, including the widely feared Grizzly Bear. Monsters may defeat him by appealing to his selfish nature, by offering sex, or by demonstrating special abilities that he wants for himself, but he manages to overcome them in the end. They are all threatening in some fashion either as killers or as destroyers of critical resources. Monsters who threaten key resources such as the salmon and the river itself are defeated without being killed. Monsters who are killers of other characters are in turn killed by Coyote. After defeating or killing a monster, he typically remarks that he has changed things to benefit the coming human beings. It is obvious, however, that he has also improved things for himself as well by eliminating threats to his own desires or to his life. Once he defeats monsters, he typically transforms them, rendering them harmless. Coyote's interest in making the world safer reflects his unique concern for the future human beings whom he creates by transforming parts of the defeated Kamiah monster.

Where such reflections occur, the myths reflect the archaic, pre-horse Nez Perce culture with few exceptions. Our descriptive method recognizes that the myths operate according to their own rules. We must emphasize that although Coyote exhibits many human qualities, he does not represent a traditional Nez

Perce person. Likewise, the mythical world in which he lives is not a direct or systematic reflection of the traditional Nez Perce world. Coyote's interactions with other mythic characters reveal consistencies in his behavior and motivation. Together these consistencies comprise his character. Our examination of Coyote's character in Nez Perce myth involves only a portion of Nez Perce mythology. A similar treatment of other mythic characters is a necessary step in discovering the deeper meanings of these narratives. Moreover, a character–by–character analysis will permit more systematic and precise comparisons with the mythologies of other tribal cultures of the Northwest and elsewhere. Our analysis is a first attempt to describe Coyote's character in sufficient detail to discover what makes the Nez Perce Coyote unique in comparison to his character as represented in the myths of other tribal cultures of Native North America.

Bibliography

Abrams, D. M. 1977. "The Development of the Trickster in Children's Narrative." *Journal of American Folklore*, vol. 90.

Ahenakew, Edward. 1929. "Cree Trickster Tales." *Journal of American Folklore*, vol. 42.

Allison, Carol. 1982. *Coyote and the North Wind*. Indian Reading Series, Book 5, Level 4. Washington, D.C.: U.S. Government Printing Office.

————. 1981. *Coyote and the Stars*. The Indian Reading Series, Book 1, Level 1. Washington, D.C.: U.S. Government Printing Office.

Aoki, Haruo, and Deward E. Walker, Jr. 1989. *Nez Perce Oral Narratives*. University of California Publications in Linguistics, vol. 104. Berkeley: University of California Press.

Arlee, Johnny. 1981. *Coyote and the Man Who Sits on Top*. Indian Reading Series, Book 12, Level 2. Washington, D.C.: U.S. Government Printing Office.

Auck, Frederick. 1982. *Coyote and the Old Lady*. Indian Reading Series, Book 9, Level 3. Washington, D.C.: U.S. Government Printing Office.

Ballard, Charles Guthrie. 1982. "The Boas Connection in American Indian Mythology: A Research Narrative on Ethnocentrism." *American Indian Culture and Research Journal*, vol. 6, no. 3: 47–68.

Ballinger, Franchot. 1985. "Sacred Reversals: Trickster in Gerald Vizenor's 'Earthdivers: Tribal Narratives on Mixed Descent.'" *American Indian Quarterly*, vol. 9: 55–59.

Basso, Ellen B. 1978. "The Enemy of Every Tribe: 'Bushman' Images in Northern Athapaskan Narratives." *American Ethnologist*, vol. 5: 690–709.

Beck, Mary L. 1979. "Raven: Benefactor, Transformer, Trickster, Thief." *Indian Historian*, vol. 12, no. 2: 50–53.

Blue Cloud, Peter. 1982. *Elderberry Flute Song: Contemporary Coyote Tales*. Trumansburg, N.Y.: Crossing Press.

Bright, William O., ed. 1993. *A Coyote Reader*. Berkeley: University of California Press.

————. 1978. *Coyote Stories*. Monograph, no. 1. International Journal of American Linguistics, Native American Text Series. Chicago: University of Chicago Press.

Bright, William O., 1954. *The Travels of Coyote*. Publications, 11, Kroeber Anthropological Society.

Calkowski, Marcia. 1975. "Cannibalism and Infertility: Sexual Imbalance in Interior Salish Mythology." In Jim Freedman and Jerome H. Barkow, eds., *Proceedings of the Second Congress, Canadian Ethnology Society*, vol. 1. pp. 47–64. Ottawa: National Museums of Canada.

Callaghan, Catherine A. 1977. "Coyote the Imposter (Lake Miwok)." In Victor Golla and Shirley Silver, eds., *Northern California Texts*. pp. 10–16. Chicago: University of Chicago Press.

Clark, Ella E. 1952. "The Bridge of the Gods in Fact and Fancy." *Oregon Historical Quarterly*, vol. 53: 29–38.

————. n.d. *Indian Legends from the Northern Rockies.* Norman: University of Oklahoma Press.

Cuadra Downing, O. 1955. *The Adventures of Don Coyote.* New York: N.p.

Curtin, Jeremiah. 1974. *Wishram Texts: Together with Wasco Tales and Myths.* New York: AMS Press.

————. 1971. *Myths of the Modocs.* New York: B. Blom.

Daklugie, A. 1955/1956. "Coyote and the Flies." *New Mexico Folklore Record,* vol. 10: 12–13.

Deans, J. 1889. "The Raven of the Northwest Coast." *American Antiquarian and Oriental Journal,* vol. 11: 297–301.

Devereux, George. 1948. "Mohave Coyote Tales." *Journal of American Folklore,* vol. 61: 233–255.

Dixon, Roland B. 1900. "Some Coyote Stories from the Maidu Indians." *Journal of American Folklore,* vol. 13: 267–270.

Doueihi, Anne. 1984. "Trickster: On Inhabiting the Space Between Discourse and Story." *Soundings,* vol. 67, no. 3: 283–311.

Edmonds, Margot and Ella E. Clark. 1989. *Voices of the Winds: Native American Legends.* New York: Facts on File.

Erdoes, Richard, and Alfonso Ortiz, eds. 1984. *American Indian Myths and Legends.* New York: Pantheon Books.

Evening, Evelyn A. Teton. 1982. *Coyote and the Cowboy.* Indian Reading Series, Book 16, Level 4. Washington, D.C.: U.S. Government Printing Office.

Gatschet, Albert S. 1879. "Mythologic Text in the Klamath Language." *American Antiquarian and Oriental Journal,* vol. 1: 161–166.

Gilliland, Hap. 1972. *The Flood.* Indian Culture Series. Billings: Montana Council for Indian Education.

Golla, Victor, and Shirley Silver, eds. 1977. *Northern California Texts.* International Journal of American Linguistics, vol. 2, no. 2, Native American Text Series. Chicago: University of Chicago Press.

Graves, C. S. 1929. *Lore and Legends of the Klamath River Indians.* Eureka: N.p.

Grinnell, George Bird. 1893. "A Blackfoot Sun and Moon Myth." *Journal of American Folklore,* vol. 6: 44–67.

Gwydir, R. D. 1907. "Prehistoric Spokane: an Indian Legend," *Washington Historical Quarterly,* vol. 1: 136–137.

Hecocta, Laura. 1982. *Coyote Arranges the Seasons.* Indian Reading Series, Book 12, Level 5. Washington, D.C.: U.S. Government Printing Office.

Hill, Willard Williams. 1945. "Navaho Coyote Tales and Their Position in the Southern Athabaskan Group." *Journal of Folklore,* vol. 58: 317–343.

Hines, Donald M. 1984. *Tales of the Nez Perce.* Fairfield, Wash.: Ye Galleon Press.

Hubbard, Patrick. 1980. "Trickster: Renewal and Survival." *American Indian Culture and Research Journal,* vol. 4, no. 4: 113–124.

Hultkrantz, Ake. 1986. "Mythology and Religious Concepts." In Warren L. d'Azevedo, ed., *Handbook of North American Indians,* vol. 11. pp. 630–640. Washington, D.C.: Smithsonian Institution.

————. 1972. "An Ideological Dichotomy: Myths and Folk Beliefs Among the Shoshoni Indians of Wyoming." *History of Religions,* vol. 11: 339–353.

————. 1955. "The Origin of Death Myth as Found Among the Wind River Shoshone Indians." *Ethnos,* vol 20: 127–136.

Hymes, Dell Hathaway. 1987. "Tonkawa Poetics: John Rush Buffalo's 'Coyote and Eagle's Daughter.'" In Joel Sherzer and Anthony C. Woodbury, eds., *Native American Discourse,* Cambridge Studies in Oral and Literate Culture, 13: 17–61. Cambridge: Cambridge University Press.

———. 1984. "Bungling Host, Benevolent Host: Louis Simpson's 'Deer and Coyote.'" *American Indian Quarterly,* vol. 8: 171–198.

Jacobs, Melville. 1959. *The Content and Style of an Oral Literature: Clackamas Chinook Myths and Tales.* New York: Wenner-Gren Foundation for Anthropological Research.

———. 1952. "Psychological Inferences from a Chinook Myth." *Journal of American Folklore,* vol. 65: 121–137.

Jacobs, Roderick Arnold. 1976. "The Rabbit and the Coyote." In Margaret Langdon, ed., *Yuman Texts.* International Journal of American Linguistics, vol. 1, no. 3: 107–112. Native American Texts Series. Chicago: University of Chicago Press.

Jones, Hettie. 1974. *Coyote Tales.* New York: Holt, Rinehart and Winston.

Jose, Cecil T. 1981. "A Cross-Cultural Content Analysis of Nez Perce Tribal Legends and Selected Anglo–American Children's Stories for Value–Attitude Factors of Achievement Motivation." Paper presented at the Indian Participation in Educational Research conference sponsored by the National Institute of Education (Washington, D.C., April 1–3, 1981). N.p.

Keaveney, Madeline M. 1983. "Humor in Navajo Coyote Tales." In Isabel W. Crouch and Gordon R. Owen, eds., *Proceedings of Seminar/Conference on Oral Tradition.* pp. 44–57. Las Cruces: New Mexico State University.

Kendall, Martha B., ed. 1980. *Coyote Stories II.* Ann Arbor, Mich.: University Microfilms International.

———. 1979. "Wolf and Coyote: An Upland Yuman Text." *Amerindia,* vol. 4: 127–147.

Kootenai Cultural Committee for the Confederated Kootenai Tribes. 1984. *Kootenai Legends.* Elmo, Mont.: The Committee.

Kroeber, Henrietta R. 1909. "Papago Coyote Tales." *Journal of American Folklore,* vol. 22: 339–342.

Laird, Carobeth. 1978. "The Androgynous Nature of Coyote." *Journal of California Anthropology,* vol. 5, no. 1: 67–72.

Landar, Herbert J. 1961. "A Note on the Navaho Word for Coyote." *International Journal of American Linguistics,* vol. 27: 86–88.

Linderman, Frank Bird. 1931. *Old Man Coyote.* New York: n.p.

Lopez, Barry Holstun. 1977. *Giving Birth to Thunder, Sleeping with His Daughter: Coyote Builds North America.* Kansas City and New York: Sheed Andrews and McMeel and Avon Books.

Lowie, Robert Harry. 1986. "The Northern Shoshone." In David Hurst Thomas, ed., *A Great Basin Shoshonean Source Book.* pp. 163–308. New York: Garland Publishing,.

Luckert, Karl W. 1984. "Coyote in Navajo and Hopi Tales." In Berard Haile, *ed. Navajo Coyote Tales.* American Tribal Religions, vol. 8, Lincoln: University of Nebraska Press.

Lyman, W. D. 1904. "Myths and Superstitions of the Oregon Indians." *Proceedings,* n.s., 16, American Antiquarian Society: 221–251.

Malotki, Ekkehart, and Mechael Lomatuway'ma. 1984. *Hopi Coyote Tales.* American Tribal Religions, vol. 9. Lincoln: University of Nebraska Press.

McLean, J. 1893. "Blackfoot Mythology." *Journal of American Folklore,* vol. 6: 165–172.

———. 1890. "Blackfoot Indian Legends." *Journal of American Folklore,* vol. 3: 296–298.

Milford, S. J. 1941. "Why the Coyote Has a Spot on His Tail." *El Palacio,* vol. 48: 83–84.

Morgan, William and R. W. Young. 1949. *Coyote Tales.* Washington, D.C.: N.p.

Nashville, Bernice G. 1979. *Trickster Tales from Prairie Lodge Fires.* Nashville, Tenn.: Abingdon.

Navarro, A. C. 1979. *Coyote After the Flood.* Cortaro, Ariz.: N.p.

Northwest Regional Educational Laboratory. 1982. *Coyote Gets Lovesick.* Indian Reading Series, Book 15, Level 4. Washington, D.C.: U.S. Government Printing Office.

———. 1981. *Coyote and Trout.* Indian Reading Series, Book 10, Level 3. Washington, D.C.: U.S. Government Printing Office.

———. 1981. *How Wildcat and Coyote Tricked Each Other.* Indian Reading Series, Book 4, Level 2. Washington, D.C.: U.S. Government Printing Office.

Old Coyote, Sally, and Joy Yellowtail Toineeta. 1971. *Indian Tales of the Northern Rockies.* Indian Culture Series. Billings: Montana Council for Indian Education.

Packard, R. L. 1891. "Notes on the Mythology and Religion of the Nez Perce." *Journal of American Folklore,* vol. 4: 327–330.

Palmer, Gary B. 1980. "Persecution, Alliance and Revenge in Shuswap Indian War Legends: A Formal Analysis." In Lucille B. Harten et al., eds., *Anthropological Papers in Memory of Earl H. Swanson, Jr.* pp. 1–7. Pocatello: Idaho Museum of Natural History.

Parks, Douglas R., ed. 1981. *Arikara Coyote Tales.* Roseglen, N.D.: White Shield School District.

Phinney, Archie. 1934. *Nez Perce Texts.* New York: Columbia University Press.

Plume, Bull. 1933. "Blackfoot Legends," *Masterkey,* vol. 7: 41–46, 70–73.

Radin, Paul. 1969. *The Trickster: A Study in American Indian Mythology.* New York: Greenwood Press.

Ramsey, Jarold. 1981. "From 'Mythic' to 'Fictive' in a Nez Perce Orpheus Myth." In Karl Kroeber, ed., *Traditional Literatures of the American Indian.* pp. 25–44. Lincoln: University of Nebraska Press.

———, ed. 1977. *Coyote Was Going There: Indian Literature of the Oregon Country.* Seattle: University of Washington Press.

Reichard, Gladys Amanda. 1947. *An Analysis of Coeur d'Alene Indian Myths.* Memoirs of the American Folklore Society, [s.l.] 41.

Rockwell, David. 1991. *Giving Voice to Bear: North American Myths, Rituals, and Images of the Bear.* Niwot, Colo.: Roberts Rinehart.

Roessel, Robert A., Jr., and Dillon Platero eds. 1968. *Coyote Stories of the Navajo People.* Chinle, Ariz.: Rough Rock Demonstration School.

Sapir, Edward S. 1960. "Preliminary Report on the Language and Mythology of the Upper Chinook." In Frederica de Laguna, ed. *Selected Papers from the American Anthropologist, 1888–1920.* pp. 411–422. Evanston, Ill.: Row, Peterson.

Sayre, Robert F. 1985. "Trickster." *North Dakota Quarterly,* vol. 53, no. 2: 68–81.

Schler, Bo, ed. 1984. *Coyote Was Here: Essays on Contemporary Native American Literary and Political Mobilization.* Aarhus, Denmark: University of Aarhus, Department of English.

Shaul, David Leedom. 1987. "The Hopi Coyote Story as Narrative." *Journal of Pragmatics,* vol. 11, no. 1: 3–25.

Silver Otter. 1983. "Coyote and the Tourist." *Many Smokes,* vol. 17, no. 1: 17–18.

Simpson, Ruth de Ette. 1958. "The Coyote in Southwestern Indian Tradition." *Masterkey,* vol. 32: 45–54.

Skeels, Dell R. 1954. "A Classification of Humor in Nez Perce Mythology." *Journal of American Folklore,* vol. 67: 57–64.

———. 1954. "The Function of Humor in Three Nez Perce Indian Myths." *American Imago,* vol. 11: 248–261.

———. 1949. "Style in the Unwritten Literature of the Nez Perce Indians." Ph.D. diss., University of Washington, 2 vols.

Smith, Patricia Clark. 1983. "Coyote Ortiz: *Canis latrans latrans* in the Poetry of Simon Ortiz." In Paula Gunn Allen, ed., *Studies in American Indian Literature.* pp. 129–210. New York: Modern Language Association of America.

Spencer, Robert F. 1952. "Native Myth and Modern Religion Among the Klamath Indians," *Journal of American Folklore,* vol. 65: 217–226.

Spinden, Herbert Joseph. 1971. "Three Songs of Mad Coyote." *Alcheringa,* vol. 2.

———. 1917. "Nez Perce Tales." *Folk–Tales of the Salishan and Sahaptin Tribes.* Memoirs of the American Folklore Society, 11. New York.

———. 1908. "Myths of the Nez Perce Indians." *Journal of American Folklore,* vol. 21: 13–23; 149–157.

Stern, Theodore. 1963. "Ideal and Expected Behavior as Seen in Klamath Mythology." *Journal of American Folklore,* vol. 76: 21–41.

———. 1956. "Some Sources of Variability in Klamath Mythology." *Journal of American Folklore,* vol. 69: 1–12, 135–146, 377–386.

———. 1953. "The Trickster in Klamath Mythology." *Western Folklore,* vol. 12: 158–174.

Stewart, N. 1941. *Meet Mr. Coyote.* Victoria, B.C.: N.p.

Stross, Brian. 1971. "Serial Order in Nez Perce Myths." *Journal of American Folklore,* vol. 84: 104–113.

Swann, Brian, ed. 1983. *Smoothing the Ground: Essays on Native American Oral Literature.* Berkeley: University of California Press.

Tafoya, Terry. 1979. "Coyote in the Classroom: The Use of American Indian Oral Tradition with Young Children." Paper presented at the Annual Meeting of the National Association for the Education of Young Children (Atlanta, November 8–11, 1979). Washington, D.C.

Teit, James Alexander. 1975. *Mythology of the Thompson Indians.* New York: AMS Press.

Toelken, John Barre. 1976. "The 'Pretty Languages' of Yellowman: Genre, Mode, and Texture in Navajo Coyote Narratives." In Dan Ben–Amos, ed., *Folklore Genres.* Austin: University of Texas Press.

Townsend, Anna Lee. 1977. "Shoshone–Bannock Legend." *Idaho Heritage,* vol. 1, no. 10. N.p.

Trejo, Judy. 1974. "Coyote Tales: A Paiute Commentary." *Journal of American Folklore,* vol. 87: 66–71.

Walker, Deward E., Jr. 1994. "Nez Perce." In *Native America in the Twentieth Century: An Encyclopedia.* New York: Garland.

———. 1989. "The Nez Perce Indians." In *The World Book Encyclopedia,* vol. 14: 395.

———. 1985. *Conflict and Schism in Nez Perce Acculturation,* 2d ed. Moscow: University of Idaho Press.

———. 1980. *Myths of Idaho Indians.* Moscow: University of Idaho Press.

———. 1978. *Indians of Idaho.* Moscow: University of Idaho Press.

———. 1973. "American Indians of Idaho." *Anthropological Monographs of the University of Idaho,* no. 2. Moscow: University of Idaho Press.

————. 1967. "Nez Perce Sorcery." *Ethnology,* vol. 6, no. 1: 66–96.

————. 1967. "Measures of Nez Perce Outbreeding and the Analysis of Culture Change." *Southwestern Journal of Anthropology,* vol. 23, no. 2.

————. 1967. "Mutual Cross–Utilization of Economic Resources in the Plateau: An Example from Aboriginal Nez Perce Fishing Practices." *Washington State University, Laboratory of Anthropology, Report of Investigations,* no. 41.

————. 1966. "A Nez Perce Ethnographic Observation of Archaeological Significance." *American Antiquity,* vol. 31, no. 3: 436–437.

————. 1966. "Some Limitations on the Renascence Concept in Acculturation: The Nez Perce Case." In Stuart Levine and Nancy Lurie, eds., *The American Indian Today.* Deland, Fla: Everett/Edwards, Inc.

————. 1966. "The Nez Perce Sweat Bath Complex: An Acculturational Analysis." *Southwestern Journal of Anthropology,* vol. 22, no. 2: 133–171.

————. 1964. *A Survey of Nez Perce Religion.* New York: Board of National Missions, United Presbyterian Church in the U.S.A.

Walker, Deward E., Jr. with Virginia Beavert. 1974. *The Way It Was--Anaku Iwacha: Yakima Indian Legends.* Yakima: Franklin Press.

Walker, Deward E., Jr. with Allen P. Slickpoo, Sr. 1973. *Noon Nee-Me-Poo: Nez Perce Culture and History.* Lapwai: Nez Perce Tribe of Idaho.

Walker, Deward E. Jr. with Allen P. Slickpoo, Sr. and Leroy Seth. 1973. *Nu Mee Poom Tit Wah Tit: Nez Perce Legends.* Lapwai: Nez Perce Tribe of Idaho.

Welsch, Roger L. 1981. *Omaha Tribal Myths and Trickster Tales.* Chicago: Sage Books, Swallow Press.

Wheelwright, Mary C. "Notes on Some Navajo Coyote Myths." *New Mexico Folklore Record,* vol. 4: 17–19.

————. 1985. *The Myth and Prayers of the Great Star Chant and the Myth of the Coyote Chant.* Tsaile, Ariz.: Navajo Community College Press.

Whirlwind Singing Wolf Woman. 1984. "Old Man Coyote and the Medicine Road." *Many Smokes,* vol. 18, no. 2: 16.

Wissler, Clark, and D. C. Duvall. 1976. *Mythology of the Blackfoot Indians.* New York: AMS Press.

Wood, Nancy C., ed. 1981. "Ute: Creation Legend." *Plateau,* vol. 53, no. 2: 4–7.

Wright, Gary A., and Jane D. Dirks. 1983. "Myth as Environmental Message." *Ethnos,* vol. 48, nos. 3-4: 160–176.

Index